Poland Challenges a Divided World

POLAND CHALLENGES A DIVIDED WORLD

John Rensenbrink

LOUISIANA STATE UNIVERSITY PRESS
Baton Rouge and London

Copyright © 1988 by Louisiana State University Press
All rights reserved
Manufactured in the United States of America
10 9 8 7 6 5 4 3 2 1

Designer: Sylvia Loftin
Typeface: Electra
Typesetter: The Composing Room of Michigan, Inc.
Printer: Thomson-Shore, Inc.
Binder: John H. Dekker & Sons

Library of Congress Cataloging-in-Publication Data
Rensenbrink, John C.
    Poland challenges a divided world/John C. Rensenbrink.
       p.   cm.
    Bibliography: p.
    Includes index.
    ISBN 0-8071-1446-4 (alk. paper): $19.95
    1. Poland—Politics and government—1980– 2. NSZZ "Solidarność
(Labor organization) 3. Rensenbrink, John C.—Journeys—Poland.
I. Title.
DK4442.R46 1988
943.8'05—dc19   88-1393
                                                                         CIP

The author makes grateful acknowledgment to St. Martin's Press, Inc., and to
the Macmillan Press, Ltd., for permission to reprint the translation of the
Gdansk Accord published in Anthony Kemp-Welch, *The Birth of Solidarity*,
© A. Kemp-Welch, 1983.

The paper in this book meets the guidelines for permanence and durability of
the Committee on Production Guidelines for Book Longevity of the Council
on Library Resources. ∞

To the men and women of Poland, both in and out of prison, who defend human dignity, often to the uttermost. Among their many gifts to me I count one most precious—that they, looking reality in the face, have not flinched but have found within its deceptive depths the power to live and prevail.

Contents

Acknowledgments

When I think of the help I have received on this book, my most immediate thoughts are of my wife, Carla, and of our three daughters—Kathryn, Margaret, and Elizabeth. The five months we spent together in Poland in 1983 remain an integral and powerful part of our family experience. Without their support, their camaraderie, their criticism, and their counterpoint, this book could not have been written.

I think next of Suzanne Theberge, Virginia Linkovich, and Sarah Jensen, staff members of the Department of Government at Bowdoin College, who worked assiduously on the manuscript: typing, proofreading, reorganizing, and retyping. In this regard I also express my appreciation to three Bowdoin students: Claire Curtis, research assistant for portions of the manuscript; and Penny Palevsky and Kevin Hawkins, who both worked diligently on bibliographical entries and indexing.

Then I move away, in my mind's eye, from the immediate, and I think of all those, especially in Poland, who in some way, large or small, contributed to my pool of information and to my thinking. I cannot list them here both for reasons of space and for subtler, political reasons. Yet my deepest thanks goes to each one.

Furthermore, several people have read all or part of the manuscript and have given me valuable critical commentary and suggestions. They are Wladyslaw Adamski, Andrzej Bryk, Adrian Hayes, Andrzej Korashevski, Marian J. Kostecki, Roman Laba, Henry Norr, Antoni Pospielszalski, and Jan Radomyski. I salute each of them for the independent and serious way in which they perused the manuscript. Needless to say, whatever errors of fact, concept, or judgment may be found in this work are entirely my responsibility and no fault of theirs.

I also extend my thanks to three institutions: Bowdoin College for financial and moral encouragement that helped make possible the visit to Poland in 1983 and a follow-up visit in 1985; Lock Haven State University for choosing me to lead its group of scholars and students at Marie Curie Sklodowska University in Lublin in 1983; and the Institute for European Studies for including me in their first seminar in Poland, whose topic was "Contemporary Problems of Poland," in 1985.

I save for last an acknowledgment to Beverly Jarrett, Associate Editor and Executive Director of Louisiana State University Press. By her steady encouragement and unremitting confidence in the work from the beginning, she was a very critical force in bringing this book into being.

Preface

The significance of Poland today lies in the presence there of a double paradox: the paradox of a communist state presiding over a nation that is in the Soviet orbit of power and yet not of it; and the paradox of a substantial social movement that is, and yet is not, revolutionary. This double paradox raises compelling questions about East-West relations and about the nature and future course of social change in a nuclear-stalemated world.

In Poland we are face to face, surely, with irony, and if with irony, then also with the tears of tragedy, of sweet hopes denied, and of bitter resignation, and with helpless laughter at the salient, ever more outrageous humor arising from the tangled travesties of daily existence.

But irony recedes, I discovered, as one understands the forces poised in conflict. Or perhaps it is more accurate to say that irony's tragedy and dark humor, though it does not disappear, gives way to another, more hidden aspect once one strives to look deeply into the Poland of today. Then one glimpses the promise contained in the irony: the promise of peace among nations instead of extinction, and the promise of nonviolent, transformational politics within nations.

In the twentieth century so much has been said about irony that the world now interprets it one-dimensionally and wallows in it. Scholars reinforce this interpretation because of a peculiar modernist tendency to transform "objective" fact into an icon and then, on bended knee, worship its brute image. Artists reinforce it because of their anger at duplicity and hypocrisy and because of their remorseless critical spirit, which requires them to scrape off all facades to reveal the incontinent mess beneath. The mess is often portrayed in their work as a cesspool of human contrarieties in which the gleams of truth, honesty, love, and purpose are allowed to flicker only to highlight more dramatically the descent of artist, and reader, into self-justified despair. Politicians trade in irony because they live in a world of fear and ego and, following Machiavelli, believe only in what they "see."

But the world of scholars, artists, and politicians hears too little about the promise revealed in apparently impermeable fact, in the seeming cesspool of real life, or in the crucible of immediate political action. That world resists turning irony around to see its other, more promising side. Perhaps what we need is the intellectual equivalent of a journey to the other side of the moon.

Beneath the irony of a social force that is and yet is not revolutionary, I see a deeply unified, nonviolent movement, confident in its inner meaning and purpose and seeking a settlement with the dominant structures of Polish Communist power. Beneath the geopolitical irony—and because of the nonrevolutionary revolution expressed in Solidarity—I see the possibility for East and West to wrench themselves free of constant confrontation. For neither side needs to feel that its nonnegotiable interests are at stake if it backs off politically and militarily from border regions such as Poland.

Depending on one's point of view, the changes each side is asked to accept in such situations as the one in Poland are negative to some extent, to be sure, but they are also positive. On the negative side the Soviets must accept changes in the practice and to a degree in the concept of the Party's hegemony in society. And the Americans must back off from visions of untrammeled freedom for capitalism. On the positive side each power can recognize in the proposed changes something that it prizes highly: the Soviets, the furtherance of social and economic rights; the Americans, the advance of civil and political rights.

So Poland, if such a backing off were to take place, could graduate to a new historical level: it could be a society containing structures that defend and facilitate both social and economic rights on one hand and civil and political rights on the other. Instead of being a threat to both sides, such a development could as readily be seen, and indeed nurtured, as a fresh answer to old and corrosive conflicts. Such experimentation in a border region could produce a historical model for the peaceful evolution of the systems of both sides toward their own unique mix of socioeconomic and civil and political rights.

Solidarity's colors, like those of Poland itself, are red and white. They symbolize the fate and the faith of a people poised in this historical moment between two camps, the red and the white. Polish society is both red and white—and neither. Its citizens are in the "great between."

Yet, Poland is not "between" one side and the other in any nicely juxtaposed way, as, for example, in the story of the donkey positioned equidistant between two stacks of hay. Poland is securely fastened to the Eastern power bloc. Even more significant, Poland has undergone a profound reconstruction of its society under Communist rule since World War II, and thus, any movement for substantial social and political change must, and inevitably will, take that reconstruction as its point of departure. I therefore make two arguments to critics of Solidarity, one intended primarily for a Western-oriented person and the other for an Eastern-oriented person.

To the Westerner I say that Solidarity is a red movement. Its redness (and note the lowercase "r") is revealed in many ways: It was, and in shadowed ways still is, a union, or series of unions throughout Poland, defending fundamental workers' rights. Second, its members are working people in a great variety of occupations, including some that extend beyond industrial work to those normally thought to belong to the intelligentsia, but all have in common the experience of being workers in a society in which virtually all production has been placed under state control. Third and most decisive, Solidarity breathes the air of ordinary people whose outlook in life is shaped by the fact that they are employees, not managers or administrators or entrepreneurs, and whose core consciousness is a workers' consciousness. It is a red movement. This may not be popular or even prudent to say out loud in circles consisting of admirers of Ronald Reagan and Margaret Thatcher. But that is what it is.

To the Easterner I say that Solidarity has learned a fundamental lesson: that a workers' union or a workers' society and state cannot realize itself or be successful unless there are basic civil and political guarantees for individuals and groups. These guarantees must not only appear in documents, but they must be practiced, and they must not only be practiced but institutionalized. This is the meaning of Solidarity's bid for independent, self-governing unions in 1980 and of its continuing challenge to Jaruzelski's regime to provide real channels of participation that protect workers in their civil and political being. This is not popular or even prudent to say in high Soviet circles. But, again, that is what Solidarity is.

Poland, through the long and continuing struggle of Solidarity and through the gradual and recently achieved victory of the moderates and liberals over the Stalinists and other hardliners in General Wojciech Jaruzelski's regime, has reached a point of historical readiness for a society that, on a red basis, can mix social and economic rights with civil and political rights. It is time for the world to understand that. The intention of this book is to show that this is so and to draw its consequences both for geopolitics and for the meaning of social change.

The words *Red* and *White* have had enormous significance in the world since the Bolshevik revolution of 1917 and the ensuing civil war. Red came to mean "real existing socialism" (a favored Soviet phrase) in a communist system of power. White came to be associated with a capitalist economy and a pluralist system of power. Following the Second World War, when two great blocs of nations formed under the leadership of the Soviet Union and the United States, there emerged two camps that were ideologically, militarily, economically, and geopolitically hostile to each other. Some border areas, such as Eastern Europe, were "assigned" to, or allowed to come under the aegis of, the Red, or Eastern, bloc. Other border areas, such as Iran and Greece, were understood to be within the White, or Western, bloc's sphere of influence. These arrangements have not stopped either side from playing destabilizing politics in the other's areas of vulnerability.

Relations between the Red and White blocs have had their relatively moderate moments, but the ingrained pattern of confrontation has not altered. It is an impasse that locks the world into a tightening spiral of destructive enmity.

Almost everyone agrees that prospects for peace in the world would improve if both superpowers could back off from sensitive areas of intense confrontation. These areas should be called border regions, not buffer zones. However, for such a backing off to become a live option in Moscow or Washington, each side must have some minimal confidence that a degree of letting go in a border region would not lead by overt or subtle stages to its absorption by the other side. Each side must also be convinced that such a course would not bring so much chaos that one or both sides would be sucked back into the vortex of the region's politics.

Thus, a mutual guarantee of the neutrality of a border country or region by the superpowers, though necessary, would not in itself be sufficient. In addition, the internal situation in that border region needs to be of a certain kind. Its politics and institutions, first, must pose no threat of pushing it over to either side and, second, must reveal a capacity to deal with its own problems effectively. For these circumstances to be present, there must be in turn some firm indication that a society is emerging in the region that is substantially different from either superpower's institutions and ideological orientation. And, a closely related point, this newly emerging society must have found within itself sufficient coherence to stand on its own.

There is at least one more vital condition that must be satisfied, especially in a border region that is already dominated by one side. The *method* pursued by the forces of change must be one that poses as small a threat as possible to the strategic interests of the dominating superpower, one that arouses its paranoia as little as possible. This method of change must also hold within itself the promise of future stability.

Solidarity, for all its historical modesty, has opened a new chapter in the book of political change. It has struck for the recovery, perhaps the attainment for the first time anywhere, of authentic subjectivity for ordinary people. Solidarity has sought to do so by stretching and bending, but not breaking, the general structures of "real existing socialism." It is a movement that anticipates a society different in politics, outlook, and institutions from that of either of the superpowers. But Solidarity also anticipates a society that incorporates elements that each superpower recognizes as something precious in its own society. Simultaneously, Solidarity conducts its campaign in a manner that strives to extract maximum adaptation of the dominant system with minimum strain and trauma. It resolutely pursues a policy of nonviolence.

In other words Solidarity satisfies those minimal conditions not only for renewal in Poland but for the development of a genuine, problem-solving, autonomous border region in a sensitive geopolitical area of superpower confrontation. By so much it invites the superpowers to think about backing off and to find the confidence to do it.

But there is one other enormous qualification: Solidarity must be *seen* to be this kind of movement. Unfortunately, it still tends to be viewed in terms of the old fixed hegemonical and ideological positions, by the politicians and pundits on both sides and by many scholars. I therefore seek to help create a new vision of Solidarity. Even if this vision, too, falls short of fully portraying Solidarity, as I am sure it does, it at least opposes the pervasive hegemonical and ideological viewpoints. By offering a new perspective, it may challenge those who are attentive to rethinking those viewpoints.

PART I

A FAMILY TRIP TO POLAND

1

Questions Before Departure

We waited in the morning chill of Brunswick, Maine, for the Greyhound bus that would take us to New York City on the first leg of our journey to Poland. It was early February, 1983. There were five of us: my wife, Carla; our three daughters, Kathryn, Margaret, and Elizabeth; and myself.

Poland! It was a strange country that lay somewhere over the horizon, and we felt that it was beyond our power to imagine what it would be like. Some of us had been to Europe, and in the 1960s some of us had spent three years in Africa. But the prospect of Poland was different, somehow more distant and more baffling. We had taken Polish lessons, enough to realize that this language was not like French, German, or Dutch. Not even Swahili seemed as different or as demanding as Polish. There was something about the language that amazed and bemused us: not only the new sounds and strange combinations of letters; and the intricate agreement, and therefore bewildering changes, in the endings of words; but also the way that the totality of a sentence or passage would seem to carry additional nuances and a range of meanings. The language challenged and often defeated our skill. It piqued our curiosity, making us wonder about the nature of the country, its people, and their history.

Furthermore, Poland, as a communist country, seemed in some ways a forbidden land. The relations between our government and the Polish government had been severely strained since the imposition of martial law in December, 1981, and had lately been getting even worse. Just after Christmas we had been informed by our stateside sponsoring institution, Lock Haven State University in Lock Haven, Pennsylvania, that their educational exchange program with the State University in Lublin was "on hold." A few weeks later we learned that it had been taken off "hold." With that knowledge, but not yet with the necessary visas, we were going to New York City. At that point we had little choice, having rented our house. Carla and I had each taken a leave of absence from our respective places of work. Kathryn, a junior at Brown, had similarly cut her material ties to that university.

Our mood of wonder tinged with anxiety was further heightened by the warnings we had received of the hardship of life in Poland. Food was scarce, and particular items, including medicine, soap, toothpaste, and toilet paper, were hard to obtain. So we had packed, and repacked, with an eye both to our minimal clothing needs and to devoting as much room as possible to these other items. The five of us ended up with fifteen relatively small bags, all stuffed to the gills. We were a somewhat amusing sight to our friends as we stood huddled among our bags at the bus stop on Pleasant Street.

On the curb the station master had placed several large bundles of newspapers, mostly the New York *Times*, ready for the bus to pick them up and take them we knew not where. A friend who spotted us on her way to work that morning later related that she had been surprised at all the bags and especially at the newspapers. She had thought that we were taking all those *Times*es with us to Poland!

Although this idea is wildly absurd, it nevertheless, with its theme of cross-cultural messages, fits well into the picture of us waiting there among the Maine snowbanks (there had been a blizzard the day before) and, with something of a shiver, looking into a future that would take us, by bus, taxi, plane, bus again, and then train, to Warsaw. For there lay before us a country in ferment. A powerful movement of revolt against the government had taken place only to be overwhelmed by military force. To go to Poland under such circumstances was more than a scholarly affair, more than a journey of adventure, more than "a junior year abroad." It had about it a strong whiff of politics. As we rode the bus to New York, had our visas granted at the last minute by the Polish consulate, and boarded an Icelandic Airways jet for Luxembourg and points east, we became increasingly aware that, as American citizens in a communist country in ferment, our words, manners, and actions would inevitably carry more messages than we might intend. On the other hand, we felt that we could learn much not only about a very different language and culture and about life "over there" in a communist nation and about whether we could take some harsh, "gray" living, but also about the ferment.

Looking back, I feel that the social and political ferment in Poland was the reason that finally and truly drew us there. We had all been caught up in various crosscurrents of social change in the 1960s and 1970s and had been marked by them. When the momentous events took place in Poland in 1980, I was first astonished, then intrigued. Here was a phenomenon, I felt, that might yield understanding of the contemporary human predicament, East and West. It might lead to new knowledge that could be applied to one's own life and politics.

Or so I hoped. I was frustrated with American politics. There seemed to be a cloying immaturity about the progressive forces in American society. They expended themselves in protest movements, in piecemeal reform activities, or in doctrinaire politics that spawned sectarian rivalries. It seemed that neither the protesters, the reformers, nor the sectarians were able to translate their remarkable energy and intense activity into an effective, responsible political force; nor were any of them even able to have a steady impact on the policy makers who ran the government or the economy. Neither protest, reform, nor doctrinaire prescription seemed adequate.

Perhaps if I looked over "the Wall," I might at least discover something about attempts to change the structure of "real existing socialism"; that is, I would start from the other side to see what was involved in changing *their* system. Communist countries, Poland and Hungary and China, for example, were trying to encourage and integrate market conceptions and mechanisms into their state-run economies. Leftist critics in America, on the other hand, were arguing over the need to do something about the ideology and practices of our market economy. What did this something entail? Was the insistence, by some of the more ideological voices, on the socialization of property or the nationalization of industry really an answer? Was the counterinsistence by self-styled pragmatic liberal reformers to keep the market basically intact any less inadequate?

So I went to Poland interested in "economic reform." The government there had been touting this phrase for some time, and it seemed worth examining, at least as a beginning point. But, as I knew, the focus could not remain limited to economic reform. It had to include the ferment, and the center of that ferment, the Solidarity movement.

Solidarity had been in the news. As we boarded the bus, it was in fact world famous. And as with all superstars, Solidarity was already as much a myth as a movement.

But in spite of the myths about Solidarity conjured up by friend and foe on both sides of the Iron Curtain, I felt that I knew a few significant things about the movement. I had been following the Polish situation in the newspapers, going to lectures, talking with Poles recently back from Poland, and reading journal articles and books. I believed that Solidarity was basically a movement of industrial workers, led by a gallant, charismatic figure. Its demands for autonomy of labor unions, for a kind of collective bargaining, and for the right to strike had been surprisingly, even miraculously, granted in the famous Gdansk Accord of August, 1980. Those demands had then escalated into the political realm, precipitously, I felt, and in spite of Lech Walesa's efforts at moderation. This escalation had continued to a point where the communist party-state felt vulnerable enough to resort to a long-planned military crackdown. The crackdown, I supposed, was carried out more or less on direct orders from Moscow, but it was also an action taken by Poles themselves to preclude the overt intervention of Russian troops and tanks.

To my mind *Le Monde* and the *Guardian* generally described these events quite well, and they reinforced my thinking about what had happened in Poland. In *Le Monde* André Fontaine wrote of the crackdown of December, 1981: "Things would probably not have got to this point if some sections of the Polish population had not been intoxicated by success in the past few months; if they had not thought to ignore the sad geographical reality that turns their country into a stepping-stone of the Soviet empire; if they had taken time to digest the many concessions they had wrested instead of continuing to press on even harder with their challenges to the government and the Party and, over them, to the Great Protector." And the *Guardian* wrote: "The increasingly political challenges to the legitimacy of the regime were genuine enough. The weekend demands [made prior to the institution of martial law] from Gdansk for a referendum on whether the people accepted the government, wanted free elections for a new administration, or whether they were prepared to guarantee Soviet 'military interest' shoved too hard against a decayed and unstable structure."[1]

This perception of a headstrong Solidarity was and is more widespread than I realized. It dominated and continues to influence heavily the image Solidarity has among its enemies—and among many of its friends. The latter are often in disagreement on important aspects of the movement, but many are united in perceiving it as a volatile and imprudent movement. Later I was to learn more about the *Guardian*'s report. It was written by the paper's Warsaw correspondent, Hella Pick, an admirer of former leader Edward Gierek and later of Jaruzelski. She had heard the demand of a few members of Solidarity for a referendum on Poland's Soviet connection and mistakenly made it seem that the entire movement was making that demand.[2]

Jaruzelski's defenders used the image of Solidarity as a radicalized movement to explain and justify the resort to martial law. They thought that Solidarity had gone to extremes, as is typical of a disjointed, undisciplined mass of working people who, after gaining redress on certain legitimate bread-and-butter demands and issues involving the unions, had been led astray into the complex world of politics by ambitious, self-appointed leaders. Many of these leaders were alienated intellectuals. Lech Walesa, a moderate, had become their virtual prisoner. Jaruzelski, by moving as he did and when he did, had saved Poland from anarchy and from the bloodbath that would surely have followed a direct Russian intervention.[3]

For their part, Western bankers used the image of a headstrong Solidarity to defend their refusal, in the period before martial law, to negotiate Poland's mounting, massive debt. The Warsaw government owed some five hundred Western banks $16 billion and Western governments $11 billion. After the imposition of martial law, the bankers used the same image to rationalize the unseemly haste with which they then proceeded to negotiate the debt with Jaruzelski's government. Bankers felt that Solidarity's rise and its mounting pressure on the government provoked too many strikes, lowered production, and destabilized the economy. With Jaruzelski in control, there would be, they assumed, greater labor discipline, reduced consumption, increased prices, and thus a more solid basis for guaranteeing interest payments and repayment. In January, 1983, the *Nation* quoted the remark of a West German banker: "I now see the chance for Poland to return to a more normal working schedule and this could be a good thing for the banks." Yves Laulan of the French Société Generale called martial law "a way of getting out of the impasse." The Bank of America's Bernard Butcher said, "Whoever is running the country, we must wish them the best and hope there's some return to a productive economy."[4]

The intimation is clear enough. Solidarity gets blame, perhaps the major blame, for the condition into which the country had fallen. Yet, such a conclusion is not self-evident. Jadwiga Staniszkis, for example, argued in my interview with her in Warsaw in May, 1983, that few if any more man hours were lost on the job in Poland in 1981 because of strikes than in Western European countries. She and others have also noted that job performance since the crackdown has been in a severely depressed state largely because of the catastrophic loss of morale. They cite, for example, the increased consumption of vodka and the growing incidence of alcoholism, phenomena that were in abeyance during the days of Solidarity.

But it is not only enemies and skeptics who took, and continue to take, this posture with Solidarity. Many of its friends do likewise, as is evident from the judgments of *Le Monde* and the *Guardian*. I have chosen four other examples to show how pervasive is this tendency, which Czeslaw Milosz called "getting angry at the losers."[5] Writing of the period after World War II in Poland, he noted that many writers and scholars, in bowing down to "history," turned their frustration on the losers, and on themselves, in order to rationalize the new order and their own ultimate acceptance of it.

The first example is a book I read that was passed hand to hand in a clandestine fashion while I was in Poland—Leszek Szymanski's *Candle for Poland: 469 Days of Solidarity*.[6] Szymanski, an intellectual and an activist, was pushed out of Poland in 1968 and is now living in California. The study tries to show the forces and personalities in conflict as the situation evolved to its stark denouement in December, 1981. He concludes that Solidarity overreached itself. Although he brings the major factors into view, including the turgidity and prevarication of the party-state regime and the prickly sensitivity of the Kremlin, nevertheless the final impression left by the analysis is that the blame lies with Solidarity: it was overly headstrong, too zealous, too politically inexperienced.

The second example is the myth of heroic action that supposedly lodges deeply in the Polish character. Poles are tragically fated to rush into defiance of the oppressor against impossible odds—so goes the myth. One's mind flashes back, for example, to the picture of dashing aristocratic figures on horseback sharing the field of battle with German tanks at the beginning of World War II. The struggle of Solidarity is made to seem yet another evocation of the myth. The judgment that emerges from this mythologizing of the movement is that once again the Poles were too impulsive, that they had more passion than common sense. Some will toast in praise; others reprove in blame.But the underlying point is the same: it was Solidarity, the Polish opposition, that failed.

A third example arose from the visit to Poland in the fall of 1984 of a leading Western politician and democratic socialist, Greek Prime Minister Andreas Papandreau. After being feted by Jaruzelski and having avoided any meeting with Lech Walesa, he stated: "Solidarity had all the elements that could lead to peaceful reform, which would have required considerable time. . . . Movements that are revolutionary, that aim for change of great scope, should know when to do what. If the progressive, radical movements are not in a position to operate within the existing framework of historical possibilities, then they become negative and dangerous, because then there is regression. Unfortunately, that is my opinion of Solidarity."[7] This opinion is more widely shared than one might think among democratic socialists in Western Europe, though it is not often expressed so overtly. One sees the sentiment reflected in Willy Brandt's visit to Poland in the fall of 1985, especially in his refusal to meet with Walesa. Brandt was not so abrasive as Papandreau in his excuse. Yet it is clear that part of his motivation derived from a set of ambivalent feelings about Solidarity that makes western Europeans on the left suspicious of the movement and therefore less unwilling to deal with the communist government. Witness as well French President Mitterand's reception for Jaruzelski in Paris in the fall of 1985.

A final example is an article by A. M. Rosenthal in the *New York Times Magazine*.[8] In May, 1983, he had returned to Poland for a visit after an absence of twenty-four years. He had been New York *Times* correspondent in Warsaw in 1958–1959, and had been expelled for what the Polish Foreign Office described as "exposing too deeply the internal situation in Poland." As Rosenthal observed, "That was an indictment in Polish Communist terms, a citation in Western."

Since Rosenthal was in Poland during my stay there and since I had just gotten back to the United States when his article appeared, I was eager to see what he thought. I certainly recognized his description of the dreariness of life, the lack of prospects, and the failures of the economy dressed up as "shortages." I identified with his anger at the blatant inequality among consumers that is institutionalized in the Pewex stores (650 of them throughout Poland), in which one can buy coveted goods and high-quality merchandise, but only if he or she has dollars or other hard currencies available to the few. I laughed ruefully with him at a joke current among Poles, which he had heard from a writer and I from a hospital intern. The joke opens with the assertion that living under Polish communism contributes wonderfully to longevity. To the inevitable question "Oh, how so?" comes the answer: "After you become an adult, you have to wait fifteen years for an apartment, eight years for an automobile, seven years for a telephone, fourteen for a refrigerator, twenty for a passport," and so on. "So all in all," goes the conclusion, "in order to live a full Polish life, you have to live to be at least 110."

But most of all I recognized something of myself in the overriding question with which he came to Poland, which he reports as having asked again and again: "So every place I met Solidarity people or their sympathizers—and that was almost everywhere—I asked the same questions: Did you really expect the Russians to allow Poles to shape their own society in freedom? Didn't you know they never have and never will? And how did you think you would succeed without Russian permission? Have you come to believe you really live on the moon?"[9]

I believe Rosenthal's article is an important one. It is well written and was widely read and favorably commented on. The man himself was at the top of the hierarchy of the New York *Times*, a newspaper with enormous influence throughout the Western world, indeed the whole world. His thinking reflects an enlightened and sophisticated cold warriorism that dominates the minds of many in the Western establishment. It was a bemusing experience for me, on my return from Poland, to read Rosenthal's article. For had not his question been my question, too?

Both of us had been seized by a similar impulse: to pose to the members of Solidarity the primary question, to put them, as it were, on trial before the court of history, and to hold in the mind's eye all other forces as unchanging and unchangeable (and hence nonresponsible) monoliths in the background. True enough, Rosenthal saw "all other forces" as meaning the Russians and only the Russians, whereas I, to some degree then and much more so now, took into consideration a whole range of other forces, including especially the dual role of the United States and the Soviet Union.

All of these examples suggest that across the spectrum of interests, perspectives, and ideologies there was, and continues to be, a widespread inclination, West and East, in and out of Poland, whether in praise or blame, in pride or shame, to score Solidarity as the element that in the final analysis failed the test of—call it what you will—political savvy, pragmatic realism, or suitable caution and prudence. And however convinced I was that Solidarity was on the right track, however much I identified with it in my political imagination as a new and creative force in the world, however much I abhorred the actions of Jaruzelski and the oppressive paranoia of the Kremlin and the feeble maneuverings of Washington, nevertheless the bottom line for me was that Solidarity (perhaps not unexpectedly) had failed to understand the processes of social change, that it had not sufficiently studied the Czech example of 1968, and that in short Solidarity's political ineptitude cost the movement its historic opportunity. Fundamentally, I agreed with Rosenthal that the people in Solidarity must have thought they were living on the moon.

So I went to Poland wanting to find out if this was so.

I also wished to find out what I could of the social philosophies that inspired Solidarity or were inspired by Solidarity. I wanted to see if perhaps they might reveal the contours of a new approach to socioeconomic organization and correlative political formations—a third way significantly different from both communism as practiced in the East and capitalism as practiced in the West. I reasoned that Solidarity would have interesting and possibly instructive ideological and programmatic offshoots, which might prove useful in a general way to the theory and practice of a new political economy, one neither capitalist nor communist.

Was Solidarity too headstrong? What were its social doctrines? In asking these questions, I was not totally off the mark. Perhaps they were as good as any other questions to start with. Yet, the questions themselves changed profoundly under the impact of being in Poland. What changed as well was my view of change itself: the relation of force to social change and of the oppressed to the oppressor, the relation of theories and doctrines to practice and of intellectuals to social movements, the relation of the state to society, and perhaps above all the relation of subject to object. This relation between subject and object became much more real for me as I observed Solidarity's epochal demand for genuine subjectivity and as I wrestled in Poland with the subject-object dualism in myself that I had to understand if I was ever to grasp the meaning of what I saw and experienced. Out of it came what I feel is a more critical and at the same time more passionate appreciation of Solidarity. I came to believe that the lesson Solidarity has to offer is not only crucial to Poland's fate but to the future political evolution of our species.

2
Questions Overturned

"Poland teaches you lessons you didn't come here to learn," said Alma Yoray, an American friend, about a month after our arrival. A performer of modern dance, she had arrived the previous November to work with Polish artists. She became ill and had, in fact, been near death in a hospital in Wroclaw, a city in the southwestern part of the country. We met her in Warsaw at the apartment of some Polish friends just before her flight home. She looked frail but deeply animated. Alma has the aura of a seer, and her words on that bone-chilling Sunday afternoon in March had the bite of prophecy.

We lived in Lublin, a city of several hundred thousand people in southeastern Poland. We had arrived in mid-February in a blizzard after a twenty-three-hour train ride from Frankfurt to Warsaw and a ride in the wee hours in a van the rest of the way with Leszek Kolek of our host university's English department. At Warsaw station we had been met by friends of a friend in the United States. They had insisted on a midnight repast with them in their Warsaw home, complete with brandy and vodka. It was a brilliant introduction to Polish hospitality and friendship. A similar scene took place the next day—actually less than twelve hours later—at the home of Professor Grzegorz Seidler, the Polish godfather of the educational exchange program between Lock Haven State University and Marie Curie Sklodowska University.

Lublin is an ancient provincial capital, more staid and more traditional than Warsaw. The latter is rife with the rumor, intrigue, and rapid swings of mood of a national capital. In that sense Lublin may be closer to the general or typical life and mood of the country as a whole. Lublin's population had changed with the coming of World War II. Before the war almost half its population had been Jews, but now only a small plaque remains in the city to recall their presence and their achievements. However, nearby is Maidonek, the Nazi concentration camp, now a museum honoring the Poles, Jews, gypsies, and many others who suffered and died there.

Lublin's population swelled with the great industrial and commercial expansion that followed the war. People from the countryside and from eastern areas given up to Russia flocked to this important city. Lublin had been the temporary seat of the provisional government of Poland set up by Polish Communists who returned from Russia with Stalin's troops as the war was coming to an end. Partly for this reason I expected pro-Solidarity sentiment not to be as vigorous there as, for example, in Gdansk or Wroclaw. This expectation turned out to be wrong.

We visited several cities and towns: Krakow, Wroclaw, Poznan, Gdansk, Radom, and Zamosc, as well as Warsaw. I made five trips to Warsaw, twice for extended visits of a week to ten days. We five were each involved in Polish life in somewhat different ways. We constantly compared notes and each of us kept a journal, so we received a varied impression of the people and the country. It was not a single impression nor merely a series of discrete impressions, but a multiple exposure that continuously changed, growing as the weeks and months went by.

Our two older daughters, who quickly came to be known as Kasia (Kathryn) and Gosia (Margaret), studied Polish culture, history, and politics at the university. They lived together in a small room in one of the university dormitories. Our youngest daughter, Elizabeth, was also soon endowed with her Polish name, Ella. For the first six to eight weeks she had little to do and was bored. Gradually, however, she became involved in helping high school students learn conversational English. Several became friends. She was also invited to the parties and other activities at the university among her sisters' friends. Her life—from being a boring affair—became very busy, and consequently she learned much Polish.

Ella, Carla, and I lived in a small third-floor apartment on a once elegant street, now a busy thoroughfare whose air is thick with the daily discharge of a thousand trucks and buses. We were a brisk twenty-minute walk from the university. Carla took the lead in learning the tortuous art of shopping for our daily needs, which involved communicating in a difficult tongue and visiting shops where paucity and bureaucracy often unite to thwart the most persistent and patient character. Fortunately, such staples as bread (extremely good and very cheap even by Polish standards) and milk and eggs were readily available in a store on the first floor of our apartment building. Later, when I became ill, Carla would have to shop at apothecaries for medicine. This is an especially daunting task, for though medicine is inexpensive, it is hard to get. The lines are long at all times of the day and the seemingly ingrained "nie ma" ("there is none") attitude of the attendants often leaves you in a daze of stupefaction and despair.

After a while it seemed to us that the shortages, the lines, and the "nie ma" attitudes, though doubtless induced by the virtual collapse of the economy in an objective sense, were nevertheless also part of a general policy pursued by the authorities. Their intent, or rather what may have been their surrender to the easiest way consistent with the retention of their dominance and privileges, seemed to be to reduce the dimensions of life as much as possible to a permanent condition of banality—colorless, shapeless, and pointless. This was the texture of the crisis as we felt it in February and March.

Carla teaches in an ungraded, open-school program that began in the public school system of Freeport, Maine, in the early 1970s. She was eager to learn about the general character of Polish education. She worked her way through certain layers of bureaucracy and was able to visit classrooms in different primary schools. She got to know a number of the teachers well enough to have some good conversations, mostly comparing primary school education in Poland and the United States. Some of the exchanges touched on politics, the "forgotten" subject. She also took a lot of pictures and traveled extensively, more than I was able to.

All five of us worked with the Polish language. We had daily two-hour sessions with an inspiring teacher, Teresa Ochab. Carla and I were both disappointed that more did not rub off on us. We remained neophytes. But our daughters gained a degree of proficiency in reading and speaking that was the envy of their parents and a source of great satisfaction to many Poles.

When we first arrived and for many weeks thereafter, we heard nothing of Solidarity or of Lech Walesa. We did not mention these names in our conversations, nor did our hosts bring them up, though on occasion there seemed to be allusions and glances referring to their existence, together with significant pauses. There was a poster with the forbidden word SOLIDARNOSC on the bulletin board of the Catholic University in Lublin one day in late February when I went to do my first interview. It was gone the next day. That interview was the first time in public or private that I had a political discussion with a Pole. A week earlier, on a crowded train from Warsaw to Lublin, a young Canadian had talked openly about Solidarity. My wife and daughters shot me reproving glances, trying to get us to shut up. Later they said they had been watching people's faces and bodily attitudes. There had been plenty of suppressed interest, even across the barrier of language, they felt, but they had been afraid that some of the passengers were special or secret police. A group of soldiers sitting quietly not far off added to that impression.

We assumed that our apartment was bugged. Later an American assured us that some person among the people we had gotten to know was surely a spy whose job it was to report on our activities. On one occasion Carla and I were having lunch in a restaurant with a Polish colleague. He was telling us about his experiences during the German occupation in World War II. Suddenly the direction of his conversation changed, though his tone remained the same. "Just behind you," he said, meaning me, "behind that pillar, there is sitting a spy who is listening to every word." So we lived in an atmosphere of reticence and doubt. There was a silence about politics that seemed very political. There was also a suffused sense of surveillance. This, along with the frugality and privation of daily living, the dour, shabby look of winter, and the sheer absence of color and variety in public places, made life seem dreary, forlorn, and threatening.

But we were sustained by the hospitality and ebullience of individual Poles—and by the fact that they could show such spirit in the face of suffering. They dressed surprisingly well, perhaps because they still had good clothes left over from the 1970s, perhaps because they make black-market visits to Budapest (and even Frankfurt), or perhaps because they have a knack for elegance. Or it might have been because they are "naturally vain," as I once observed jokingly, noticing the mirrors that seem to be everywhere, in front of which both men and women will unself-consciously check their appearance and even preen a little. We had been prepared for the displays of Old World manners, such as the greeting ceremonial in which men lightly kiss the hand of the woman. This and other survivals from the eclipsed aristocratic culture seemed to be practiced gracefully by this new generation of Poles who had been reared in a new, antiaristocratic, industrial age presided over by the comrades of "real existing socialism" and their vision of the new pro-

letarian man. Only later, and gradually, did we realize that kissing the
hand of a woman and other manifestations of gentility are subtle ways in
which Poles express their opposition to the prevailing regime and by so
much sustain a sense of themselves and their own history. These simple
gestures were, we discovered, themselves symptoms of a crisis in the body
politic.

In 1984 Michael T. Kaufman wrote in the New York *Times* that the
Polish ceremony of hand kissing had developed into a political act. He
quoted a Polish writer who stated, "Obviously, to some extent hand
kissing is a profession of nationalism." The writer went on to observe that
the practice has been discarded as archaic or snobbish in all of Poland's
communist neighbors. In the Soviet Union, he emphasized, "No one
kisses women's hands." So of course the Poles do. But the ceremony also
has a deeper political significance than this immediate, anti-Soviet one.
It signifies the blend of ancient or traditional culture, which is aristocratic, and the egalitarian or leveling impetus that has taken place under
communism. Kaufman noted that "in Poland truck drivers, coal miners,
police officers, professors, journalists, party sympathizers and Solidarity
activists all kiss the hands of women upon meeting, and women all
routinely extend their hands to be kissed." Kaufman quotes the writer
again: "It is a brilliant irony that under forty years of communism, in
terms of manners at least, classes have not so much been levelled as
elevated, so now we all try to behave like princes." This includes even
Jaruzelski. During the campaign for local elections in June, 1983, Kaufman reports, the general "was often shown on television kissing the hands
of female shoppers and workers, just like a Polish noble of the 18th
century." He, too, thus seemed to be "adjusting" to the national and
subtly anticommunist nuances of such kissing.[1]

In addition to such displays of Old World manners, we were enlivened
by the adventures with vodka that our hosts encouraged us to undertake.
Their gentility could turn to force in this regard, as they waved away our
protests and filled our glasses for the second, third, and fourth time. We
were also sustained by a small but omnipresent antidote to the system's
banality—the daily multitude of cut flowers available on every street
corner. These are gaily, often tenderly, displayed in homes, shops,
schools, offices, factories, and churches and on carefully scrubbed grave-
stones.

Most of all we were sustained by the fact that this was for us an unusual adventure, and much of the impact of the experience had to do with the silence about politics. We felt this silence. It was like a mask, even though we did not know exactly what was behind it, who wore it and who did not, or when it might, however briefly, tilt this way or that or come off altogether.

On Thursday afternoons we attended informal seminars on Polish life and culture and on the response of individual Americans to being in Poland. These seminars were proposed by Professor Seidler at that first gathering at his apartment twelve hours after we arrived. He suggested that Elizabeth, our youngest daughter, start things off at the first seminar with a short statement about her first impressions of Poland. She readily agreed, captivated by the persuasive powers of the old man (he wanted me to call him "Uncle," which I did) and, perhaps, by the unfamiliar but welcome spirit of vodka on a Sunday afternoon. Her sisters followed suit on successive Thursdays; later, in the spring, Carla spoke to the seminar on her impressions of Polish education.

At first it was unclear who would be attending the seminars in addition to Seidler and the small group of Americans who were associated with the Lock Haven program—four professors, five students, and several spouses and children. At the first seminar, as Elizabeth was about to begin, she noticed that with the exception of Seidler, only Americans were present, and she then asked where "everybody" was, meaning Poles. Seidler immediately sent out word for people to join us. Several junior faculty quickly came in, and at later meetings other senior faculty did, too. Seidler at that time (he is now in semiretirement and a member of the Sejm, the national parliament) was a senior professor of law and political philosophy. He had earlier been rector (president) of the university. He is an erudite, widely published scholar, a lively, brilliant thinker, and a stellar member of the Communist party. He has extensive connections with Western scholars and leaders. At the get-acquainted meeting in his apartment, he mentioned several well-known Western scholars whom he knows, including Eugene Rostow, Isaiah Berlin, and David Easton. He was, and is, one of a small group of intellectuals in Poland who actively and staunchly defend Jaruzelski. During the first four Saturdays of our stay he invited me to his home to discuss the history of political philosophy (political doctrines, as he calls them), his conception of the movement of history, and what he considers Lenin's pathbreaking role in resolving the modern conflict between elites and masses.

Several times during those early sessions of the seminar, the talk would inch up to politics and Solidarity, but then it would veer away from direct encounter with the subject, which we found tantalizing and frustrating. We were treated to the Polish art of giving "hints," a word Seidler used to describe what he said was a characteristic and ancient Polish style of communication. Junior faculty especially would give hints about whither their thoughts were drifting by speaking of "those days" or "before the war" or "the recent events"—all euphemisms for the sixteen months in 1980–1981 during which Solidarity was legal. Later, in April, an American professor boldly discussed Solidarity in his presentation to the seminar. He said that it must seem a great betrayal to Poles that Solidarity should suffer the fate of suppression. By that time, we knew that most of the people in the room, with the important exception of Seidler, had been members of Solidarity. Although it was evident that they felt some constraint, on this occasion they talked openly about the crisis. Seidler made a powerful and moving response to the American's presentation.

At first my primary activity was lecturing on international politics with the help of a very capable interpreter and fellow political scientist, Jacek Pietras. One such event was sponsored by the university's Students for the United Nations. In May I gave a lecture on the structural determinants of American foreign policy to professors in law and social science at the university's political science institute. Earlier in the semester I participated in an international relations seminar. I was told that I was the leader of the Lock Haven State University contingent at the university, but the role seemed to lack definition.

Soon after we arrived, I sought to get on with my major concern, interviewing, but an illness delayed me. By mid-April, however, I got started in earnest. My declared purpose in arranging the interviews was to explore the government's plans for economic reform. Many if not most of the interviews led to discussions of the general crisis of the country and the Solidarity phenomenon. My initial contacts were based on names obtained from knowledgeable people in the United States before I left. These led to other contacts and then to others and so on. Eventually I would interview several dozen people in government and university circles and among the general population. Some favored Solidarity, others opposed it, and still others preferred being neutral. All together they provided a great range of vantage points from which to view the crisis.

As the weeks went by, our new friends and acquaintances gradually became more accustomed to us. We likewise lost some of our own reserve and caution. Voices grew bolder and references to Solidarity more direct. We were soon amazed at how pervasive and deep the feelings about Solidarity were. We felt it as a powerful force just below the surface of the outward masks.

In April we were returning from an afternoon spent at the home of a friend. He escorted us to the trolley stop and seemed to take advantage of the noise to tell me that in Lublin alone there were seven underground printing presses. Later we learned that some four hundred Solidarity newspapers are printed in Poland. Most professors at the university had been members. The university's rector during the days when Solidarity was legal had been a strong advocate and member of the movement. He was later removed from the rectorship, but he continued to teach at the university. Seventy percent of the teachers at a leading local high school were part of Solidarity, we learned from a person who taught there. We were assured that this figure was matched at other schools. A local Communist party organization had taken a lead in the Horizontalist movement of 1980–1981, we were told. This movement had been a vigorous but unsuccessful effort within the Party to transform it into a democratic, grass-roots organization in alliance with Solidarity. Various individuals whom we had supposed were much too conservative by temperament or outlook to be mixed up with a radical labor movement had been staunch members of Solidarity.

From the students our daughters were getting to know and from other contacts, we learned how strongly students generally identified with Solidarity. But they now felt intensely frustrated because along with the crushing of Solidarity had come the diminution of their life prospects. The economic downturn seemed permanent, and the restrictions on everyday life by the regime were like a gray cloud on their lives that would never go away. Some were growing cynical. Others fought the temptation to become a part-time spy for the government. Not a few succumbed. Still others seemed to maintain a spiritual liveliness and determination and a scarcely concealed defiance that we marveled at. One young man told us of a friend of his who had been called up to serve in the army. He was with several others from Lublin at an officers' training school. One day a leading figure in the army gave a lecture to the officer candidates. He got carried away with his attempt to underscore the danger of the Western threat to Poland's sovereignty. West German intelligence, he maintained, was trying to infiltrate western Poland with a view to taking it over someday; the British were doing the same in central Poland, he went on, and the Americans were aiming for control of eastern Poland. At the mention of the Americans, there was a sudden burst of applause from the Lublin contingent. (Lublin is in eastern Poland.) Our friend did not tell us what happened next. Perhaps the story is merely apocryphal; still, the bite of anger and defiance beneath the laughter goes deep.

I spent Good Friday (April Fool's Day, as it turned out) in an empty hospital room. I was in the hospital for a checkup to determine if pains I had been having were indications of heart trouble. It turned out they were caused by a hiatus hernia in the stomach—benign but troublesome. My two Polish companions in the adjoining beds had left. The hospital staff was at a minimum, since everyone who was able was spending the evening with their kin. A doctor came to see me, and after some talk about my physical state he quickly turned the conversation to politics. Gradually I realized he was taking advantage of the situation—no one was around. He bluntly and powerfully expressed his disgust at, and defiance of, the present regime. He recalled the scores of injuries he had had to treat during and since the crackdown following the declaration of martial law. He sought words to show his determination to continue his resistance. "They are two million," he said, "or three at most, and we are thirty million." As he spoke, I observed him closely. He was a successful professional, a man whom I would have pegged as ambitious and career-oriented. Would such a man as this in America be so political? Yet here he was, a brilliant, busy professional, pouring out his yearnings for freedom and dignity. I felt I was face to face with the elemental, the irreducible. What was life for—my life, his life, any life? What was it if it had to be lived in fear and cringing, if there were no hope at all of reaching a life of freedom and dignity, for oneself and with others, together in a self-respecting community? I felt a bond. I also felt helpless. Eventually he stopped talking, and we parted, he to his rounds and I to the emptiness of my room.

We were learning, as much through inadvertence and the experience of daily life as from conscious effort to find out, that Solidarity was no fledgling movement. Although young, it had hardly been "born yesterday." Its antecedents stretched back through the decades of Communist rule and before, to centuries of rebellion against internal and external oppression. We learned how closely the Poles link Solidarity's struggle with all the previous uprisings in Communist Poland: the anti-Stalinist outburst in 1956; the protests of students and intellectuals in 1968; the rebellion of industrial workers in 1970; and the combined protests of students, intellectuals, and industrial workers in 1976. To the people we saw around us and with whom we rubbed shoulders, Solidarity was the natural heir to those movements.

It became clear to us that Solidarity was not limited to one social stratum, class, or group, such as industrial workers. Instead it embraced most segments of the society: blue- and white-collar workers, farmers, scholars, clerics, professionals, and students. Nor did it seem to be a movement pieced together out of an accumulation of many separate, particular grievances that just happened to spring up at the same time. We were familiar with grievance politics, having participated in several single-issue protest campaigns in the United States. We were familiar with efforts to achieve a coalition of such protest groups. But here the particular grievances of individuals and groups spilled over and into a demand that, though it included a particular grievance, extended beyond it and beneath it into broader territory—into fundamental political concerns. For a while we thought it could be expressed as a demand for selfhood, for that is the way it struck us. Such a demand could mean selfhood for the country of Poland, for the nation as a people with a language and a culture going back a thousand years. It could mean the right of every person to be treated with a basic respect by the authorities. Or it could mean the selfhood of unions and associations, of universities and churches. All of these meanings seemed to be present in almost all cases and to be connected internally with one another.

Later I would drop the word *selfhood* in favor of the term *subjectivity*, a word that emerges from a tradition of Marxist humanism, even leftist

Hegelianism, and that seems more appropriate to the Polish context and Solidarity's struggle. It is not accidental that Pope John Paul II repeatedly used the word *subject* in the many stirring sermons he addressed to ten million Polish people during his halcyon visit in June, 1983.[2]

We saw that in each case of grievance and protest and in each implicit demand for selfhood, the target of anger was the same. That target was the state, as the omnipresent employer and wielder of coercive force, and simultaneously the Party, as the dominant force in the State. And the anger carried beyond the Polish party-state to what was perceived to be the real hegemony, the Russian party-state.

We sensed that the phenomenon we were daily encountering was a politically self-conscious, albeit diffused and decentralized, and now muted and suppressed sentiment of the great majority of Polish people. They were agreed about their opposition to the existing system of power. They demanded—when and where they could—a substantial change in the ordering of the state, a change in the direction of greater respect for selfhood, or subjectivity, for the nation, for the union and association, and for the social person.

Such thoughts began to push themselves into our minds as April's balmy weather continued into May. But I was still on the track of my original question—why had Solidarity been so pushy and headstrong? In other words, I sought evidence to demonstrate the contrary. I sought evidence of caution. Actually, I wanted to show that it was Jaruzelski who had acted with unnecessary haste and arbitrariness in his sudden imposition of martial law in December, 1981. I wanted to make a case that if he had tried harder to negotiate in good faith with Solidarity, he and the movement could have worked out a satisfactory compromise. Indeed, some of the people I interviewed, though only some, staunchly argued this. Bitter at Jaruzelski, they were convinced that he could have waited at least until the spring of 1982. He could have given Solidarity somewhat more time and scope, and some genuine recognition as a force to be reckoned with, and thus eased some of the pressure on Walesa from his left wing. This would have allowed a gradual softening of Solidarity and a corresponding shift in the matrix of forces in which Jaruzelski was himself embedded. A Polish solution acceptable to all sides might have been the result. Such an interpretation, I felt, would be strengthened by evidence of Solidarity's own prudence and sobriety.

But staring us in the face was evidence not of prudence but of intoxication—and not from vodka. Nor was it an intoxication just of "some
sections of the Polish population," to recall Fontaine's judgment in *Le
Monde*. It was an intoxication of most sections of society. The vestiges of
it were all around us in 1983. We could readily infer, and more and more
Poles confirmed the inference, that "in those days" there was rampant in
the land a spirit of confidence and certainty of purpose that at the time
must have seemed overwhelming. Even loyal party careerists, seeing
which way the wind was blowing, were joining Solidarity.

A person whom we all grew to like and respect, and who was especially
close to Carla, told her in a moment of candor that, however cautious or
concerned about consequences they had felt they ought to be, there had
been no doubt in their minds where they belonged: with Solidarity. The
reality of the Russians would have to fit in to some degree, however
minimally. One could not just wave a magic wand and reverse history.
But in a way it had felt as if ordinary Poles had joined history and that as a
nation of people, and as people of the nation, they were finding themselves. Renewal was for them already happening—not something to be
gained in the future.

A man who had been a student "before the war" spoke to me at length
of a powerful tide that caught up almost everyone. You could feel it, he
said, as if it were gripping the whole country. There seemed to be no
stopping the movement, since virtually everyone was with it or running
fast to catch up. The thought of the Russians, though important, took
second place to this vital fundamental affirmation. It was a heady, contagious discovery that was made by the great majority of the people as the
months of 1981 rolled by. True, there was a wearying of mood as fall
advanced into winter, he recalled. The stalement of forces had created a
virtual political vacuum in the country, which blunted the confidence
that something positive could happen. But there was no decline in the
people's sharply aroused desire for basic political change. This impression of his (and many others we talked to shared it) is confirmed by
opinion polls conducted by Polish sociologists during the latter months of
1981.[3]

I was beginning to see—or feel, in the sense of "feeling my way"—that
the question I had brought to Poland (Rosenthal's question, everybody's
question) had been merely one of tactics and strategy. The question of

why Solidarity acted in such a headstrong way was a typically instrumental question. It was actually an obstacle to looking directly at the substance of the phenomenon, at what the phenomenon was in itself and for itself.

In Warsaw in early May I was staying with friends in their apartment. A Polish man, a friend of theirs, came over one evening. As we lingered over dinner, the talk started out on pollution, nuclear bombs, and the Green movement in Western Europe (they were skeptical). But soon it shifted to Solidarity, Jaruzelski, Russia, and the boredom and harshness of everyday life in Poland. "What's happening is a gradual and insidious Sovietization of our life," said our host. His guest explained that he could not find an apartment. Consequently he and his wife were forced to live in two separate rooms many blocks apart, he with their dog and she with their child. He then described with biting satire the oppression, the banality, the insipidity of life in his country. He was vituperative in his anger and brilliantly eloquent. I finally asked him if he was more anti-Russian or anticommunist. He paused for a long moment and replied, "More anticommunist."

By itself that exchange was not more significant for me than many others. But when added to all the others, it made me stop and think, or rethink. I realized that I did not know what I had thought I knew. I felt that I needed to go back over all that I had observed and learned since my arrival in Poland. I felt I should look again with fresh eyes. The experience of my illness was still very much with me. Just as other parts of me— the unconscious, my body—had forced me to listen to their needs and their logic, so now Poland itself was demanding that I, the Western social scientist, listen to Poland as a subject in and for itself.

So I laid aside my question about tactics and strategy, my concern about prudence and the virtues of pragmatic adaptation. I did not attempt to answer it. I just put it on the back burner, for I might need it again, once I had satisfied myself that the thing I was trying to understand, this phenomenon of Solidarity, had revealed to me a measure of its meaning.

The dinner guest said that he rejected communism more than he rejected the Russians. Why was that such a triggering moment for me? I remember clearly that it was such a moment, but I am not sure why. One side of me perhaps registered the surface contradictoriness of his statement. Was not Russia the citadel of communism? How then can one distinguish between them in practical or even theoretical terms? But another, less logical side of me registered *him*, the real person sitting in my friends' kitchen, facing an impossible life and knowing how trapped he and his countrymen are. In the midst of his fervor and his anger he had made a vital and profound distinction. He knew his enemy. It wasn't people, but a system, the communist system.

Does this mean he hungered for capitalism? Some might leap to that conclusion. It is a possible inference, and since I did not immediately ask him whether he favored capitalism, I cannot absolutely set aside such an inference. But is it the only possible one or even the most likely one? It is so only if one is possessed of a certain double inclination—an inclination, first, to see the world defensively with Western or Eastern eyes and, second, to treat the world solely in syllogistic terms, presuming all that is not communism to be capitalism or vice versa. Nothing I gleaned from our conversation that night, or at other times with my host, supports the inference that either he, his wife, or the guest thought that their universe divided itself between communism and capitalism.

During that same journey to Warsaw I was fortunate enough to have a lengthy interview with Jerzy Wiatr, a well-known Polish sociologist, at that time director of the Communist party's Marxist-Leninist Institute. At one point he asserted that Solidarity had strong capitalist elements. I asked him for an example. He named a person who had been a leading adviser to Solidarity. Later I interviewed this person. Indeed, in many ways, as that interview proceeded, I was surprised at the vehement and far-reaching arguments he was making on behalf of antiplanning and free markets. I think he even used the word *capitalist*, and not pejoratively. It seemed that Wiatr was right, at least in this case. At the end of the interview I asked this person what he proposed to do about his society's fundamental social guarantees, meaning full employment and support for the basic needs of life, such as food, medicine, shelter, transportation, and clothing. He looked at me quizzically and said that of course these guarantees should stay in place. I left saying to myself that if this was capitalism, then it was of a species I could hardly recognize; indeed one might be excused for confusing it with socialism.

Still, what did the dinner guest's anticommunism mean? Perhaps it was in line with Solidarity's own stance, which sought to reassure the Russians that their workers' movement was not aimed at rejecting Russia and joining the West but rather at accomplishing important changes in the communist system of power in Poland. True enough, such a stance is not easily comprehended or appreciated by those whose minds, East or West, are attuned to doctrinal categories and code words. Thinking in terms of doctrines readily becomes a mental straitjacket. The notion that a person must be a capitalist if he adopts an anticommunist stance carries with it the idea that one simply must have a doctrine, no matter what, whether he likes having it or not. Thus, it is further assumed that if a person rejects one doctrine, he can only be doing so for the sake of another.

But perhaps the whole point about the dinner guest's rejection of communism is that he did not mean it doctrinally at all. I saw clearly his rebellion, the pain caused by his deprivation, his disgust with the banality around him, his anger at political oppression, and his own personal encounter with "the barrier of fear," a phrase Poles use to describe the private terror that must be faced by each person who contemplates resistance to the authorities. I also believed in his capacity to distinguish hatred of a system from hatred of people. And I felt a living contact with a desire to treat oneself and to be treated as a human being, a historical subject, not an object. What did doctrine have to do with this—any doctrine, communism, or capitalism, or some other? True, as I ruefully recalled, I had come to Poland with the search for some other doctrine clearly in mind. It now seemed that this other doctrine was the doctrine or set of doctrines supposedly set forth by Solidarity. The movement's ideology might reveal the shape and contours of a new way, a third way that lay between communism and capitalism. That had been my hope, my ambition.

But it also seemed that doctrine, or the idea of doctrine itself, was becoming discredited in my eyes. I saw the need to deconstruct this notion of doctrine, to pare away its layers and show the reality underneath. Doctrine was the creation of that propensity of the Western ego for rational system and rational control (hegemony) over the body, over all bodies, physical and politic. Doctrine, I saw more clearly than ever before in my life, was a way of forcing reality into a mental construct and then foisting that construct upon the world as if it were reality. Communists did it, backed up by the state, and called it building socialism. In a similar fashion Westerners converted capitalism into an all-encompassing doctrine and called it progress. Was Solidarity doing it, too, devising an articulate, complete doctrine, neither communist nor capitalist, one that would sum up and integrate the many strands of a people's rebellion and effectively compete for doctrinal supremacy with the ideologies of the world?

I had looked for such articulate ideological expressions. I had encountered no dearth of social theories that claimed to explain and set forth the position of Solidarity in the world. Their variety, and in some cases their mutually contradictory positions, caused some of my interviewees to shake their heads. Solidarity was so crisscrossed with different ideas and philosophies that one could be pardoned for wondering if it was a movement at all. So said several, both friends and foes of Solidarity. Someone would tell a new variation of the joke that when you ask five Poles to say a word on an issue, you get at least six opinions.

But to me, for whom the idea of doctrine was shattered, this joke was exactly the point—or part of a larger point that was forming in my mind. The deepest meaning of a real and successful social movement is not the unity and coherence of its doctrine. Nor does it even lie in doctrine, whether one or many. A successful movement inspires ideas and programs that then in turn help shape the movement, but the sources of the movement are not made up of doctrine. The sources are embedded in a political consciousness that lies deeper than doctrine.

To decipher the meaning of Solidarity, I would have to look at something other than its doctrine, just as I had had to look at something other than its tactics and strategy. I now knew that Solidarity was more politically self-conscious and more inclusive of the Polish people than I had imagined, but I urgently wondered what made it go.

3

Springtime: The Beginnings of a New Outlook

Spring in Poland was a revelation. Suddenly, it seemed, the world turned green, and spirits long subdued by the harsh privations of winter rose to meet the balm and brilliance of the new season. Even the multitudinous crows lost some of their menacing mystique. Their big black shapes, crouching in trees and on rooftops and flying in massive formations overhead, had given winter an even darker, starker edge. We learned that the Polish word for crow, *wrona*, was also approximately the acronym for Jaruzelski's Martial Council for National Redemption (WRON). In the Polish imagination these hapless dark creatures became constant reminders of the dark forces of WRON.

But in April and May the spring enveloped the *wrona* and gave these creatures counterpoint. They seemed to lose some of their maniacal aspect, and one could laugh a little at their raucous cries. So it was, too, with WRON: there was the feeling that one might risk a spasm of laughter now and then at its suppoesdly overarching and pervasive power.

The small park between the flat where our friends the Jacobses lived and Chatka Zaka, the student union, blossomed with flowers and shrubs and green grass. It was a pleasure to sit on the benches before or after our daily Polish lesson, luxuriating in the spring sunshine and watching the people go by. They seemed less stolid, less weighted down, less furtive. There was almost a lilt in the air, though perhaps it only seemed to be so, compared with the bleakness of winter. Politics emerged from its protective shell. It was a presence more felt than put into words, much like the air itself, invisible and everywhere. The government braced for trouble. This was apparent to us from our conversations with Polish friends, and reinforced by reading between the lines of the translations of articles and interviews of Polish authorities provided by the American and British embassies.

An incident took place. It took place because it was spring, because young people are ebullient when exams are over, because the government was jumpy (or were so divided that some of them may have wanted to create a provocation), and because most Poles despise their government. It could have happened in Lublin, Radom, Wroclaw, Gdansk, Poznan. It happened in Warsaw in May. A young man, Grzegorz Przemyk, finished with a round of examinations, was celebrating with friends in Warsaw's meticulously restored Old City. For some reason he was picked up by the police. He was taken to the station house and beaten. Perhaps he was insufficiently penitent, or perhaps he was even defiant. Or perhaps the police knew his mother was Barbara Sadowska, a well-known poet active in Solidarity. They beat and beat the young man, then took him to a first aid station where he died. The news of this event traveled swiftly all over Poland. We had friends who knew Barbara Sadowska and worked with her. We knew this could easily have happened to any one of several friends of our daughters at the university. It drove home to us the bitter and dangerous truth about life in Poland. And it made us wonder anew at the spirit of pride and resistance in the people.

Grzegorz Przemyk became a martyr. On the day of his funeral scores of thousands of young people, most of them from high schools, walked in frozen silence from church to cemetery in Warsaw. Along the way thousands more raised their hands in the V-for-victory sign, a token of their defiance of the government. The government made a half-hearted, public effort to investigate the murder. It put several policemen and attendants on trial and, a year later, could not find sufficient evidence to punish even them. Almost everyone felt both at the time of the murder and during the trial and final judgment that higher officials had been involved but were being protected by powerful politicians in the Party's Politburo. Perhaps the certain politicians had even instigated this action and others to discredit Jaruzelski, provoke Solidarity, or both.

These same factors came into play again eighteen months later, with the kidnapping and death by beating and drowning of Father Jerzy Popieluszko. Then, too, thousands—this time hundreds of thousands— marched, and the country was again locked in the great drama of an unfinished struggle. It is the struggle of a state in ludicrous pursuit of a nation that it cannot seem to find. And *mutatis mutandis*, it is the struggle of a nation trying to find a way to meet the state, not in the posture of supplicant or avenger, but in the posture of free citizen.

*   *   *

As spring advanced, I continued to grope with the question of what makes Solidarity go. What is its driving force?

The way to an answer came partly through the interviews, which now took place with greater frequency, and partly through the convergence of two kinds of inquiry in which I had become engaged. One was historical and cultural, and the other was sociological.

My illness had led me to spend quite a bit of time reading Polish history, and I thus gained some general grasp of the change and continuity of the Poles' political traditions and of their cultural and national experience. Professor Seidler proved to be a provocative guide in these matters. My daughters at the university were pursuing these subjects in their courses, and we had many conversations. Two American friends, Fred and Ava Jacobs, who were teaching at the university, are Polish theater enthusiasts, and through them we learned much about the connection of the political and the personal in Polish theater and in Polish literature generally.

A powerful witness to the power of Poland's past in the consciousness of its people came from our visits to other cities—to their libraries, museums, churches, bookstores, town squares, and monuments. We also went to two concentration camps, Auschwitz-Birkenau and, just three or four miles from our apartment, Maidonek.

One day I emerged from the magnificent St. Mary's Church on the great square in Krakow. I had felt myself immersed in the centuries of Polish history in that church, as I had been in so many other churches and would be again. The enormous square, as I squinted hither and yon in the spring sunshine, everywhere evoked the glories of Poland's history. All at once I was overwhelmed, and in that moment all I could see was the past seeping into and looming over one's consciousness. There was such a thing as too much history, I reflected. Too much history can weigh one down. I remembered Nietzsche's observations on the problem of having too much history. After paying his respects to what he called antiquarian history and monumental history, admitting their importance, he turned to critical history, which he portrayed as a necessary solvent of the encrustations of the past. Critical history provides the power to rise above the past and act creatively and effectively in the present.[1]

I walked back to the hostel where we were staying. En route I passed the entrance to a smaller church that stood off the square, tucked away behind St. Mary's massive walls. There was a service in progress, and the church was jammed with worshipers. I stood at the entrance watching for a while. Several hours later I returned to the square by the same route to meet members of my family. The church was still jammed or newly filled, and once again a service was in progress. Perhaps it was the same one. It was not the Sabbath. I was struck, as I was again and again, at the intimacy between the Poles and their church. Like all Christians, they went to church for succor and condolence and the sweet joy of spiritual blessing. But they also went because the church is the living embodiment of their history, the record of their sufferings and triumphs, the assurance and protector of their identity.

Going to church is in the deepest sense a political act for Poles. It is the place where their history is renewed and made rich and fruitful in their consciousness. I knew enough Polish and Latin to realize that the many hymns they sang were both Christian and Polish, the two elements being melded together in a profound spiritual feeling. At the end of the service they sing their national hymn. In it is a line that originally went, "Fatherland and freedom bless, O Lord." But today they change the words to the defiant "Fatherland and freedom return to us, O Lord." When they would sing the forbidden words, and for some the tears would start down their cheeks, I, the Western observer, knew that the religion of the Polish people was indeed spiritual, but I knew, too, that it was also directly and irrevocably political. History, the history of Poland, was the touchstone. Embedded in that history lay the unquenched fire of resistance to oppression. That fire is nurtured deep within the church. It is a people's institution.

This matter of history—initially so prosaic to an American sensibility—came home to us in many ways. Auschwitz-Birkenau and Maidonek were searing encounters with the reality of genocide. We saw the awful record of the attempt by the Nazis to exterminate millions of Jews and Poles (and gypsies and homosexuals), the evidence of a weird, frenzied attempt to obliterate not only individuals by the millions but to expunge from history what they were as a whole, what they represented as a people, a nation, and a culture. It was, as Hannah Arendt described it, a fateful, horrible experiment in "radical evil."[2]

In Warsaw, in the great Lazienka Park, stands a statue of Chopin, at once magnificent and sensitive. There was almost no one else in the park when I saw it early one Sunday morning. It was May Day. I was told that when the Nazis marched into the city in 1939, they not only toppled the statue but ground it into powder. This act impressed me. It symbolized the diabolical—the radical evil Arendt speaks of. It was a perverted effort not to suspend or reverse history but to destroy it. This is what the Nazis had in mind for the Poles—to grind their history into powder. The Polish response after the war was swift and forceful. They restored the statues and reconstructed Warsaw and all the many cities destroyed by the Nazis. They restored what had been—practically brick for brick, building for building, and monument for monument. Their intention, their passion, is clear: they were not going to allow anyone to deprive them of their history. By rebuilding, they rebuild their culture. As I realized this passion, something fell into place for me. I saw that Solidarity is the inheritor of that passion, that will to history on the part of the Polish people.

The claustrophobia of the centuries I had felt in Krakow's great public square was solely my own. The Poles' sense of history is not a heavy burden that limits their vision. History is alive in them, and by identifying with their history, they both preserve and renew it in the present moment. The Poles are conscious of their "being in history," precisely because it has for so long and so often been threatened, even to the point of total destruction. For them history is not merely antiquarian, heroic, and monumental, but it is first and foremost a powerful cutting edge that arouses them to action in its defense, which is defense of themselves, their meaning, and their own movement forward. The church is a key agent in this process: it permits, even nurtures, in the consciousness of the Polish people a daily awareness of the magic of their history, of their "being in history."

Other significant aspects of this historical sense drew my attention. I became reacquainted with Poland's constitutional history and realized the vital part that constitutionalism has played in the Polish political tradition. And it is a somewhat different kind of constitutionalism than that of the West. It lies much further back than the highly, and justly, touted constitution of 1791, which has been heralded as the second republican (nonmonarchical) constitution in the world, preceded only by that of the United States. Long before that time, Poland had developed a rich political and constitutional tradition. It contained an emphasis both on strong governmental rule (the Piast dynasty, then the Jagiello-nians, and, beginning in 1573, elected kings) and on the need to protect the basic rights of the people and of the various regions of the realm. As early as 1505, the king and a constitutionally aroused Sejm agreed to a document known as *Nihil Novi*. It prescribed that "nothing new," *i.e.*, no new law or policy, could be decided on without the consent of the Chamber of Deputies, the Sejm's lower house. Previously the decisive vote had been in the Senate, whose members were chosen by the king. In 1652 the famous (and eventually infamous) liberum veto, whereby one deputy of the Sejm could block the passage of a piece of legislation or overturn it, was put into effect, though it was sparingly used at first.

These political conceptions suggest that a combined respect for deci-sive government and for the substantive rights of the heterogeneous parts of the realm is more characteristic of Poland than of the West. In the West the constitutional tradition is overlaid with a prevailing formalism of law, with majority rule (winner take all), and often with self-imposed governmental inaction in the face of private corporate laissez faire. On the other hand, constitutionalism is certainly more at home in Poland than in the East, where the spirit of constitutionalism, though not en-tirely absent, has never had much of a chance to manifest itself in face of the fatal sequence of authoritarian rule, wild rebellion, and return to authoritarian rule.

May 3 is the date on which Poles commemorate the constitution of 1791. It follows hard on May Day, the great day of workers' international-ism, a day taken over by communist regimes as a time of special celebra-tion. The Jaruzelski government promotes May Day, as the Party tries to whip up the people's enthusiasm with marches, parades, bunting, and speeches. But the results are usually disappointing. On May 3, however, Poles go to church and afterward lay wreaths on monuments to mark the acceptance of the constitution and, one may surmise, to rededicate themselves to the renewal of constitutional liberty today.

On a public square in Lublin, not many yards apart, stand two monu-ments. One is an imposing figure erected to celebrate the liberation of Lublin, and all of Poland, from the Nazis by the Russian army in 1944–1945. The other is a small granite block, put there in the days when Solidarity was legal, commemorating the constitution of 1791. The first is almost always totally ignored. The second never lacks wreaths of flowers, and on May 3 the wreaths are legion, which does not please the authorities.

We stayed at home on May 3, but student friends of our daughters described their experiences that day. Militia and Zomo (special riot) police units sprayed the people who were bringing flowers with blue-colored water that left a stain that would make them easier targets on streets as they headed home. Some were arrested on the spot, and others were beaten. Many fled. But because of the blue stains, they found it hard to elude their pursuers, and several were caught. As a tactic the spraying was probably used as much as an additional means of intimidation as it was actually to catch people. Next day a friend told me that his father, now old and weary with years, and his mother had gone together to the Solidarity monument to lay a wreath. The father had dressed himself in his old full army uniform, proudly displaying the many ribbons bestowed on him by the state. The elderly man and his wife were arrested, taken to the police headquarters, interrogated, humiliated, and finally allowed to go home. Telling this tale, my friend was near tears and almost beside himself with anger and with frustration. It was the humiliation that was the worst part, he said, the stricken look on his father's face.

These events demonstrate that, once again, the connection between religion and the church on one hand and politics—in this case the spirit of the constitution—on the other cannot be overlooked. And neither can the vital role of Solidarity. One goes to church and then places flowers on a certain monument. Both acts are part of a single ceremony. The day is a *political* commemoration, both ancient (in honor of the 1791 constitution) and contemporary (in honor of Solidarity), but religion is also part of the observance. Just a few weeks later came Corpus Christi Day—this time, on the face of it, a purely religious holiday. But many people performed the same actions: attending church and placing flowers on the "right" political monuments, such as Lublin's granite slab erected by Solidarity. As before, monuments such as the imposing one on the same square heralding the Russian liberators were pointedly ignored.

On Corpus Christi Day Carla went for a walk about the city and mingled with the throngs in the churches and on the streets. On such a day the entire country seems to shut down in order to be with family, to go to church, and to parade and promenade and lay wreaths. It was a very colorful event, solemn and exciting at the same time, she reported. The crowds, the elegant church services, and the often gorgeous pageantry are remarkable. But these visible things reflect an invisible unity of religious and political sentiment that is wondrous to feel, especially for Westerners accustomed to the secularism and atomized indifference of public life in the West. Such a day must also seem deeply intimidating to the authorities of Poland's party-state, who are in the ludicrous position of being hopelessly in pursuit of their nation.

Another critical aspect of the Poles' creative historical sense is their close relationship with their intellectuals and artists. We received intimations of this relationship from the plays we were seeing, the comments on these plays by our friends the Jacobses, and the works of poets and artists that we became acquainted with through conversations with Polish professors. One theme in particular continually struck me: It might be termed the posture of the Polish artist. That posture is somewhat akin to that of the bard, the seer, or the moral interpreter. There is about it something of Homer's relation to the Greeks. In Poland there is a deep and quite explicit feeling that poets, painters, film makers—all artists and intellectuals—have a vocation. That vocation is to take the whole Polish experience, especially the anguish of its political tragedies, and transmute it through art into forms that reveal its meaning to the people. So Adam Mickiewitz, who has been dead for more than a century, speaks as a guide and moral authority in his people's political struggle of today. So, too, does Nobel Prize winner Czeslaw Milosz, even though he, like so many other Polish intellectuals for generations, is forced to live and write in exile from his native land. Milosz' words are engraved in the great Gdansk monument to the striking workers of 1970, a monument erected by Solidarity in December, 1980, during the early days of its legality. The art and politics of resistance to oppression are interwoven into a single brilliant and tragic tapestry that is part of the everyday lives of the Polish people. Art thus takes its place alongside religion as an incalculable force shaping, and being shaped by, the Poles' political consciousness.

There was also a sociological dimension to the factors shaping my perceptions of my Polish experience. This sociological dimension had to do with the nature of the communist state and its impact on the shaping of Polish society and consciousness.

One day in March, I was told by telephone of the existence of a sociological journal called *Sisyphus*.[3] Volume III, number 2, my caller said, carried articles about "those days." I asked Polish friends to try to find it for me, since because of my illness I could not go out much. Only one of them had heard of it. Another friend, however, an indefatigable searcher, finally located a copy in an obscure corner of the library at the Catholic University in Lublin. I read it in snatches but had to return it before I had absorbed its contents, which included several learned articles on the Solidarity phenomenon by Polish sociologists, results of opinion polls taken during late 1981 just prior to martial law, and essays by workers about their experiences in the strikes that led to the Gdansk Accord in August, 1980. Several weeks later I found a copy I could buy (the last copy, I was more or less surreptitiously told by a clerk) in Warsaw's largest bookstore. Later I was given a copy by the editor. The volume was written in academic sociological prose (with the exception of the workers' essays) and printed in a very limited edition in English. Even so, it had had a difficult time getting past the censors, I was told by authors of the articles, many of whom I was able to interview. After I returned to the United States, a Polish friend told me an anecdote about this *Sisyphus* volume on Solidarity. It seems that a copy found its way into Russia, probably sent by one of the authors to a friend in Moscow. The KGB discovered it. In due course Jaruzelski's office received a cautionary note from somewhere in the Kremlin remonstrating about the publication of the volume and "suggesting" that as many copies as possible be recalled and put out of circulation.

From interviews with authors of these *Sisyphus* articles and from the contents of the volume itself, I obtained additional perspective on the wellsprings and the meaning of the Solidarity movement. I appreciated, as never before, the sharp break with the past inaugurated by the new communist state following World War II, and I saw the demographic, economic, and sociological factors that combined to push the Polish worker toward confrontation with that state. The *Sisyphus* authors put these factors together in various ways that inspired my thinking in a new direction.

Gradually there formed in my mind a hypothesis of historical irony or dialectic. While still in Poland, I only sensed it, but after a time I was able to express it. This hypothesis holds that the very success of the Communists in rebuilding Poland and shaping society in a certain way has helped to bring into being—unintentionally but inexorably—the force that now opposes them with such a strong and implacable spirit. Under a system of authoritarian Party rule that combined ideological, political, and economic hegemony, the Communists created, for perhaps the first time in Polish history, a competent, administratively effective state, albeit a grossly overbearing one that was also vulnerable to corruption; they raised the standard of living and the material expectations of the hitherto suppressed classes of Polish society; they opened the doors of overall cultural development (and thereby historical knowledge) via universal education to that same hitherto suppressed two-thirds of Polish society; and in so doing, they forced the former social, economic, religious, and military elites to soften, if not abandon altogether, their hierarchical, paternalistic, and racist view of society and history. By pushing economic, social, and cultural development for ordinary people, but at the same time withholding correlative changes in the pattern of authoritarian rule by the Party elite, they had only themselves to blame for the pent-up pressures that steadily increased as the decades passed.

Confirmation of this perception of historical irony came from my conversations with articulate supporters of Jaruzelski, especially Professor Seidler and Jerzy Wiatr, director of the Communist party's Marxist-Leninist Institute in Warsaw. A third was Professor Artur Bodnar, who heads the Political Science Methodology Institute of Warsaw University. Bodnar said that he spoke neither for nor against Solidarity but as a dispassionate observer and expert. All three men made arguments that gave credence to my emerging sense that the Communists had accomplished important historical tasks for Poland, especially in breaking down the earlier semifeudal, semicapitalist class structure; in strengthening the efficiency of the state; and in providing for the basic needs of every person or at any rate creating the public expectation that to do so is a fundamental function of the government. In reciting these impressive accomplishments, Seidler and Wiatr became almost plaintive in their exasperation with the people. They felt that the masses lack an appreciation of the enormous costs required for Poland to reach its current level of development. It was the Party and the state, they pointed out, that created the social, economic, and cultural conditions that today enable the people to speak up and make their demands. The masses want everything right away, Seidler and Waitr maintained, and they have no realistic, unified program. Furthermore, they allow themselves to be manipulated by self-serving, anarchistic intellectuals and malcontents, some of whom are probably employed by the CIA.

All three thinkers, despite their sincerity and influence, overlooked, I felt, their own, and the Party's, paternalistic assumptions about the relation of leaders to led, and of the Party to the masses. They also overlooked certain implications of their own argument. If indeed the Party-state has enabled the masses to improve their conditions, should there not also, then, be a corresponding shift in the *political* evolution of the Party-state? And is this not what "the masses" are doing—pounding on the doors of power for access to the state so that the state can be joined to the nation?

Thus, I began to understand both the outer conditions and inner substance of the people's quarrel with their Communist regime. I saw that Solidarity had become the magnet and the catalyst that focused the grievances and aspirations, the angers and hopes, of the people caught up in that quarrel. I had located the struggle in its true context, in the real life of the people: in their religion, art, and sense of history, and in their experience with the Communist-inspired transformation of society. It became clear that the struggle drew both its sustenance, and its limits, from that context.

Solidarity was no ideological movement replete with analysis and finished doctrine; nor was it an instrumental, vanguard movement sporting the latest in revolutionary tactics and strategy. It had its ideas and principles, of course, and its tactics and strategy. But these were secondary to the call for action to provide structures for the defense of historic rights and to demand that the state rule in accordance with them. I was reminded of the Burkean view of the American Revolution as a revolt on behalf of received rights sanctified by tradition and renewed by the spirit of struggle and sacrifice. Perhaps more to the point, I saw here a close kinship with the post-Marxist view of revolution expressed by Walter Benjamin. Marx thought of revolution as history's locomotive. But Benjamin said: "Maybe it is just the opposite. Perhaps revolutions can be better understood as the people's way of reaching for the emergency brake on the train."[4] In 1981 Polish society was in a convulsive condition. A political vacuum yawned, and both state and nation teetered on the edge of it. Under the circumstances, Solidarity acted, again and again, with resolution and restraint. And in the crucible, so did the government, in the person of the new leader, Jaruzelski. The pity of it is that these two great forces cannot find a settlement.

My last interview in Poland took place in Warsaw two days before our return home. I talked with a leader of the once vital Horizontalist movement, which in 1981 swept through the Polish Communist party only to be first domesticated and then suppressed by Party moderates under threat from Party hardliners and the Kremlin. He spoke of the goals and the roots of the Horizontalists, most of whom either were also members of Solidarity or favored close Party association with Solidarity unions. He invoked the spirit of the constitutional traditions and of nineteenth-century Polish socialism. These traditions, he said, were the wellsprings of their movement, in contrast to Leninist democratic centralism and revolutionary vanguardism. To me these considerations were significant, because they lead to a new view of Poland, a Poland floundering, to be sure, but one also trembling on the threshold of a renewed beginning that is neither communist nor capitalist. Poles had arrived at this juncture not through ideological leaps, vanguard strategies, or charismatic incantations, but through the slow forging of historical conditions, through their own appropriation of their history, and through their recognition of what it means to be a subject of history and not merely its object.

We left Poland by a south-bound train to Budapest. Five months earlier we had arrived by train from the West. We made no summings-up as we rumbled through Poland's green countryside in the long evening twilight. Leaning out of the windows, we sang songs, including some we had learned from our Polish friends. Often we looked at one another and smiled. The smiles were both glad and rueful; they were the smiles of persons who have shared an intense, varied, and deeply human experience and been changed by it. Poland was more than a place, more than a project. Poland was individual persons into whose lives we had entered briefly. And though we were leaving, their lives had, by some mysterious process of spiritual osmosis, entered into us. We could never forget their pain, their courage, their humor, and their hope. Most of all we could never forget their stubborn insistence on self-respect and the dignity of the human spirit in the face of established wrong.

PART II

WHY SOLIDARITY?

4

Forces Shaping Solidarity

Before and for a time after my arrival there, Poland had been to me, an outsider looking in, an interesting, even compelling, object of study. But it had taken me where I had not thought to go, had grasped and shaken me and turned me around to look at the Poles' situation as if from the inside. Once that happened, though I was still a foreigner, indeed was consciously a foreigner perhaps for the first time, I looked carefully and soberly all around me. It had become my hope "to see Poland steadily and see it whole."[1]

This hope became my settled aim once we had returned to the United States and reflected on what we had seen and heard and felt. I focused on the Polish situation, and for a period of four years of writing and lecturing, which included a return visit to Poland in the summer of 1985, I strove to understand the meaning of Solidarity as if from the inside. To put this goal in language appropriate to Solidarity's own quest, I would say that I strove to perceive Poland, in its otherness, as also a subject. My question became, Why Solidarity, *i.e.*, why this kind of movement and not some other?

This chapter describes the major structural, or shaping, forces active in the Polish situation. The next chapter treats the major psychological, or generative, forces. Chapter 6 focuses on the breakthrough itself: the action of Solidarity and the counteraction of the government. The intent is not to write a history but to pose and probe the problem facing Solidarity, and Poland, on the critical issue of political participation.

The Gdansk Accord of August, 1980 (see Appendix), was an agreement between Solidarity and the government, after intense negotiations in Gdansk, Szczecin, and Jastrzebie, on twenty-one demands made by the union. Any effort to understand the meaning of Solidarity must begin with these demands.

The first and foremost demand was that the government "accept free trade unions, independent of the Party and employers." One should note that the union sought independence from both Party *and* employers.

One should also note that the demand was not for workers' councils (*i.e.*, self-management). Workers' councils became part of a separate movement in 1981 that was subsequently linked with Solidarity.[2] It must also be emphasized that with reference to this first demand the new union accepted "the principle of the social ownership of the means of production," acknowledged "the leading role of the Polish United Workers Party in the state," and agreed not to question "the established system of international alliances." The agreement went on to say that Solidarity's "purpose is to provide working people with appropriate means for exercising control, expressing their opinions, and defending their own interests." In other words, despite its determined stand for the rights of working people, Solidarity accepted much of the established order in Poland. The Gdansk Accord was an agreement among reds. This highly significant passage concerning the first demand would figure prominently in the subsequent trials of strength between the government and Solidarity.

The second demand was "to guarantee the right to strike and personal safety for strikers and their supporters," and the third was "to uphold freedom of expression and publication as guaranteed by the Constitution." This demand, which in the West is considered a civil liberty, follows hard on the demand for independence for unions and the right to strike. But in Poland a civil liberty is closely conjoined with, and becomes integral to, the economic rights usually associated with trade unions.

The fourth demand called for ending repression for beliefs and opinions (another civil liberty); the fifth for full public information about social and economic conditions; the sixth for all social groups to participate in discussion of reform to end the economic crisis. Point 7 assured the workers of strike wages equivalent to vacation pay; points 8 and 9 raised their basic pay and guaranteed raises in accordance with the price of commodities and the value of money. Points 10, 11, and 13 demanded that in the distribution of food the domestic market be given priority and that only surpluses be exported; that "commercial prices and sales for hard currency" in special shops for the privileged be abolished; and that until the market was stabilized, there would be rationing of meat.

Point 12 abruptly switches from economic issues to an absolutely critical structural issue—the omnipresent workings of *nomenklatura*, which, in a communist state, is the means by which the Party hierarchy dominates selections for all vital positions in the economy, the government, and the Party. Point 12, without mentioning the word *nomen-klatura*, nevertheless in effect called for its abolition, by demanding the introduction of the "principle that people in leading positions" be "chosen on the basis of qualifications rather than Party membership."

The final eight points addressed particular details, calling for the lowering of the retirement age, increases in pensions and annuities, improvement of working conditions in the health service, improved day-care services, "paid maternity leave for three years while a mother brings up her child," the reduction of waiting time for flats, increased travel allowances, and the laying down of rules about Saturday work.

These twenty-one demands, struck off in the heat of a tense struggle, are remarkable for their lack of ideology and ringing rhetoric and for their correlative ability to express principle through the particular, and the fundamental in the form of the historically concrete. Later, in April, 1981, Solidarity promulgated its *Theses for Discussion*, and in September and October of the same year its First National Congress of Delegations adopted the Program of the Independent Self-Governing Trade Union Solidarity. These documents, as we shall see, reflected the changing character of the struggle. Yet what became explicit in these later documents—that it is a *system* that must be changed, for example, and that Solidarity is a social movement as well as a trade union—is already implicit in the twenty-one demands. The evolution of concept and program came in response to the development of the crisis, especially the twin phenomena of economic catastrophe and the equally catastrophic decline of the Party. The additional concepts and program goals came out of historical experience based on the principles of Gdansk.[3]

THE MEANS OF PRODUCTION

Seven structural forces have shaped present-day Polish society. These forces, of course, have also done much to shape Solidarity. The first of the seven is the form of ownership and control of the means of production. According to Marx, the purpose of the revolution of the proletariat against the capitalist class is to inaugurate a process leading as rapidly as possible to the abolition of a state standing over against society and bearing down upon it with its coercive weight. In his scheme he foresaw that after the revolution there would be a first, or preparatory, phase in which actions would be taken by a state under control of the proletariat in order to hasten the coming of a second and final phase in which the public or social ownership and administration of the means of production would replace the state. He did not specify how long the first phase would take, but it is clear that he felt it would be brief. Yet he thought a strong and even coercive state would be necessary during this period.

The question of who owns and controls the means of production during this interim period is a critical one. It is doubly critical when, as it turns out, this phase extends itself forward in time as "real existing socialism" to such a degree that the second phase—supposedly the *raison d'être* of the first—is soon pushed onto an eschatological plane, as if it were a heaven to be contemplated and mythologized, a place that the faithful will reach "someday" in the far future.

In answering this question, there is room for vast equivocation. Marx is too general. Communist leaders seem to fancy the notion that, under their regimes, ownership is "social," but there is no doubt that they locate the control, and indeed the ownership, of the means of production in that semiodious institution that according to holy Marxist writ is slated for the dustbin of history—the state. It is true that the Party has a fundamental role, but the central point is that in practical terms the ownership and control of the means of production are lodged securely in the hands of the state. From this fact flow several consequences for a resistance movement in a communist country.

First, communist revolutions against capitalism and feudalism have created historically new problems and opportunities for working people not encountered before under the two earlier systems. The communist revolutions of the twentieth century not only nationalize industry. They go further, abolishing the fundamental separation between the state and civil society that characterized the semifeudal and semicapitalist societies they overcame. This separation continues to be an almost sacred feature of contemporary capitalist countries. Some capitalist nations experiment with nationalization of various industries. But such efforts are piecemeal and pragmatic and not systemic. They do not alter the decisive dichotomy between a private realm (civil society) and a public realm (the state). Civil society is the arena for private judgment and conscience, private property, and egoistic striving. The public realm is the arena of state institutions and political mechanisms, such as political parties. Action for common or general purposes is supposed to occur in the public realm. But these purposes must be limited. They must not contravene, at least not seriously, the fundamental dichotomy between state and civil society. The realm of private egoism must be sustained.

Few thinkers articulated the separation of capitalist society and politics into the realms of civil society and state more trenchantly than Karl Marx in such essays as "On the Jewish Question." In some ways he only carried forward the classifications already developed by Hegel in *The Philosophy of Right*. Hegel saw a juxtaposition of three realms: family, civil society, and state, and he celebrated what he conceived as the historical evolution toward a state that would unite (in the sense of transcending dialectically) the "organic" bonds of the family and the "artificial" or merely "contractual" bonds of civil society. The works of Hannah Arendt, especially *The Human Condition*, show how contemporary these notions still are. Yet, the assumption that civil society is the arena of egoistic striving and legalistic (formal) contracts guaranteed by an objective state remains intact throughout her formulations.

In communist countries the dichotomy has been abolished. It is very questionable, however, that it has been transcended. For what has ensued from this abolition is a lopsided, top-heavy relationship between a state (and a directing force called the Party) on one hand and on the other a "society" shorn of its own self-organization. Under modern communism "society" is nothing more than a discrete, rudderless, passive heap of individuals and forces—that is, unless and until it is organized from above.

In this situation, the organizing and controlling force in society is not private, as in the West. But neither is it social or truly public. Instead it takes the form of the state administration. It is necessarily coercive in its essential being, instinctively seeking to bar any other organizing or controlling force, whether private or social.

The point of departure for a resistance movement in a communist country must be based on the results of the communist revolution there. The movement has certain options. It can attempt to turn the clock back to capitalism or feudalism. But it is doubtful if that could work, given the radical reconstruction of the communist period. More interesting, but romantic, would be an attempt to complete the thrust and the stated goal of the communist revolution. This would be an effort to overcome the administrative power and other state coercive power by introducing means for the self-organization and self-defense of society. The state would be abolished, and society would regain control over the means of production. Thus, in keeping with Marxist categories, the state of the first phase would be replaced by the "democracy of producers" of the second.

Another option is to seek a new settlement that would aim not to replace but to modify the existing structure. This might be accomplished in either of two ways: by delegating real power and authority to plant managers and even to a number of small private entrepreneurs; or, going much further, by introducing a new principle—self-governing unions and associations.

Solidarity has sought to put Poland on this latter path, demanding the introduction of self-governing unions and associations. Instituting such unions and associations would not just create a greater role for ordinary people on bread-and-butter issues and on a piecemeal basis, which is as far as unions in the West can go, if indeed they even get that far. Instead it would mean, because of the already accomplished communist revolution, that ordinary citizens would have a stake in the effective disposition and control of the means of production and in the civil and political freedoms such a cause requires.

Unfortunately, this point is lost on many if not most Western observers. They persist in seeing Solidarity as a labor union in a Western sense of a bargaining agent (another private egoistic force) or as a proletariat class striving for hegemony against a ruling class. They do not see, or they refuse to see, that in Poland there already has been a thoroughgoing communist revolution and reconstruction that has become part of the country's history.

A second consequence of the state's ownership and control of the means of production is that nearly everyone is an employee. In addition, nearly everyone works for the same employer—the State. This means that there are often rapid ripple effects throughout society once a disturbance occurs in one part of the economy. There are indeed differences between peasants, urban workers, and the so-called intelligentsia, and within various ranks of the intelligentsia.[4] Nevertheless there is no capitalist class of owners and managers who dominate civil society through the power of their vast wealth and property and are themselves divided according to many different industries, sections, and regions and often carry "their" portions of the working force with them on any given issue. Nor is there a feudal class of landowners with similarly disproportionate power based on property and personal prerogatives. Nor is there any substantial number of small business people and entrepreneurs. This latter group, in the West, for example, often acts as a buffer between embedded (corporate) capital and a fairly disparate and sometimes militant labor force. But it also often acts as a solvent of a working-class consciousness. The "self-employed" mystique of this group may lure many workers away from solidarity with their fellows. But no force with a correlative position in the structure of society can be found in "real existing socialism."

In contrast to these sharply etched divisions in property and labor, a communist society puts almost everyone in a decisively similar relation to the means of production: everyone in some crucial sense is a worker. This holds true across the board, be they industrial workers, blue- or white-collar, or be they intellectual and professional workers—writers, scholars, journalists, teachers, artists, musicians, technicians, technologists, students, doctors, medical workers, lawyers, engineers, managers, etc. It holds true for agriculture as well. Even though most of Poland's three million farm families are individual proprietors, they do their work under the direct aegis of the state, which controls prices, allocates investments, and lays down quotas for production. Formal ownership may be lodged with the farmer, but everyone knows where the real control of the productive process lies. Indeed, in 1980–1981 the farmers organized themselves into unions (Rural Solidarity, Peasant Solidarity, and the Union of Agricultural Producers) and sought to enter into negotiations on issues of union autonomy, prices, and investment with their common boss, the state.[5]

It must be stressed that not only is the boss ubiquitous, essentially the same for all, but the boss is a political entity. Workers in a communist society do not sell their labor in the same manner as under capitalism. The policy of full employment (or, as anticommunists prefer to call it, compelled employment) divests the worker of his or her status as a free commodity. There is no labor market in Poland or any other state under "real existing socialism." Workers obtain, hold, and lose jobs as a result of administrative decisions conducted by the ultimate power, the state.

Thus, the communist state and the people encounter each other simultaneously in two sets of relationships: as government and citizens and as employer and employees. Any dividing line between political and economic is extremely vague, if it exists at all. As Anthony Kemp-Welch said concerning the Gdansk negotiations of August, 1980, in strikes in which "the employer is also the state . . . the distinction between an 'economic' grievance against an employer and a 'political' demand of the state is thus narrowed, if not obliterated."[6] And though such an arrangement makes the state sovereign in both political and economic relationships—in both the law court and the workplace—it also makes the state immediately vulnerable to economic pressures that might otherwise have been contained in a different sphere. The state becomes a clear target for the dissatisfactions, the anger, of virtually all the people—both in their role as workers and in their role as citizens.

A resistance movement, therefore, in a communist society cannot be a working-class movement of the sort that is familiar to Western scholarship, whether liberal, Marxist, or conservative. The structure of society and its political economy are fundamentally different. All differences in society stemming from the relations of production are subsumed under one major difference—that between the immense majority, who as workers encounter the same ubiquitous employer, and the small minority of virtual "owners" who direct and supervise the operations of the political economy from the commanding heights of the state.

There is a third major consequence of the fact that the means of production are owned and controlled by the state: the structural relationship between intellectuals and industrial workers is different from in the West.

Many in the West know that some intellectuals took a stand side by side with Solidarity as members of KOR, the Workers' Defense Committee, originally organized in 1976 to give professional assistance and bread-and-butter support to striking industrial workers and their families. Such actions forged crucial links between intellectual workers and industrial workers, preparing the way for the successful strikes in the summer of 1980 from which Solidarity emerged.

But it is a mistake to look at this phenomenon through typical Western eyes, which see intellectuals acting from the goodness of their hearts to bring succor to the downtrodden or out of ideological zealotry or hidden and frustrated desire for power. Such a view misses the point, though there may be a few Polish intellectuals who correspond to these stereotypes.[7] The whole matter of the relation of intellectuals to society in Poland is but poorly understood in the West. Intellectuals in the West are privatized in civil society just like every other individual; what they say or do is understood to be only their own idiosyncratic utterances or actions, no matter whether they can get a market for them or not. But in Poland there is still a tradition of the intellectual as a social critic whose *vocation* it is to speak the truth to the state and the nation. In KOR, because of the Marxist humanist notion of praxis, this tradition is taken one step further, so that the vocation of the intellectual embraces the responsibility actually to side and work with any element of society permanently abused, especially those whose skills do not include the crucial arts of effective speech backed up by training in law and the social sciences.

The point at issue is a very real one, with numerous practical consequences. In communist systems intellectuals work for the same employer as everyone else and receive their bread and butter in exchange for doing what they are supposed to do as intellectuals—to think, speak, write, teach, publish, communicate, etc. This is their *material* activity, and in terms of trying to do that they encounter the very same master as do the industrial workers in Lublin, Gdansk, and Wroclaw. Furthermore, the incomes of intellectuals and of other professionals, including even doctors and lawyers, are typically lower than those of many industrial workers, a fact that serves to erase differences of status and motivation that in the West are used to divide various social strata from one another.

When the industrial workers went on strike and stayed on strike to win the fact and principle of independent, self-governing unions, these events obviously struck a powerful reverberatory chord in all other workers in this society of workers—blue-collar, white-collar, professional, peasant, and intellectual. So along with the small number of intellectuals who provided expert assistance as advisers to industrial workers (in addition to doing their own work in their professional careers), there were many layers of intellectual workers of all kinds who, after August, 1980, quickly moved to press for independent, self-governing status for *their* associations, unions, or universities. Most of them were already in unions that had been approved by the state. Many such unions were simply taken over by members who endorsed the goals of Solidarity. Other groups of intellectuals, such as teachers, imitated the shipyard workers of Gdansk and formed new unions. Students successfully prodded the government for their own independent unions. Medical workers did the same, and the peasants formed Rural Solidarity. Universities were beginning to press for and receive autonomous status. [8]

The prestigious Union of Writers became autonomous, a heavy blow to the established Party assumption that it must be the Party that takes the leading role in this vital area. The members of the Union of Writers so savored their newfound autonomy that, even after the crackdown following the declaration of martial law, they refused to submit. The Jaruzelski government, after a year and a half of alternately coaxing and attempting to coerce the union to accept once again the priority of the party, finally gave up and dissolved it. At one point the government had sought to get the writers to agree to accept "communist values" in their work. This wording was offered in place of the earlier requirement to acknowledge "the leading role of the Party." The union overwhelmingly rejected the new phrasing as a mere rhetorical ploy. [9]

The move to limit the definition and application of censorship came from the Gdansk industrial workers in August, 1980, as point three of the twenty-one demands. The government agreed to do so in the Gdansk Accord. The industrial workers saw that without a broader and freer opportunity to express themselves in public, they could not expect to protect their right to independent, self-governing unions. In the West it is commonly thought that such demands for civil liberties are of primary interest only to the intelligentsia. But in Poland, at least in this instance, such a demand was a priority for "ordinary" workers.

Thus, in the Poland of Solidarity, intellectuals and other members of the intelligentsia joined the movement for self-governing associations out of a practical concern for their own livelihood, and at the same time, the so-called common man argued fiercely, and won a battle, for greater civil liberties. This is not to say that either kind of worker ignored either demand. But these facts suggest that one must be wary of applying Western concepts and assumptions about the "nature" of "workers" versus "intellectuals," or of "material" versus "spiritual" motivations, to the people of Poland and other non-Western countries.

THE PARTY IN A COMMUNIST STATE

The second major structural force that has shaped Solidarity has been the location and character of the state's power and authority. In Poland, as in every communist nation the world has seen to date, that power is located in the Party (which, however, is not mentioned in Marx's writings). For the Polish United Workers party (PUWP), as for the Party in every communist regime, the overriding goal has always been the creation and fostering of a historic directing agency. The role of this agency is to integrate the "preorganized" spontaneities and longings of the masses into a coherent program of social transformation and construction in line with the direction of history.

The Party must not be confused with parties in a Western parliamentary system of two or more parties. Western parties take turns providing marginally different sets of leaders and policy emphases within an established framework of governing institutions that are themselves limited in the role they play vis-à-vis a supposedly self-regulating civil society.

In a communist country the Party's vision and role is much grander than that. It is the central institution in the totality of relations in the entire complex of state and society. This point is essential if one is to grasp the significance of the Solidarity phenomenon. In the communist conception, the Party is not only the agent of economic development, the mover and shaker on the political frontier, and the initiator of social organization (both in its parts and as a whole), but it is also the nurturer and directive agency in the creation and re-creation of the culture of the people. What is at stake is the attempt not only to raise the standard of living and meet the problems of order and security, but to mold a "new man."

In this scheme of things the state is necessary until social conditions are ripe for it to wither away. It is necessary in order to expedite the journey of postrevolutionary society toward the higher phase of social relations. The state is the instrument of the Party par excellence, the means through which the building of the new society and the new man is to be accomplished.

Thus, there is a three-way relationship of society, state, and Party. There is the actual society—the multitude of the people in their relations and activities, living and laboring in an historically developing milieu toward the accomplishment of the task, the fulfillment of the vision. Second, there is the state, whose job it is to direct society authoritatively toward the goal and defend it from enemies within and without. Finally, there is the Party, the keeper and nurturer of the vision, the supreme agent of social and economic activity, the motivator and educator of the people, and the supervisor and catalyst of state action.

Solidarity, with its central demand for independent, self-governing unions, undercut this theory of Party hegemony, and its practice. The union's initially victorious demand—replicated throughout society— was a thunderclap in a system in which "everything is political"—and is supposed to be. The right of unions to full autonomy cut deeply into the role and status of the Party as the mediator between society and state.

After all, in a communist system, the Party is the central institution in the totality of society and state. The whole is like a giant circle. At any given point in the circle, a group of workers, acting through the official unions established for the purpose, can go in one of two directions for redress of grievances—toward the state (their direct employer) or toward the Party. But since the Party and the state are closely conjoined, it does not really matter in which direction one goes, for the circle always leads back to the same authority. The Party's internal organization, based on the Leninist doctrine of democratic centralism, guarantees a strict hier- archical control of its lower and middle by the top. Pressures are always at work confounding strict hierarchical control, perhaps more so in Poland than in the Soviet Union. Yet the doctrine and the practice both tend to a monopoly of direction from above. Such direction is further guaranteed by the practice of nomenklatura, whereby all Party secretaries at all levels, save at the very top, are virtually appointed by the next-highest Party apparatus (though the form is one of election) and whereby all of the important posts in state and society are filled by an appointment process dictated by the highest echelons of the Party. Thus, the top Party people have a hammerlock on the Party, the state, and society, and it is this hammerlock that guarantees the system's stability and its authoritar- ianism and oligarchic rule. But the principle of self-governing unions breaks into the giant circle and causes significant tremors if not severe wrenchings throughout. The system of power would have to be recon- stituted to accommodate this intervention, if only to the degree that henceforth the PUWP would have only *a* leading role, not *the* leading role.

The Gdansk Accord therefore went considerably beyond both the direct and indirect consequences of collective-bargaining struggles in Western capitalist countries. There, collective bargaining affects a single plant, perhaps a single industry at most, and may have some faint ripple effects in other industries. In addition, it may erupt into a serious confrontation involving strikes, lockouts, economic disruptions, and even armed struggle. But these events remain occurrences within civil society. The state may be forced into the struggle, from the outside, but only to "restore" the rights of property, to balance these rights with other economic rights, and to maintain order.

But in Poland, Solidarity's bid for self-governing unions challenged the combined economic and political authority of the Party-state, threatening the monopoly of the Party-state in making decisions. It was a move to change the structure of the nation's political power. Struggles over collective bargaining in a capitalist context are not carried on for such high stakes.

On the other hand, Solidarity's bid for self-governing unions is considerably short of class-struggle scenarios present in much liberal and Marxist analysis. Such analysis posits a general strike of industrial workers against the capitalist class, and in the showdown there is an either-or struggle in which the aim of the proletariat is to "expropriate the expropriators." This model does not fit Poland. Solidarity does not confront capitalists or capitalist modes of production. Nor does Solidarity correspond to an image of vanguard industrial workers leading other "orders" of society as hangers-on. Instead, Solidarity embraces the immense majority in an immediate sense, who by the logic of the communist system are all employees. In this situation industrial workers are first among equals. Finally, Solidarity does not regard itself or act as if it is in an either-or adversarial struggle of total revolutionary combat in which either the union or the Party must destroy its foe. The Solidarity movement is an attempt on the part of its members to modify the structure of power, not replace it. This is a position far more consistent with their real situation than would be the imaginary positions invented for them by eager Western intellectuals or by jaundiced Eastern intellectuals and Party bureaucrats.

THE GEOPOLITICAL RIDDLE

A third significant structural force shaping present-day Poland is the geopolitical milieu within which the state exists and operates. "With our bodies we are in the East and with our souls we are in the West." These words were spoken to me by a scholar of note who is also a dedicated Party member, committed Marxist, and eloquent defender of the Jaruzelski regime. He went on to say that the Yalta conference had fixed Poland's fate in 1945. There was no doubt in his mind that Poland must fully embrace its connection with the Soviet Union. Only thus can Poland be secure. Only thus can it sustain the gains made by Communist rule since World War II, gains such as providing for the basic needs of all the people, providing jobs for all, and creating access to culture for all—accomplishments made possible by the institution of a socialist basis for the productive forces of society and by mass education.

A strong Party is necessary, he argued, both to tap and organize the spontaneities of the people and to prevent the disorganization and paralysis that mere spontaneity leads to. In this view Lenin's concept of the organized, disciplined Party leading the masses is the best answer in modern life, East or West, to the challenge of a mass society. Thus the connection with the USSR is both politic from the standpoint of security and creative in the sense of enabling Poland to develop a stable, prosperous society. The Party makes serious mistakes, he acknowledged, and constantly needs reforming. But it is the linchpin of both Poland's progress and its security. So the Party needs to be defended against the anarchic tendencies uncorked by Solidarity. Events in Hungary in 1956 should be warning enough to Poland that the West will not and cannot provide Eastern European people with basic physical security, he maintained. Nor can the West, given its checkered economic performance, provide the steady assistance needed for an effective political economy.

These arguments, made by this man and supported by several other leading figures whom I interviewed, are compelling. But they are compelling only on the basis of three assumptions: first, that there can be no change in the geopolitical structure laid down at Yalta (as interpreted and successfully acted upon by Stalin); second, that a communist system cannot evolve beyond the principles of Lenin; and third, that Solidarity is anarchic and represents disparate forces that at best need to be rechanneled into the Party and into Party-sponsored bodies and at worst provide a cover for Western intrigue and capitalist counterrevolution.

None of these assumptions fits Solidarity. Its call for renewal is a call for rethinking and rejuvenation in social theory and practice and for realigning theory and practice with the historic subjectivity envisioned for working people by Marx. Solidarity has carefully eschewed any intention or appearance of joining the West or of advocating a policy that would lead Moscow to suppose that, if Solidarity were in power, it would seek Western protection for Poland.

Yet Solidarity continues to find the geopolitical issue a dilemma.[10] Its leaders wish carefully to separate the Warsaw Pact issue from the issues of worker autonomy, the right to strike, the reduction and redefinition of censorship, and a renegotiation of "the leading role of the Party." But as is evident from the arguments of leading thinkers whom I interviewed, the Jaruzelski forces inevitably see these issues as closely intertwined. This structural fact of life is Solidarity's greatest single problem. It was not created just in Moscow and Warsaw (though Moscow, by the iron laws of superpower contestation must, and enthusiastically does, enforce the pattern). The structure was created by the two superpowers together. It is a knot that ultimately only they can untie, acting together.

In the meantime, the geopolitical dilemma remains an insuperable obstacle for Solidarity. Try as its leaders might to cajole, peacefully coerce, and humor the Jaruzelski government to treat with them on the basis of the agreement and principles negotiated at Gdansk, they always run up against the suspicion and—for the Jaruzelski forces—the useful rationalization that the union's demands are but the entering wedge for counterrevolution and capitulation to the West.

This structural conundrum has also had the effect of quelling any tendency to violence on the part of Solidarity. It has made the union wary of a romantic, "man the barricades" mentality. The Solidarity insurgents, however moved to anger, and frequently with just cause, are reminded by cooler heads and by their own other inner voices that violence is folly in the face of the overwhelming force of the modern state, backed up by Russia's many divisions in Poland and on three sides of its border. There are other sources of Solidarity's commitment to nonviolence (see Chapter 5), but this structural feature of the situation is a telling influence.

ECONOMIC ORGANIZATION

The fourth structural force that has shaped Solidarity consists of the institutions and mechanisms that run the economy on a day-to-day basis. Under a communist system the economy is an arm of the state, controlled and managed from above. According to the principle and practice of nomenklatura, the Party controls the personnel and supervises the performance of the planners, administrators, and managers of the economy. Given the geopolitical milieu within which the Polish state exists, the economy is closely tied to the East, even though Poland frequently bargains gingerly with the West to gain particular economic advantages and avoid disadvantages.

From 1971 to 1975 Poland accepted huge loans from the West.[11] Thereafter, with the downturn in the Western economy—which meant that Poland fell far short of its expected levels of sales to the West—the government tried desperately to stave off Western pressure for the repayment of the mounting interest on the accumulated debt and of the debt itself.

These are some of the brute realities of the international economic environment within which Poland's economy must operate. But the economy has itself been organized and dominated by a coercive state in tandem with an imperious and jealous Party. In the years following World War II and the establishment of the Communist state, the economy was organized in Stalinist fashion as a command economy in which decisions travel downward from the heights of state and Party organs and information is supposed to flow upward. This pattern hardly changed under Gomulka from 1956 to 1970, though the state planners began to rethink Stalinist concepts in the direction of autonomy for plant managers and creation of genuine market mechanisms as one way to measure managers' performance. These intimations of a more flexible state-run economy mirror the Kosygin reforms in the USSR in the mid-1960s, and though they went further than Kosygin's concepts, they suffered a similar fate—partial acceptance and half-hearted implementation. But these ideas of the Polish economists and planners migrated to Hungary, where they were taken up with considerable seriousness and success by the Kadar regime. While in Poland, I was told by Polish planners that Hungarian economists had first learned of market reforms for a command economy from the Poles, as early as 1959. Later, in Budapest, I reported this, somewhat jokingly, to Hungarian economists. They gravely assured me that it was so.

From 1970 to 1973, during Gierek's early years, there seemed a moment in which the "progressives" in the state planning agency were being heard. Schemes got under way to open up the economy to the greater play of market forces. But the moment was short-lived, and as an economist in the planning agency assured me, the technocrats, as he called them, soon reasserted themselves. Presumably, he meant both the less progressive faction of planners and the administrators in the various ministries who control the country's industries and the plants within those industries.

Later in Gierek's decade there was an attempt to "coordinate" plants into WOGs (Wielke Organizacje Gospodarcze, or large economic organizations), presumably to give their leadership greater scope in dealing with Western capitalists and with the ministerial bureaucrats. But even this effort backfired, for it put more administrative restraints on the individual managers and facilitated meddling by politically motivated and well-placed administrators and planners in the government and in the correlative sections of the Party apparatus. Indeed, as one editor in Warsaw took special pains to point out to me, the truly significant feature of the Gierek years, and a phenomenon that persists under Jaruzelski, was the formation of "lobbies" of well-placed people from various power centers in the Party and the state. These lobbies intervene both in any reasonably coherent plan (whether tight or loose) that emanates from the planning agency and in any scheme to give market forces freer play. They intervene, to the detriment of either administrative patterns or market patterns, to frustrate the effectiveness of the economy and to corner for the privileged the lion's share of state produce and power. Of these lobbies, the most powerful and pervasive is the "heavy industry lobby."[12] Married to the concept of "bigger is better"—to a quantitative instead of a qualitative approach to technology, production, and consumption—and possessed of an extractive, domineering attitude toward nature, this entrenched lobby continues to be a major obstacle to economic and social regeneration in Poland—and in the Soviet Union as well.

Gierek himself played the game of lobbies most assiduously. There emerged in the 1970s the reality and then, more and more, also the appearance of a corrupt machine hogging the good things of life. Meanwhile, the daily fortunes of most Poles improved steadily from 1970 to 1975 under the impact of Gierek's wholesale borrowing of petrodollars from the West and as a result of his apparent desire to buy favor from the people through consumerism. But the second half of the decade saw the average citizen's fortunes decline, first relatively and then for many even absolutely, relative to what they had been before the boom. A J-curve theory of revolution could, to some degree, be applied in this case. This theory holds that revolution is likely to occur when a period of rising satisfaction, both apparent and real, is followed by a sudden downturn both in the level of satisfaction and in the assurance of continued satisfaction. The suddenness of the downturn, as much as its extent, helps to trigger revolution. [13]

But this state of affairs was exacerbated for the Gierek regime by some additional factors. The immense majority of Poles, being all employees of the state and as consumers all equally subject to the state's manipulation of prices, logically traced the source of their troubles to the same target, the increasingly visible privileged elite in the Party-state. Furthermore, the privileges of the elite were doubly offensive. Their life-style became more and more luxurious in comparison with that of the immense majority (though the contrast was not as extreme as between the superrich and the middle class in Western countries). But what especially galled was that these same privileged Party and state bureaucrats laid claim to a philosophy and ideology of egalitarianism. This blatant hypocrisy was as much a cause of the revolt as was the disparity in income, privilege, and power.

Finally, it should be noted that the regime, in its haste to industrialize and modernize, and because of its mania for the gigantic, concentrated much of its effort on a relatively small number of industrial sites around the country. Thus were formed enclaves or concentrations of industrial workers. These enclaves, by the 1970s, were made up of the second and third generations of Poland's industrial work force. They were more highly skilled, better educated, more independently minded, and more experienced than their fathers and grandfathers had been. They were increasingly restive under the rigidities and bureaucratism of the state-managed economy. They had learned to know from whence came the orders and who profited and who did not. The rebellion, when it came, launched itself from among these workers centered in these enclaves, and it soon engulfed the entire society.[14]

A highly ironic element in this picture is the posture of the Communist state itself toward "the worker." In its propaganda the government constantly assured the industrial workers—and reassured itself—that "real working people," the bone and blood of the proletariat, were the apple of its eye. This was a significant psychological factor in the rise of Solidarity.

THE FAMILY CONNECTION

The fifth structural force that has shaped the Polish society of today is the position of the family in daily life. In Poland the concept of family is not quite the same as that in the West. The family in Poland is more stable, has greater historical depth, occupies a larger and more significant area of social space, and is rooted more securely in the ontological foundations of human experience. In America the family is like a fort on the plain trying to protect itself from hostile forces. In Poland it is itself a force that helps shape the social and cultural landscape. The Western family seems atomized, always vulnerable to the disintegrating effects of capitalist markets and the constant technological shifts. Attempts to control these effects through more and more regulation and centralization further corrode family life.

In Poland technology and industrial development also harass and tend to erode the family, especially its more traditionally rooted aspects. Yet the pace of things is different there and more in keeping with family stability. The family continues to constitute a powerful structural force in Polish society. It dominates the many national and religious holidays that Poles enjoy. It unites people in city and country. As a carrier and re-creator of ancient Polish traditions and values and as a transmitter of the knowledge of Poland's political and cultural past, it joins past and future. It is a strong nurturing force, a haven, for all workers. The family is a training ground for social responsibility and social unity on a basis other than Party ideology. It is essentially separate from the Party and the state and, though often under intense pressure from them, nevertheless remains an area of limited but fundamentally autonomous behavior and experience.

On the other hand, the family is changing. In some senses it is changing negatively. The lines of kinship are stretched thin or broken under the impact of modernization and the rationalizing and authoritarian demands of Party and state. A certain alienation or indifference sets in, and the family relationship becomes less important and also less supportive. So the family loses social power. Furthermore, women are now in the double bind of being workers both in the world and in the home, with a dual responsibility and a dual weight of the weariness and frustration of daily life.

But other changes are positive. The harder, hierarchical edges of traditional patriarchy are gradually softening. Women have greater opportunities and wider orbits and are on a more nearly equal basis with men in the world and in the home. Men, whose culture derives directly from traditional aristocratic roles and values, and not from any thoroughgoing capitalist culture such as that of the West, seldom seem to fit the stereotype of the aggressive, manipulative male that one finds so many embodiments of in the Western corporate world. Thus, there is more openness within the family because of modernization, socialist values, and the socialization of the economy.

The probable future course of the family is hard to anticipate, but it will likely remain a strong structuring force. Without its strength, both as a conserving influence and as a repository of the fiercely autonomous spirit of Polish traditions, it is doubtful that the workers of Solidarity would have made such remarkable progress or that they would have made it with such a keen sense of balance—within an explosive situation—between violent disruption on one hand and cautious reformism on the other.

THE CHURCH

The sixth major structural force is the church. How a society organizes its religious life is a crucial matter. In Poland religious life is tightly organized as a defense against the frontal attack on religion by Marxism. It is organized in a body that embraces the overwhelming majority of the population, and its hierarchy is a dominion of a large and powerful international body, the Roman Catholic church.

Consequently, pressure is exerted on the church in Poland from at least three sources: the Roman hierarchy, headed by the pope, albeit at present a Polish one; the Communist regime, from which it strives to attain some independence of action; and the political, social, and economic aspirations of its parishioners. The fact that these parishioners encompass virtually the entire Polish nation makes them a powerful influence on the character of religion practiced by the church. For the same reason, of course, the church is in a position to influence strongly the Polish nation and society. For example, the independence of action sought by the Polish church against the Party's hegemonical policies suggests by so much a general principle of social autonomy vis-à-vis the state that could be more generally applied in other areas. Promotion of such a principle has not necessarily been the intention of the church, but intentionally or not, it teaches by example. When Solidarity arrived on the scene, advocating independence for working people's associations, the parallel was obvious, and it seemed clear that Solidarity and the church have some common interests. However, these common interests have not prevented the church hierarchy from now and again making deals with the Jaruzelski regime that have hurt Solidarity, as for example, in the pope's diplomatic maneuverings with Jaruzelski and Walesa in June, 1983 (see Chapter 8). On the other hand, the pope's visit in June, 1987, seemed designed to help push the hierarchy of the Polish church toward more support for Solidarity. So the church, it appears, gives with one hand and takes away with the other.

Other evidence of the church's influence lies in the daily impact of its priesthood on Solidarity. It is as if through its own grass roots the church connects with the political and social strivings of the people for justice, freedom, and renewal. Indeed, many priests seem more Polish and national than religious. They identify with the popular struggle, giving it inner, conscientious strength, and through counsels of nonviolence and patience, they help channel popular feeling into politic directions. Thus, there is an inherent contrast between local priest and hierarchic prelate. Even so, both priesthood and hierarchy, the former from faith, the latter from considerations of prudence, combine to act as a buffer between Party-state authority and the nation. In this fundamental structural sense they condition the course of the revolution. They help to prevent the intransigence of either side and promote the readiness of both to find room for negotiation.[15]

THE POLES AS SINGULAR NATION

A seventh and final structural force that has shaped Solidarity lies in the fact that Polish society is essentially one and only one nation. Although there are small populations of Germans, Ukranians, Armenians, Jews, and Lemke, the overwhelming majority speak a single language and belong to a cultural group with a common history, heritage, and symbols and with a common, compact territory. The results of the Second World War were cruel in the extreme, and crucial. Almost all Polish Jews, nearly three million of them, were exterminated by the Nazis. Both the eastern and the western boundaries of prewar Poland were pushed westward. Vast resettlements took place, and Poland is now, with small exceptions, a homogeneous people. The state presides over one nation, not several. This structural feature interacts with and supports the other structural features, especially the emergence of a worker society in a socialized economy and the almost universal Roman Catholicism. At the least it poses no obstacle to different social and economic sections of society making common cause. In a positive sense it nurtures a cross-sectional love and respect for the same traditions and heroes and memories of suffering and struggle, including memories of the deaths of martyrs.[16] And even as it arouses people's spirit to revolt against internal and external attempts at domination, it also inculcates a constitutional conception of politics that runs far back into Polish history.

These seven structural features of Polish society have powerful effects on any movement there. Some of the seven are major continuities from the past: a virile family life with considerable social depth, a strongly embedded national church, and a vigorous national and cultural life going back a thousand years.

Another feature is geopolitical. An understanding of the geopolitical dimension obviously starts with the fact of the close proximity of the Soviet Union, ever watchful and always ready to intervene should it feel the need. But there is also the legacy of the Yalta agreement, by the terms of which Poland remains uneasily situated between the two blocs created by the superpowers.

Finally, there are features that are direct products of the revolutionary changes that swept Polish society in the wake of World War II. These changes not only brought new and different structures into being in economic and political life but also deeply affected the abiding structures of family, religion, and nation. A command economy emerged, managed and run by the state and extending to almost all aspects of economic, social, and cultural life. Within and behind the state is the Party, which rules in the name of the workers and has taken upon itself the sole responsibility and right to lead. Its avowed goal is to transform Poland into a fully industrialized, modernized, and progressive nation. The Party has claimed a monopoly on leadership. It has persistently sanctioned the rule of a small group, especially in terms of a Leninist model. This model assigns to this special group of leaders initiative, organization, and conceptual reasoning and assigns to the masses spontaneity, feelings, a sense of particular grievances, and a capacity for comprehending leadership's conceptual reasoning.

The fact of this monopoly, and the mistakes made by those upholding it, triggered revolts beginning in 1956. Eventually, as mistakes compounded themselves and reverberated throughout the structures of society, and as the fact of monopoly became ever clearer, there grew up a counterforce, a resistance movement aimed not so much at the particular mistakes but at the monopoly itself.

These structural features help account for the growing dissonance or imbalance in Polish life and for the emergence of resistance in the many and seemingly diverse sections and strata of Polish society. They help account for the special importance of three social elements especially: industrial workers, priests, and intellectuals. Finally, they help account for the underlying unity of the resistance: there was a common target; there were few surrogate enemies that those in power could throw into the breach to divide and conquer the resistance, *i.e.*, few hostilities that could be based on ethnic, national, religious, or even class differences; and finally, the cry first adumbrated by the industrial workers for self-governing unions naturally struck a responsive cord throughout society, since virtually all citizens have so much in common as employees of the state.

What the workers responded to was the sane but forceful cry for an effective end to the Party monopoly on leadership. This is the meaning of the demand for the "self-organization of society" first publicly articulated by the industrial workers on the coast in 1970 in their movement for free unions. This demand was later voiced by KOR intellectuals, beginning in 1976.[17] It later crystallized into the Interfactory Strike Committee's demand for independent, self-governing unions, which led to the formation of Solidarity in 1980.

Thus, these seven structural forces help to account for the birth, direction, and pervasiveness of the resistance movement. But they are not a wholly sufficient explanation of the Solidarity phenomenon. Structures such as these seven are powerful governors of human existence. But however much they consciously and, more often, unconsciously mold behavior and thought, they are of themselves without motive force. What moves them is energy—human energy. In the ordering of things it is this energy, or psychological force, that presses human beings forward in pursuit of the fundamental interests through which the appropriate structures are constituted and reconstituted.

Whereas structural forces suggest determinateness, system, pattern, and predictability, psychological forces exhibit negativity, critical impulses, creative imagination, and the side of human behavior and experience that perceives variation, contradiction, and potential. Psychological force is not by nature antistructural, any more than structure is by nature antipsychological. Each seeks the other. The two belong together. But as we shall see, they do not always fit together in harmony.

5
Forces Generating Solidarity

A fundamental tendency in modern philosophy and science is to inspect, dissect, and divide things up for analysis. Another such tendency, often a companion of the first, is to put all things together through the operations of objective mind, thus creating mental systems. These two tendencies trade on dichotomies such as those between body and mind, the particular and the whole, the spontaneous and the rational, the material and the cultural. Through such adversarial categories reality, life itself, can be understood only in terms of an intellectual system describing it either as a series of discrete phenomena or as a totality of these phenomena. The celebration of the molecular confronts the apotheosis of abstract form. A great deal of scholarship—and politics—veers between these two poles or tries to make them coincide in some meaningful way. [1]

Applied to social movements for change, such as Solidarity, these tendencies of scholarship and political analysis can result in severe misunderstandings. Some profess to see the source and thrust of Solidarity's political consciousness in "the workers" (plus or minus other sections of "the people"), whereas others profess to see it in "the intellectuals." The difference between the two positions is assumed to be a dichotomy, an either-or question: either body, emotion, spontaneity, particular insight, and particle of consciousness, or mind, formal logic, planning, comprehensive understanding, objectivity, and strategic clarity.

In February, 1985, I attended a symposium organized by Roman Laba of Harvard University's Russian Research Center and entitled "KOR: Intellectuals in Democratic Movements—The Polish Experience." It was attended by an outstanding group of leading American and Polish scholars and journalists and by persons active in the Polish resistance movement. True to form, the key issue at the symposium was whether the source of Solidarity's political consciousness lies in the workers or the intellectuals. In spite of efforts by Laba and some members of the audience, such as Abraham Brumberg, to clarify this issue and move on, the discussions remained fixed in a mode of arguing either-or, either the workers or the intellectuals. Beneath the surface of the sophisticated commentary lurked the usual stereotypes. The celebrators of worker spontaneity were pictured by their opponents as romantic populists, and those who defended the role of the intellectuals were seen as the equivalent of Leninist ideological manipulators and worse. Some tried to make pragmatic adjustments between the two views. The symposium was a vigorous and useful experience. Yet this talented group could not extricate itself from the unproductive intellectual game of either-or.

The debate can be fierce. On one side the workers are lauded. In their spirit or soul or gut they have the power of insight into the unique truth of their situation. And according to their partisans, they had it well before intellectuals ever arrived on the scene. On the other side the Polish intellectuals are lauded. The emergence of political consciousness is found in the educational works of the activist members of the intelligentsia. They prepare the way by developing and propagating the necessary conceptions and connected understandings that others (the workers, the people) can thereafter imbibe. Failure comes when the workers have not successfully imbibed the political message. The movement is then fragmented and riven by factions. The movement becomes erratic—now adventurist, now overly cautious.

But the debate between the two sides is probably a spurious one. Both sides are composed of persons who, in terms of their own dichotomizing, would have to regard themselves as "intellectuals." Furthermore, in the real world spontaneous, particulate behavior and the exercise of intelligence are almost never totally separated. Only a science that has already decided to dissolve social reality into "particles" over here and "constructs" over there would insist on seeing them as totally separate.

It is possible to avoid such mechanical juxtaposition, such dichotomizing, and to do so without falling into a fuzzy intellectual pragmatism that merely seeks a middle ground. One must first unburden oneself of unexamined assumptions about mind versus body, the particular versus the whole, and the spontaneous versus the rational. Then one must look closely at the actual deeds and demands of Solidarity. What then reveals itself is specific, interconnected groups of people who together through their actions are making a clear demand for change. Their goal is considerably more than amelioration of grievances and considerably less than the destruction of one ideological and political system and its replacement by another. They demand independent, self-governing unions, along with other measures, such as greater freedom of expression, that they believe are necessary for the full realization of this basic demand.

The demand for self-governing institutions lies at the center of Solidarity's quest for renewal. It was this demand that focused the workers' consciousness and mobilized their spirit. It also describes the limits of their quest, not in the sense that they never think beyond it, but in the sense that all their thinking and their increasingly politicized consciousness always returns there. To date, even when their thinking has seemed to go beyond it and even when their ideas have come to them from members of the intelligentsia who wanted them to go beyond it, the workers of Solidarity have nevertheless returned in their minds and actions to the goal of independent, self-governing unions as the touchstone of their quest. It was the point at which individual self-interest and the interests of society were in touch with each other; at which utility and what was right were, in the eyes of Solidarity, still conjoined; and at which the admittedly mystical feelings of "the movement," of redemption for the martyrs of past struggles, and of hope for the future could easily commingle with prudential calculation, estimates of realistic possibilities, and the more abstract conceptualizations of new political arrangements. Without this touchstone there would have been no unity of industrial worker and intellectual adviser, no coming together of otherwise disparate sections and ranks of the people, and no evocation of the energies and spirits of millions of ordinary citizens.

The cry "No taxation without representation" was far more than just a brilliant tactic or a fortunate slogan for the Americans fighting King George in the Revolution. It in fact expressed the "materialized" spirit of a people fighting for a say in their own destiny. Similarly, in Poland the cry for independent, self-governing unions was the concrete manifestation of a unified people determined to change decisively the circumstances under which they were governed, whether in their job or in their community. In each case the very concreteness of the demand at one and the same time evoked the deepest political instincts of a people and also decided the limits within which the struggle would be fought. And in the light of this demand there are no "workers" and "intellectuals" ranged in separate categories or ranks. There are instead people united in a common, practical political movement, people with different talents, temperaments, training, and tendencies, who often disagree but can stick together around a clear goal that is immediately, viscerally, and intellectually clear to all.

NONVIOLENCE

There are four major psychological, or generative, features of the resistance movement in Poland that became Solidarity. The first is nonviolence, a policy to which Solidarity has persistently adhered. It is best termed a *policy* because Solidarity's nonviolence does not seem to have the same philosophical undercurrent as that in the teachings of Mahatma Gandhi and Martin Luther King. There is, of course, a kinship with the ideas of the two great leaders, but Solidarity has basically adopted nonviolence as the most practical thing to do.[2]

Solidarity's nonviolence is a new thing in the history of Polish dissent. Past resistance movements have almost always culminated in action on the barricades. Poland has a long and fierce martial tradition. In the hearts and minds of Poles the ancient lure to close with the enemy on the field of battle, even against insuperable odds, is a powerful one. Still vivid in every Polish heart are memories of Kosciusko's famous campaign in the 1790s, of the heroes of the 1832 uprising, and of the Warsaw uprising against the Nazis in 1944.

Several factors are responsible for Solidarity's turn to nonviolence. First, geopolitics has a strong bearing on the way in which Poles think and feel about their situation. They are painfully aware of what happened in Hungary in 1956 and Czechoslovakia in 1968. The Soviet Union's threat of violence was a powerful sobering influence on the insurgents of Solidarity. Their movement was not destroyed by this threat, but it was restrained. The Russian threat, however, never dissuaded the insurrectionists of the nineteenth century from violence. The geopolitical element is therefore not sufficient by itself to explain the turn to nonviolence. Yet it is worth noting that the modern state—including that of Poland—can overawe society as never before in history. Because of technology and the overall rationalization of existence and because of the state's imperious claim to monopoly in the use of physical force, the disproportion in sheer power and organization of information between state and society has grown much beyond what it was in the nineteenth century. These overwhelming changes doubtless are not lost on the modern Polish rebel.

Second, it may be that the long series of defeats through violence suffered by the Polish people has made them receptive to an alternative to violence. The members of Solidarity seem to have worked around and through the romanticism of the violent deed that so captivated previous generations of Poles. Historical suffering may have made them more clever or at least more mature. They may have come to realize that physical defeat, or physical victory for that matter, is not necessarily an index to achievement or superiority.

Progress is often achieved by turning in a new direction. The new direction of the Polish people today is not the inward or "spiritual" one that in earlier times merely compensated for physical defeat. The new direction is toward physical, but nonviolent, action, it is away from violence toward politics, politics meaning the permanent will to negoti- ate a genuine strategic compromise of vital differences. Involved in this commitment is the readiness to engage in nonviolent direct action such as strikes, ceremonial vigils, unauthorized meetings, and commemora- tive gatherings like those at the workers' monument in Gdansk.

Nonviolence is more than a new method. It is, and in fact it requires for its success, a new spirit. The new spirit brings directly into politics the affirmation of basic human rights—including the rights of both sides in the conflict—and the search for new ways of doing things that will benefit the oppressed and, in time, the oppressor as well. It is of course recog- nized that the sides in the struggle are not equal in power. But the oppressed seek to turn their disadvantage to good account, on one hand by resisting cooperation with the oppressor until the latter clearly indi- cates a willingness to negotiate, and on the other hand by eschewing both violence and any ideologically motivated effort to unseat him. Although Solidarity's campaign may be similar in some ways to those of Gandhi and Dr. King, its spirit has a more political character than the almost purely moral one that lay at the heart of theirs.

Another cause for the movement's turn to nonviolence may be that in Solidarity there is a new breed of Polish rebel: a democrat, not an aristo- crat; a worker bred in the factory, shipyard, and mine, not an intellectual bred in academe or an upper-class salon or the clubs of the expatriates; a practical person, not a dreamer of impossible schemes. Such a rebel is not for that reason a clod or a pushover or a person capable of only "trade union consciousness," to quote Lenin's pejorative term for the insufficient degree of consciousness exhibited by industrial workers left to themselves.[3] The member of Solidarity, as a worker, is accorded status in a socialist society quite beyond what the prevailing culture accords ordinary people in Western society. This gives him or her a greater sense of confidence than workers seem to have in the West. Today's Poland also has a young work force, one that, as a result of the troubles of 1954, 1970, and 1976, is seasoned in its capacity to act for itself.[4] These previous trials of strength, which led to much suffering, have also bred in the workers a sense of limits. They now conduct their action where it counts—within the factory gates. In contrast to workers in previous struggles, they do not brandish slogans and commit acts of arson in street marches and demonstrations. In addition, the intellectuals, especially in KOR, have shared with the workers a newfound sense of the need for action short of violence, a feeling that may be rooted in the Marxist humanism that most of the KOR people espouse in one form or another.[5]

The church, at the levels of both hierarchy and grass roots, influenced Solidarity in a nonviolent direction. The hierarchy sought to restrain both the government and Solidarity. Unfortunately, out of a fear of violence, it acted as often to undermine Solidarity's peaceful activities as it did to calm the government's anger. However, at the grass roots, the priests were less concerned with playing such a role. They were committed to nonviolence as a philosophy, and they literally sided with Solidarity against the government. In this way the local priests contributed effectively to the new strategy of positive, nonviolent action to redress wrongs.

Yet another factor in Solidarity's pursuit of a nonviolent strategy is Jaruzelski's new government, which, following the martial law crackdown, became a buffer, a Polish buffer, between Polish society and the Soviet Union. Jaruzelski provides a space within which society can continue to press for change short of the point of violent eruption. Furthermore, since Jaruzelski himself uses violence (beatings, imprisonment, and arbitrary applications of the rules of justice), for Solidarity and society at large to insist upon nonviolence as a method of resolving conflict becomes, from some points of view, an even more necessary and more brilliant tactic than ever.

Finally, the major positive reason why Solidarity follows the path of nonviolence is that its members feel that this is the one best way to struggle to change the prevailing system of power sufficiently to guarantee the protection of ordinary people from the government, to achieve the fulfillment of their basic daily needs, and to offer some hope of continuing enhancement of their daily lives. It must be emphasized that the goal is to change the system, not abolish it. This search for revolution short of revolution, this quest for reform that is more than reform, turns the hearts and minds of the people away from violent solutions and toward, in the broad sense, political methods of combat.

SUBJECTIVITY

Marx felt that though human beings are powerfully shaped by the objective forces of history, there was nevertheless arising a class that increasingly would be able to act as a subject in history. This class is the proletariat, especially the industrial workers. Lenin agreed, but he also posited a new force, the Party, to guide the proletariat. In communist countries the Party, more and more, has taken on both the substance and the appearance of Marx's subjectivity, reversing the relationship between workers and Party that Lenin still to some degree adhered to. Indeed, since the revolutionary overthrow of the old order and its transformation through wholesale social reconstruction became the historic business of the Party, the very concept of subjectivity changed from that of acting within history, to that of acting above, in spite of, and in control of history—as it were, from a point outside of history. Subjectivity became a markedly rationalistic, reconstructionist, and ideological thing.

In the teeth of this situation the Gdansk workers, and then workers all over Poland up and down the social scale, asserted the subjectivity of unions—the unions' right to act on behalf of the daily livelihood of their members. The workers' claim is significant in several ways.

First, they asserted their autonomy—a form of subjectivity—vis-à-vis their employer, the state, and by so much also vis-à-vis the real political power in the state, the Party. On this issue they were uncompromising.

When KOR-related and other intellectuals counseled them to seek the government's agreement to a strengthening of existing unions, the workers pushed the proposal aside peremptorily and insisted on their demand for new unions that would be clearly independent and self-governing. One of the advisers, Tadeusz Kawalik, recalled the event.

> We [the members of the Commission of Experts] knew from the beginning that the demand for free trade unions was most crucial, though we did not realize that it would so overshadow the rest. Almost all members of the Commission arrived in Gdansk with grave doubts about the feasibility of this point. . . . A joint meeting of Presidium members [of the Interfactory Strike Committee] and experts was held discreetly in a distant part of the shipyard (in a disused canteen) to discuss whether the Strike Committee would be satisfied with a radical reconstruction of the old trade unions, so-called Variant B. We presented a short paper on the subject. It was categorically rejected by all who spoke. I must add that during the course of a whole week's negotiations, I did not meet a single striker or delegate who was willing to compromise on this issue.[6]

Second, Solidarity stands for a different kind of subjectivity than that to which the Party subscribes. Solidarity's subjectivity is not reconstructionist, rationalistic, ideological, or totalitarian. According to Solidarity, truth and policy must emerge from communication and negotiation between equals, not from a consensus within one organ of society—the Party—that is then imposed on every other part. What Solidarity seeks is not a wholly new order, not one that in the style of Lenin would result from a shattering of the old and the creation of something brand new out of the remaining pieces, but a renewed order in which the subjectivity of the extant parts of society, and the dialogue between them, would be given genuine political space to grow. Such a renewed order would necessarily modify substantially the claim of the Party to a monopoly of subjectivity.

Third, Solidarity rejects the Western capitalist notion of subjectivity, which stresses individualism and personal ambition. Solidarity's notion is that subjectivity inheres in social being. Thus, the individual is honored, but mainly as a member of a group or association or, indeed, as a member of the human species. The movement struggles for the subjectivity of unions, associations, and professions, seeking to give them the autonomy and efficacy through which the life activities of society can prosper and grow.

Finally, it was on the basis of this notion of subjectivity that Solidarity developed a full-scale program. But the program has remained practical and nonideological. It started, as had the programs of past rebellions, with bread-and-butter issues and longtime specific grievances: the price of meat, the "political" hiring and firing of workers, the loss of free Saturdays, the pervasiveness of bureaucratic red tape, the existence of dollar stores for the privileged. Awareness of these specific grievances, however, rapidly evolved into a widespread realization of the seemingly more general and more imperative need for independent, self-governing unions. There was no break between awareness of the particular grievances and the more general perception. The workers saw quite clearly that they needed permanent institutions of their own with which to protect their livelihood.

Furthermore, there was no break between the demand for institutional autonomy for their unions (points 1 and 2 of the twenty-one demands that led to the Gdansk Accord; see Appendix) and the demand for the right to publish and be free of prior and other forms of censorship by the Party (point 3). These demands, logically and chronologically, also led to the demand for far greater participation by workers, through their unions, in the making and operation of industrial policy (point 6). This demand in turn led to tackling the nomenklatura system, the linchpin of Party hegemony (point 12).

The evolution of Solidarity soon led beyond the social and economic realm, to which the government sought to limit the movement, and spilled over into the political realm, in which the Party-state and its bureaucratic power group are entrenched. After the Bydgoszcz beatings in early March, 1981, after the narrowly averted national general strike and the resulting threat of Russian intervention, and after the pyrrhic victory of the Party's "moderates" that spring and summer, the Party became moribund and incapable of holding up its end. Solidarity was forced more and more into a role of heir apparent, as a power that growing numbers, on each side of an increasingly polarized nation, either hoped or feared would *replace* the Party. But Solidarity was not prepared to move into a power vacuum and in effect run the state. In any event such a move was unthinkable simply on geopolitical grounds. Still, Solidarity might have moved in the direction of resolving the crisis of state power—spinning off a political group or groups that could, as one or more parties, take charge of the state—if it had had more time and if the Kremlin could have stomached it.

The point that must be emphasized is the practical, evolving nature of Solidarity's quest for the realization of ordinary people's subjectivity. The strength of Solidarity was, and today remains, as a corrective of the system, not a replacement for it. And if by a quirk of historical fate Solidarity would be forced to replace the prevailing system, it would do so by inventing a power in the state with which the movement—as a set of autonomous unions and on behalf of society—could conduct negotiations on a regular constitutional basis.

This analysis of Solidarity's subjectivity may seem to leave out of the picture those forces, fears, and feelings in the movement that could be called extremist, that pushed spontaneity beyond its practical boundaries, that would if given their head have led to the adventurism and all-or-nothing posturing that its enemies in the government pretended to see in the movement as a whole. On the other hand this sketch may seem to leave out of the picture those tendencies in the opposite direction: toward ideological definition, historic rationalism, and one or another kind of leadership from the top down.[7] But the radical center that was Solidarity hewed to a line between and beyond those twin abstractions of adventurism and ideologism. It remained resolutely and radically practical and evolutionary.

LEGAL-MINDEDNESS

"The spirit of August had a legal mind," wrote Ewa Hauser in *Poland Watch*. Another scholar, Anthony Kemp-Welch, begins his introduction to a book that reproduces the tapes of the Gdansk negotiations by pointing out, "The strikers' demands, though radical and far reaching, were also limited: they did not seek to take power but to bring it within legal jurisdiction." Adam Michnik, a KOR intellectual leader who has lived much of his life in jail, demanded to be put on trial, arguing that he had done nothing wrong in the eyes of the law. Although he was freed by the terms of the amnesty of July, 1984 (and later reincarcerated and then once again given amnesty), his demand to stand trial may itself have been one reason the government resorted to amnesty rather than be forced to deal legally and constitutionally with the issue.[8]

The emphasis on legality, due process, and structural change based on constitutional balances is deeply characteristic of the Solidarity movement—of both its industrial workers and its intellectuals. This is an enormously important point. On the basis of both expertise and instinct, the insurgents of Solidarity think in legal terms. They constantly recall and reaffirm the spirit of constitutions past, especially the constitution of 1791.

This deep belief in constitutional politics ties in very closely with Solidarity's nonviolence and subjectivity and with its emphasis on unions, associations, and professional groups. In every society there are many kinds of work that support and give expression to life. The organization of this work needs protection and the opportunity for autonomous growth, conditions that do not just happen spontaneously, by some mystical impulse to equilibrium inherent in market forces. The organizing framework of the state is needed. The state and related political groupings, such as the Party, are necessary to bring a certain coherence to the whole, to find balances among the various forms of work, and to protect the whole from attack and disorder. Thus, a premium is put on communication, negotiation, and daily politics. This in turn requires a constitutional framework, which, in a fundamental sense, is nothing but the creation and growth of a set of structures to guarantee the autonomy of each of the parts of society and to facilitate discussion, negotiation, and compromise among them. Inherent within this set-up is the need for continuity and predictability and for the protection of the individual: in a word, for legality.

Legality sums up the approach, the spirit, and the long-term implications of Solidarity. According to Solidarity, there are two sides to issues involving legality: first, the autonomy of social units, primarily unions of workers (of *all* kinds); and second, the rights of the state acting for the whole of society.

Both aspects of legality are clearly evident in point 3 of the Gdansk Accord, the one relating to censorship. Point 3 begins by affirming the need "to uphold freedom of expression and publication as guaranteed by the Constitution, not to suppress independent publishing, and to grant access to the mass media for representatives of all denominations." Four subpoints embellish this general statement (see Appendix). The first and third points are especially significant.

1. The government will submit a draft law to the *Sejm* on the control of press and publications within three months. It will be based on the principles that censorship should protect: the state's interests, that is preservation of state and economic secrets which will be more closely defined by law; matters of state security and its major international interests; religious feelings and those of non-believers; and [the law] should prevent dissemination of morally damaging material. *The draft law will also provide a right of appeal to the Supreme Administrative Court against decisions taken by bodies controlling the press and publications.* The right of appeal will also be incorporated into the Code of Administrative Procedure. . . .

3. Broadcasting, the press and publishing should express a diversity of ideas, opinions, and evaluations. They should be subject to social control. (Italics added.)

A new balance is being sought—or a genuine balance for the first time—between the rights and responsibilities of social units and the rights and responsibilities of the state. One recognizes basic liberal themes, such as insistence on independent publishing and on fair procedure and legality. But one also notes a Marxistlike insistence, and a traditional and religious insistence, on the rights of the whole. Thus, there is a fusion that points to a new approach recognizing the autonomy of social units in conjunction with the rights of the state to act for the whole, with these two different and often opposing needs being adjudicated by some such body as a Supreme Administrative Court.

There was a fine, and deliciously ironic, moment during the first meeting in August, 1980, between the Gdansk workers' representatives and the government, led by Mieczyslaw Jagielski. Florian Wisniewski, an electrical technician, said to Jagielski: "When the Americans were fighting for independence, their slogan was 'man is born free and lives free'. I consider this 'born free' is a great help to us. I think, Prime Minister, you understand me." To which Jagielski replied: "I do understand. I do."[9] Whether he did or not is not so important. Nor is it important that Wisniewski may not be altogether historically correct in his comment about America. What is important is the emphasis he is putting, as a worker, on "born free," because it contrasts so sharply with the Marxist belief that man *becomes* free through social transformation and rational reconstruction. Whether Marx himself can be altogether interpreted in this fashion is a moot question, but it is the gospel of Lenin and Stalin and of the Polish United Workers party. In contrast, the Polish workers' movement believes that workers—all people in a socialized society—are the inheritors of certain rights, that indeed they possess these basic rights by the simple fact that they are human. No history, revolution, or party has to create these rights for them. Constitutions should enable these rights to shine in the sun, not enfeeble and eviscerate them. The difference is fundamental, and workers of Poland, by instinct and by virtue of their own constitutionally rich history, have traveled a long way beyond liberalism and Marxism toward new ground. Men and women are born free, but together, not as isolated individuals. Men and women act in history to modify institutions to increase human freedom. The Marxist temptation to reconstruct the world from the top down has been surpassed; the liberal predisposition to accord freedom only to isolated individuals has also been surpassed.

PIETY AND THE NATIONAL FEELING

Between 90 and 95 percent of Poland's citizens are Roman Catholic, and they throng the churches. Furthermore, most Polish holidays, and they have many, are Catholic Christian holidays that are celebrated with a fervor and love of pageantry unexcelled in the world. On Corpus Christi Day, for example, the entire nation virtually comes to a halt: everyone is with his or her family, going to church or celebrating at home. The day may include laying wreaths of flowers on a favored monument or sacred place. And therein lies the rub—both for politics and for analysis.

There is a rub for politics because the people, after singing national hymns in a Catholic Christian mode in church, stream out of church and place their flowers at places made sacred both nationally and religiously. Most of these observances are motivated as much by national as by religious feeling.

There is a rub here for analysis as well. I have been posing this matter in the manner of a Western rationalist, who must divide things up and thereafter can no longer understand anything. The national and the religious in Poland are not divided. They blend into each other. In a decisive spiritual sense they are the same. A thousand years of Catholicism, a thousand years of Poland—these centuries form one experience, a melding together. Nor is the national feeling at its base a chauvinistic one. It has all the appearance of being a bid for genuine national subjectivity. The church supports and feeds it. The hierarchy would like to use it to enhance its control and to bend the national church to the needs and policies of the international church in Rome. The spirit of piety and gentility and of patience in suffering is instilled in the generations of Polish citizens by their religious beliefs and confessors. At the same time, the spirit of indignation at wrongs done and the church's own long struggle for autonomy in Poland bolsters and guides the workers-citizens of the nation in the direction of freedom and autonomy for themselves.[10]

Thus, there is a kind of implicit overlapping of the church's conscientious but persistent struggle for autonomy within its sphere, with the equally limited, patient, but radical struggle of the workers for autonomy in theirs. In that sense it is idle to speculate, as so many do, which force— the church or Solidarity—is leading the struggle at any particular time. Both tendencies are moving in the same direction, a political one— toward authentic subjectivity in the Polish nation-state: that is, toward the subjectivity of the nation (or of society, as some call it) and toward the subjectivity of the social units into which the nation is divided, with all at bottom unified within a framework of a constitutional, self-governing state. Thus, though political, these dynamics are also deeply spiritual. One must be careful not to counterpose religious to secular in Poland. Civil society is a social unit, a social being, not a contractual one. The nation evokes this notion of social being and therefore has a strong spiritual content. Piety is infused into the social, the worldly, realm, and worldly concerns and political themes are also present and deeply felt in the pews of every church.

The degree to which the church speaks the language of Solidarity was never clearer than when Pope John Paul II addressed millions of his fellow Polish citizens in June, 1983. Again and again he appealed to "the nation" and to "the subject."

> A state is really sovereign if it governs the community and serves at the same time the common good of the community, if it allows the *nation* to realize the *subjectivity* peculiar to it. . . .
> The Sovereignty of the state is closely linked with its ability to promote the freedom of the nation, that is, to create conditions which will enable it to express the whole of its own historical and cultural identity; this means conditions under which the state will allow the nation to be sovereign. . . .
> Why do the working people of Poland—and, after all the working people

of the whole world—have the right to such a dialogue? Because the working man is not just an instrument of production but a *subject*. He is a subject who, in the entire process of production, has primacy over capital. . . . Man is unable to work if he sees no meaning in his work, when the meaning ceases to be clear to him.[11]

Two words: *nation* and *worker*. One is from the vocabulary of liberalism, the other from Marxism. Threaded together by a third word, *subject*, a word much dearer and more familiar to political Marxist humanism than to the religious Catholic mind. But the pope knew in what context he was speaking. He adapted the message of the spirit to the political matters that were uppermost in the minds of his vast audiences, for it was because of these things that they poured out in such numbers to see and hear him.

There are other structural and psychological elements shaping Solidarity, but these seem the leading ones. All together and severally, they reveal a movement that is complex but also simple. On the surface it would seem to be extraordinarily diverse. It erupts everywhere, among miners and shipyard workers, farmers and teachers, believers and unbelievers, writers and professors, students and priests. Jews and non-Jews, among party people, professionals, housewives, druggists, grocers, consumers, etc. In other contexts, many of these groups have been in opposition to one another, often intensely, and were kept in opposition by the divide-and-conquer methods and ideologies of the powers that be. But in Solidarity there is a great coming together, even though there are still some mutual suspicions, unfamiliarity, awkwardness, and labeling. But it is as if the harder edges had worn off and people had found both negative and positive reasons to bond together in a common cause on common ground.

The structures of Polish socialist society put almost everyone in a fundamentally similar economic position vis-à-vis those in power—a position, it must be stressed, that is not in the private realm of a privatized civil society such as one in the West but is itself directly part of the public, and thus the political, realm. Also, within that realm the structure and role of the Party-state made it a clear target of blame by virtually everyone when things went wrong. The geopolitical squeeze acted upon the people to solidify their common sentiment of rage at the Soviet Union and intensify their national feeling. At the same time, it helped to quell any turn to a violent response. The family, in a modernizing epoch, acted on one hand to nurture a spirit of resistance and on the other to help channel it in practical, nonideological directions. Similarly, the church, a zealous defender of its autonomy that has held its own against the authorities for forty years, helped promote the people's quest for subjectivity.

The psychological forces underlying Solidarity tended in similar directions. The Polish people as a whole, not just the old aristocratic upper crust, have gained access to their common history and culture. They have done so not only through the mists of family traditions, but through modernizing, socialized schools for everyone—an achievement of which the Communist regime is justly proud. Contact was made with revolutionary heroes, with kings who ruled in different ways, with constitutional movements, with a tradition of balanced government emphasizing the rights of both state and citizens, and with Poland's own brand of socialism, which is rooted in the nineteenth century.[12] The Polish people have found a common basis for a unified resistance to the Party-state monopoly of power and authority. This basis is the demand for the subjectivity of social units. They found the will to pursue this goal, and the goal implied therein (that of balanced constitutional powers shared by state and society), with a pertinacity that is not pugnacious, not sullen, not adventurist, and not violent, but that is itself a constitutional style and thus consistent with the whole form and content of the movement.

If *revolution* means the attainment of one's goal by any means possible including violence, if it means wholesale social reconstruction and a unified ideological theory to direct it, or if it means wholesale and permanent replacement of the established power group in the state by another, then Solidarity is not revolutionary. If *reform* means successful protest over grievances, effective struggles over policy, or even piecemeal adaptation of structures, then Solidarity is not a reform movement. If *liberal* means the struggle for freedom and individual rights, for legal forms that alleviate irreconcilable individual conflicts, and for labor unions that defend the individual rights of workers in the private sphere, then Solidarity is not a liberal movement. Finally, if *Marxism* is the elevation to power of a proletariat class or if it is that and also the leadership of that class by a Party dedicated to social reconstruction, then Solidarity is not Marxist.

However, one could find elements from each of these definitions in Solidarity. In some way Solidarity seems to be at a later stage in the evolution of humanity than the societies that produced these definitions of political phenomena. It is clearly a workers' movement. It is also clearly a movement for freedom expressed as the subjectivity of ordinary people through the solidarity of their unions and associations. It is clearly a constitutional movement expressed in the mode of the complementarity and balance to be struck among different powers representing different political and social needs. But their constitutionalism is not the classic liberal contract struck between competing, adversarial, individual interests. In sum I would hazard to call Solidarity a movement appealing to the needs and imaginations of ordinary people that has as its fundamental goal the constitutionalization of a socialized society.

Three impressive books about Solidarity describe the movement as a self-limiting revolution. Their authors are Neal Ascherson, an Englishman; Alaine Touraine, a Frenchman; and Jadwiga Staniszkis, a Pole who participated as an expert in the Gdansk negotiations.[13] There is much truth in their descriptions and analyses.

But though I distance myself from George Sanford's harsh criticism of their thesis as "self-serving and absurd," I do believe that they misstate the case more than a little.[14] "Self-limiting" is too voluntaristic, too liberal, a concept. It implies too much the notion of a rational actor who is the all-seeing master of his or her fate. It almost implies that individuals and groups can choose their history. It gives too little weight to the structural factors identified in Chapter 4.

I see Solidarity as a trailblazer. A trailblazer may appear to be the very essence of the rational, free, self-starting actor dear to the heart of thinkers such as Ayn Rand, whose novels are the apotheosis of the thinking, egoistical hero, the "I am a rock" rational actor par excellence.[15] Nevertheless, trailblazers are deeply conditioned by the place from which they start and by the trail they begin to blaze. Applied to Solidarity, this is true not only for the solid center of the movement, led by Lech Walesa, but for the nationalists, the socialist reformers, the Catholic cohorts, and the many others that comprise it. The structures and the psychocultural milieu deeply conditioned their beginning and deeply affected how they would move and how they would evolve as they blazed the trail.

To reconnoiter for a moment: Solidarity started with grievances, grievances accumulated for years in the *Sturm und Drang*, the press and banality, of everyday existence of the sort familiar to every Pole, as worker, as consumer, and as citizen. The struggle deepened into issues of policy and nibbled at the edges of dominant structures. These policy issues became a reality of growing importance to the workers. They decided to press for structural change: independent, self-governing unions and professional associations. This decision led to the drive for legalization of Solidarity, the new law on censorship, the Bydgoszcz confrontation, the recognition of Rural Solidarity, the new law on worker participation in management decisions, and Solidarity's first (and to date last) great national convention. Beyond this point lay the more frightening prospect of having to provide state leadership because the Party, losing its last vestiges of legitimacy, had failed to be a sufficiently strong or able partner. But this problem of revolutionary responsibility was swallowed up by the great intervention of December, 1981, when General Jaruzelski struck by force of arms.

As Jaruzelski and his moderate Communists now struggle to be a government in the face of a deeply resentful nation, Solidarity's role, along with that of associated resistance efforts, continues in the same mode. There is insistence on autonomy of social units (the principle of subjectivity) and on negotiations with the state to that purpose. Furthermore, there is an insistence that Poland's problems be dealt with through a partnership of the state and the people and that henceforth there be a balance of constitutionally defined powers, in law and in fact, in an emerging Polish workers' society and state.

In all this I see a trail being blazed. I do not see "self-limiting" action; nor do I see "revolution." However, if one were to fashion a new concept of revolution as a series of practical steps, triggered by the conflicts and oppressions of daily life, that do not suddenly overturn a nation's social and political system but still lead to a fundamental alteration in the structures and balances of power, then Solidarity would indeed be revolutionary and that would be the only word with which to describe this movement "at a later stage" in humankind's evolution.

But Solidarity is not (not yet, that is) such a movement, because realization of this series of practical steps has eluded it. Although it is true, as a New York *Times* editorial observed in the summer of 1984, "that Solidarity's ideas are now deeply rooted in Polish reality," nevertheless, as the same editorial also pointed out, there must be recognition of this fact by the Jaruzelski regime in Warsaw. And, one should immediately add, there must also be such recognition in Moscow and Washington.[16]

Thus far this movement "at a later stage" has not been able to fulfill its promise. Solidarity remains a signpost to that revolution. As such, it was and is a hybrid: a coming together, into possibly a new pattern, of elements from Poland's traditional and constitutional past, from its socialistic, modernizing, Communist present, and from Western liberal influences both past and present.

It is a promising amalgam. It constitutes no fundamental ideological threat to Moscow or Washington. If knowledge of its reality were to seep into the consciousness of the policy makers in all three capitals and if, simultaneously, leaders in Washington and Moscow were at last to decide that the world's and their own interests hinged on a backing off from their intense confrontation, then the way would be open for negotiations to some purpose between Walesa and Jaruzelski. Solidarity's revolution, a new kind of revolution, would be fulfilled.

This picture of Solidarity flies in the face of several other interpretations of the movement. These include Communist views that it is at best spontaneity gone wild and at worst a perfidious, petit bourgeois, Western-financed counterrevolution; Marxist humanist views that it is a working-class phenomenon with religionational accretions—a positive struggle in the long march to a classless, humane society; Western liberal views that emphasize its trade-union character and its bid for a kind of collective bargaining with the state as employer or that stress its diverse character and consider it a cluster of interest groups jockeying for rewards and favors; and conservative views that Solidarity represents freedom in the struggle with totalitarianism and is helping the church in the latter's historic struggle with godless atheism.

One major fault that runs through these other views is the failure to place Solidarity in its context. My approach offers an alternative to these ideologically loaded interpretations.

A second major fault they exhibit is a tendency to presuppose a split between material and spiritual factors, place Solidarity in one or the other category, and reduce what is left out to an illusion or epiphenomenon. I will comment briefly on this second fault because the reader may have interpreted my distinction between structural and psychological forces as just another restatement of the material-spiritual dichotomy. Nothing could be further from my intention.

In placing Solidarity in its context, I have taken a standpoint rooted as much as possible in the totality of human existence. The structural and psychological forces I cited are things confronting, channeling, and generally influencing people in their everyday life. I have tried to draw together all the critical factors present in their daily existence so that a sense of the connections among things is communicated. This set of connections, or totality, stands revealed as such because these related forces in everyday life embrace both material and spiritual factors. They do so "from the beginning," and together, in a unity of experience. It is only "afterward" that factors are singled out, as it were, by rational analysis, as material or spiritual. But I begin with the assumption of their unity. I do not assume that people, in their actual daily being, are walking cardboard stereotypes of now material, now spiritual activity; nor do I assume that either the material or the spiritual must be the only "reality."

My effort to place Solidarity in true context is based, for example, on Marx's notions of sensuous human relationships and real human relations, on Husserl's concept of the life-world, and on Gramsci's concept of the ensemble of relations.[17] But I understand this ensemble as the full range of life activities that people in society pursue in order to express and develop their fundamental interests. These interests are not limited to economic ones but include in addition interests in physical security, in biological continuity, and in communication (self-expression and inter-self exchange).[18] These are all interests, and the various life activities they give rise to all evolve in a totality of needs and aspirations that make up "the ensemble of relations."

Conservatives can see only what they describe as spiritual forces. They mistily and ideologically invoke freedom as a "spiritual" force. But their spiritual freedom is a ghost completely abstracted from any context. And their invocation of freedom occurs in advance of actually looking at such a phenomenon as Solidarity.

Marxists come to the perception of social reality and historical phenomena with fixed notions: that matter is all that matters (a pre-Einstein-
ian, philistine, bourgeois view, the Marxists having forgotten Marx's own
acknowledged debt to Hegel); that economic relations are the only really
important relations; and that all that is not comprehended directly within
these relations of "the base" must be treated as epiphenomena, as "superstructure." There is no way that Solidarity could emerge from the embrace of these straitjackets in other than mangled form.

Liberals seem to work both sides of the street, at times taking a "hard,"
no-nonsense, materialistic view, then again taking a "soft," idealistic
view (*idealistic* being their favorite word for the spiritual). Actually their
approach has more unity than it seems. The crucial desideratum for
them is not the spiritual or the material, but the individual, or the
individual as atom. If one begins at such a point, the status of spiritual
and material is altered. All interests are interests of atomized individuals.
These interests are reduced to preferences, moods, whims, and urges.
Some seem spiritual, others seem material, but that is not as important as
the fact that each is the assumed expression of, and only of, a particular
ego. So of course Solidarity is analyzed as a collection of individuals, of
egos, striving in interest groups, unions, associations, and other amal-
gamations to maximize their "felt interests."

In contrast, my interpretation of Solidarity acknowledges the social
being of individual action. Individual action lies in the daily life activities
of ordinary people (and everyone in his or her core of being is an ordinary
person). It is there that the challenges, opportunities, problems, conflicts, and contradictions arise. From one vantage point the activity and
the conflict seem spiritual; from another they seem material. As problems
persist and deepen and grievances multiply, as opportunities seem to
open up for change, people encounter structures. As a result people
simultaneously grow more self-conscious about purposes, goals, and new
ideas. There ensues a struggle, then, both over purposes and goals and
over structures. The struggle is not over the spiritual versus the material,
the base versus the superstructure, freedom versus collectivism, or God
versus the Devil. Even though often dressed up in such terms, the real
struggle remains over the fit between the structures and the life activities
they are meant to serve and enlarge. These life activities are themselves
rooted in fundamental human interests, and the struggle is not about

them abstractly but about them as they have evolved at a certain time within a certain context.

The struggle of Solidarity is the struggle of the people of Poland to find a better fit between their state and their society. That better fit, because of the evolution of Poland, can now take the form of the self-governance of working people in unions and professional associations of their own creation, working in partnership with a state responsible for the coherence of the whole. Such is the promise and the prospect—if the world will only listen.

6

Solidarity and Communism: Opening a New Route

Solidarity burst on the international scene in the summer of 1980. Although it was instantly mythicized and endowed with universalistic meaning by friend and foe, it was born within a particular historical context and within a particular system of political economy and state power. Solidarity pursued limited but substantive goals, and its method of nonviolence led it into a step-by-step progression or evolution in close interaction with all the inner and the outer political forces that were shaping Poland's political development.

From the outset, Solidarity sought to establish the principle and practice of self-governing unions. The Gdansk Accord between the newly emergent labor movement and the Communist government in August, 1980, had self-governing unions as its centerpiece. It is true that many other demands were included, ranging from very general to quite specific grievances. Several concerned civil liberties, but most were social and economic in nature. Indeed, the government, in putting a good face on the transaction, chose to see the accord as only a set of economic and social concessions and not a matter of structural or strategic political significance at all. They deduced this, comfortingly for them, from that part of the accord in which Solidarity acknowledged "the leading role of the Polish United Workers' Party." There are some who doubt that Solidarity ever agreed to this. During the fight over the formal registration of the union in November, this issue was a hot potato. The government eventually agreed to put the objectionable phrase in an appendix to the registration document, and the workers accepted that. The agreement thus seemed to have achieved a compromise along the lines of a division between narrowly conceived economic and social matters on one hand and broadly conceived political matters on the other.

There were those on both sides who seemed satisfied, even captivated, by this compromise and firmly believed in it. It may have been a mutually useful subterfuge, entered into consciously or unconsciously in the heat of the August struggle. By its terms the government presumably would undertake to guarantee the autonomy of "self-governing unions," and the workers would undertake to accept the Party's "leading role." But efforts to put these two principles into effect led inevitably to a fundamental psychological and structural conflict in Polish society.

In the course of this conflict each side has made certain political choices. On one side is the Communist system of power and that stratum of Party and state officials defending it and themselves. On the other is Solidarity, a great resistance movement made up of the large majority of Polish citizens. The latter are making a bid not only for the redress of an extensive set of specific grievances but also for a permanent shift in the way in which decisions are made in society and state. They are bidding for effective participation by ordinary people in decisions of consequence to their personal, social, economic and political lives. For them the emphasis is on participation—the institutional affirmation of their subjectivity as persons, groups, regions, and nation.

To understand the political choices that were available to both sides, it is necessary to have some grasp of the nature and meaning of participation in countries under "real existing socialism." It is not the case that there is no participation in these countries. Examining the theory and practice of communist participation and comparing them with Western modes of participation will facilitate an understanding of Solidarity's challenge to the Communist authorities in Poland (and other countries). It will also help chart the tortuous course of the political struggle between Solidarity and the Party-state.

PARTICIPATION IN THE COMMUNIST MODE

The great preoccupation of countries that embraced communism, or had it thrust upon them, has been to organize society along a coherent path in the face of an overwhelming breakdown in the economic, social, cultural, and political institutions of the old order.[1] The motivation varied. For some people, as described in works such as Milovan Djilas' *The New Class* and André Gorz's *Arduous Socialism*, it was to catch up with the already industrialized and increasingly imperialistic West. In other cases, in addition to that motive, there was the greater one to avoid what was seen as the alienation and hypocritical oppressiveness of the so-called democracies of the West, whose civil liberties and formal representative institutions camouflaged intense, permanent social and economic deprivations suffered by whole classes of people. Lenin's *State and Revolution* best justified this line of reasoning. For still others, those inspired by such writings as Mao's *On Practice* and *On the Correct Handling of Contradictions Among the People*, the motivation has been to build a new harmonious society in which the old accumulated divisions of hand and head, farm and city, worker and boss, male and female, buyer and seller, authority and obedience, and subject and object were successfully overcome.

But whatever the motivation, the bottom line in every case has been the urgent need to create and foster a historic directing agency—the Party—that could integrate what were considered to be the spontaneities and longings of the masses into a coherent program of social construction and renewal. In this scheme the Party's role is truly a grand affair. It may be compared with the role of the Church in the traditional society of the Middle Ages. But there is an important difference. The Church claimed to be the individual's only direct channel to the next world, but it dealt only indirectly with matters pertaining to this world. The Party, believing that "the next world" is a dangerous, mystifying delusion, focuses on all things as if they were only in this world. Thus, all expressions of human activity, however spiritual and otherworldly they may appear and claim to be, are nevertheless viewed as part of this world and subject to the Party's vision and authority. The Party is central not only to politics and economics but also to culture. What is at stake is the attempt not only to raise the standard of living but to mold a "new man."

The state in this scheme is a necessary, and presumably temporary, evil, but it is absolutely necessary. It must expedite the journey of postrevolutionary society toward the higher phase of social relations. It becomes the Party's foremost instrument through which the building of the new society and the development of the new man are to be accomplished.

What has been the nature, degree, and scope of political participation in this system? First, working people in all the institutions of society, including economic, educational, and cultural institutions, are granted unions. Through them they have the right to influence their employer—the state—with regard to pay scales and working conditions. And through the union they have access to the Party, which mediates between them and the state. In this arrangement the workers are supposed to be able to ventilate the grievances they have with their boss, the state, by turning to the Party for help. But the Party's mediatory role has consistently lagged behind its role of controlling the state. So in practice there exists a severe disproportion between the Party's inclination to hear and act on workers' concerns and its responsibility to supervise the state. The Party is pulled toward and into the state functions at the expense of its mediatory role. Like the God of old, the Party gives, and the Party takes away.

Second, in addition to unions, the people have the opportunity to enter the grand institution itself, the Party. Although recruitment patterns change over time and are carefully structured, the Party is a channel for political participation for selected individuals from all segments of society. However, as already noted, the Party is organized internally according to the principles of nomenklatura. There are lists of persons whose appointment to responsible posts both within and outside the Party requires prior Party approval. Thus, though it is the case that Party officials are elected by the Party membership, the latter do so, at any given level of the organization, on the recommendation of the Party secretary at the level just above. This practice assures hierarchical and centralized direction and control from the top down. Nomenklatura is, in turn, reinforced by the Party doctrine of democratic centralism, which is also carefully followed in practice. This doctrine, though it stresses the importance of participation by the lower Party bodies and of the flow upward of political sentiment from below, also emphasizes the necessity for decision making from the top. The doctrine also provides for the closing of ranks once a decision has been made, a tradition begun in the Soviet Union's Communist party in 1921 and known as the no-faction rule, which further eviscerates the scope and meaning of political participation.

In addition to membership in unions and in the Party, the people have the opportunity to participate in nominating and voting directly for representatives in local, regional, and national assemblies. The Party-run nomination process provides limited but real involvement by the people through their membership in unions and other social organizations, organizations whose views the Party solicits. In the elections the people

vote for one, and only one, Party-designated candidate for each representative slot. The assemblies themselves, such as the two-house Supreme Soviet in Moscow and the unicameral Sejm in Warsaw, have very
restricted roles. They perfunctorily discuss and then pass unanimously
the legislation decided upon and prepared by the top organs of the Party
in concert with such state bodies as the council of ministers and the state
planning agency. One might argue that the Polish Sejm is somewhat
harder for the Party to control totally than are correlative bodies in the
Soviet Union. Its traditions go back to a time in Polish history when as a
body it ruled the nation. Yet, in general the net effect is the same: the
representative assemblies are given little power, and in only a very restricted sense are they dimly responsive to the will and sentiments of the
people.

Four significant points should be made concerning political participation under "real existing socialism." First, it is different in nature from
poiltical participation in the West. Second, it is broader in scope than
that in the West. Third, it is sharply limited in the degree of its operations, and fourth, it exists and survives in only a highly mystified form.

In communist countries the notion of participation is strongly influenced by organic views of society as opposed to the contractual views of
society popular in the West, with its liberal traditions. One might describe the difference in terms of *gemeinschaft* versus *gesellschaft*, the
former referring to an organic partnership or community of people, the
latter to an aggregation of individuals. Although Marxism prides itself on
having moved beyond such traditional or feudal notions as gemeinschaft,
it has nevertheless been more at home with that tradition than with
liberal bourgeois notions such as gesellschaft. In contrast to traditional
concepts of organic community, or gemeinschaft, Marxists believe in a
dynamic movement of historical forces, which they see as either progressive or reactionary. These contending forces dominate the processes of
society. Marxists therefore combine the concept of gemeinschaft with the
notion of a historic agent or subject that will act to bring society closer and
closer to perfection. The agent acts on behalf of the progressive forces,
obeying the laws of history. In Marx this agent is the proletariat. In
Lenin's writings, and in all communist countries, the proletariat is seen
as itself needing leadership (*i.e.*, the Party) in order to actualize its own
progressivism and dynamism.

In Lenin's view there is no room for more than one party to be the central directing element in catalyzing, cohering, and leading the spontaneous energies of the masses. For tactical purposes there may be subordinate parties, but they must gravitate around the central party. There can be no other parties of equal status, both for strategic reasons (the need for unity and efficiency, the problem of vulnerability to hostile forces, etc.) and for the deeper reason that there is only one historic progressive truth relevant to a given epoch. This truth can be discovered and known. It can be acted upon only by a unified historic agent—the Party. One may perceive how influential the doctrines of positivism are upon the core of Leninist Marxism. Its epistemological foundations—belief in purely objective, knowable, and all-encompassing truth—inexorably prepare the way for the hegemony of the Party.

Thus, individuals successfully engage in political participation by joining the Party. And whether they join or not, they can become effective participants by involving themselves in activities that contribute to the historic, common task of the Party and follow its direction and discipline. Therefore, in addition to Party activity, individuals may participate by being diligent on the job and by being members of youth organizations, unions, study groups, and various social organizations. All of life is caught up in the forward movement of history under the leadership of the Party. Every part of life is, in that broad sense, political.

Political participation is therefore more broadly conceived than in Western countries. The Party supervises and correlates all activity—whether that be economic, social, cultural, or narrowly political—to the central goals of building socialism and creating the new man. And *mutatis mutandis*, the individual can and must regard all aspects of his or her life as somehow related to a historically evolving set of political and politically inspired goals.

In the West there is a break between the state and the private sector, the state and the family, the state and the church, and so forth. It is assumed that there are principles in each nonstate realm that are separate and even greater than the state, though the state plays an ancillary role to regulate and at times facilitate the better performance of these other realms. Under the impact of capitalism, which became the norm in economic activity, all realms not part of the state have been more and more infused with, and subordinated to, the principles of atomistic individualism, egoistic behavior, and the treatment of all things as if they were commodities. The nonpolitical, even apolitical, character of this trend has reached the point at which there exists a breach of crisis proportions. The breach is between the narcissistic behavior of individuals as members of civil society on one hand and the requirements of citizenship on the other. Business activity, educational activity, consumer activity, and worker and union activity are all dominated by nonpolitical norms, which leaves room for behavior in the public interest only in a highly attenuated, rigidly formalized state sphere.

It is as if in communist countries almost everything is political and in Western countries almost nothing is political. Or private behavior in communist countries is judged by its meaning for public good, and public behavior in Western countries is judged by its meaning for private good. Both kinds of countries are in crisis, especially on the issue of political participation.

A severe problem in communist countries, in both theory and practice, is the sharply limited *degree* of political participation, even though the *scope* is broad and even though there is strong support for the public meaning of private action. Various bodies in state, economy, and society have an immediate relationship to the Party and have access to it. Nevertheless they are much more in the role of object than subject. And although the individual is given a broad range of rights and opportunities to have an impact on politics—not only at election time but in his daily life through his union and other social groups and organizations—he is permitted only mechanical responses to directive and structured signals from the higher echelons of the Party. The form of active political participation is permitted, indeed required, in all spheres. The substance, and the true subjectivity involved therein, is largely blunted and in effect denied.

Finally, one perceives the mystification of power and accountability in this seemingly participatory process. The local party organization seems to, and is said to, elect its own secretary. But the meeting always follows the recommendation of the party body just above it (actually, of that body's secretary). The same thing happens with that party body, and so it goes all the way up the hierarchy to the central secretariat and the Politburo. Similarly, citizens seem to, and are said to, elect their representatives. But in every case only the one recommended by the Party is on the ballot. Likewise, the constituted assemblies seem to, and are said to, make the laws; yet they only follow the directives of the Party. Similarly, appointments to important positions in all the organizations of society and state seem to, and are said to, be based on merit. But actually they are filled through the Party's controlled manipulation of nomenklatura, as the Party makes appointments only from a list of acceptable candidates. In short, authority is supposed to be based on participatory principles throughout society—not only in the state but in *all* economic, cultural, social, and political spheres. But nowhere are these principles realized.

One might justifiably speak of communist systems as the universalization of institutionalized hypocrisy. The core of the hypocrisy occurs in the Party itself. The claim is that all things done in society and state should conform ultimately to what the Party considers to be best. It is a large claim, and one might for the sake of the argument still make it subject to some minimal idea of participation. But the Party mystifies its own internal processes of election and accountability so that power and authority flow from the top to the middle and the bottom. In appearance, and in the rhetoric that accompanies the practice, it seems that power and authority flow in a balanced way, both from the top and the bottom through the middle echelons. The Party, finally, also mystifies its relations with other bodies. It appears to be a mediator and a catalyst, an aggregator of various interests and concerns of the greater society and state. But it, or rather the leading forces within it, puts on the cloak of authority of the state, absorbs the spontaneities of the masses in society, and uses both state and society for its own interests.

What has essentially happened is that the Party, or rather its self-perpetuating leadership, has become the self-selected, self-proclaimed sole agent of history, acting in the name of the proletariat, identifying its interests as if they were those of the proletariat. Participation as the release of subjectivity and the accountability of those in power has been distorted and emptied of meaning.

In the West the citizen is taught to believe in voter sovereignty. But the leaders he or she is asked to choose from almost always reflect only a narrow range of social classes and policy options. The actions taken by the leaders, once they are in office, extend only to regulatory and to some degree to facilitative actions with regard to the institutions of civil society. Such state actions operate to improve only the conditions of individual life and not the public situation. In almost all vital nonstate institutions, the individual is ruled by nonparticipatory principles and practices of authority, though again there are some modifications of that authority on behalf of an individual's private preferences. The profound mystifications of political life in the West, and the related mystifications in social and economic life (*e.g.*, consumer sovereignty, individual achievement, a free press, and a free market economy), are all variations of the residual myth that the maximization of individual preferences can and will add up to vital community life, citizen participation, public responsibility, and happiness. What happens in fact is the growing hegemony of some individuals, the inordinate amplification of their arbitrary preferences, primarily for money and power, and of their capacity to pass these on to their children.

CHOICE

The assertion by Solidarity of its demand for independent, self-governing unions took place within a system in which "everything is political." The unions' bid for full autonomy cut deeply into the role and status of the Party as the mediator between society and the state. With this in mind, one can more clearly understand the disbelief and panic Solidarity must have aroused in higher Party circles. One can also more clearly understand the historic limits of Solidarity's action. The easy accusation that its members acted as in a fever and without due regard for consequences is surely wide of the mark.[2]

From the Party's standpoint, Solidarity's claim must have seemed rank heresy and therefore more to be feared than outright apostasy. The Party was supposed to be the historic agent that objectively embodied the subjectivity of the proletariat. So what was this Solidarity doing—offering an alternative objective embodiment of proletariat subjectivity? This was dangerous heresy, too much to swallow. So at first the Communist leadership temporized and pretended that Solidarity's demands were only social and economic. Later it went to the opposite extreme and excommunicated Solidarity as an apostate abomination, claiming that the proletariat had been led astray into capitalism, that they were dupes of that old seductive lure—churchly religion, etc. Any explanation would do that would help the Party avoid acknowledging and accepting heresy—though, as in the case of the Christian martyrs under the Inquisition, the so-called heretics were in fact returning to the source, seeking to develop further, to apply under new circumstances, the teachings of the master.

From the standpoint of Solidarity, it was of course possible that its members could have opted for a revolutionary, violent eruption in an attempt to bring the whole system down. But there is very little evidence, either in structural or psychological terms, that this was their intention. It was not a live option. It was an abstract option. To be sure, they could have acted "abstractly." Some wanted to do so or at least revealed intimations in that old direction. But the great majority, the deep center of the movement, were not about to be trapped into abstract action: they were, and are, profoundly aware of history.

On the other hand, Solidarity could have opted for a series of protest strikes, to push the government into paying attention to people's everyday needs. But they went well beyond protest. They saw an opportunity to move between and beyond both revolutionary violence and the incremental politics of protest. They chose to press for the true politicization of a communist system of power—a system that has never totally denied proletariat subjectivity but that has greatly distorted it and mystified the distortion. The historic opportunity consisted of a chance to wrest from the monopolistic and reified Party-state the right to genuine autonomy for a non-Party, nonstate body or bodies. Solidarity seized that opportunity.

Such were the viewpoints of the two sides. They were miles apart at Gdansk, and they still are. Small wonder, then, that when faced with two nonnegotiable demands—self-governing unions on one side and the leading role of the Party on the other—and with the threats of both a general strike and Russian intervention hovering in the background—the negotiators of the Gdansk Accord seized on a seemingly objective, functional, even administrative demarcation between "economic" and "political" realms. Solidarity, it was said, would confine itself to the former, and the Party would continue its hegemony in the latter.

In most societies such a distinction is fairly artificial to begin with, though in most Western societies, epecially the United States, it has the status of a reigning myth. But in communist societies it has no such status at all, and if for administrative convenience and for the uses of political mystification there is a role for such a distinction, the degree to which it is used and insisted upon becomes itself a suspicious piece of political

chicanery and manipulation. The very fact that, under the terms of the
Gdansk agreement, Solidarity existed and was acknowledged as a self-
governing institution with, therefore, its own subjectivity constituted a
fundamental challenge to the prevailing system of power and to the
Leninist-Stalinist justification for it.

Since management is an arm of the state, if the workers within the
autonomous walls of their own union were to decide to strike over economic issues, by so much would economic issues impinge directly on the
authority of the State and the policy-making powers (the leading role) of
the Party. Perhaps one can envisage an attempt to distinguish certain
kinds of economic issues from other kinds, for example narrow versus
broad. But however narrowly one attempts to refine those economic
issues to which a self-governing union is supposed to restrict itself, the
fact remains that with respect to that "narrow" issue (suppose it were
merely the number of times a worker can go to the toilet in a day), there is
an autonomous body, legally acknowledged by the government to be
autonomous, which has the authority to stand up for the worker—to
stand up as a force between the worker and the state, a force that is *not* the
Party. The issue, therefore, is not what kind of problem (economic or
political) or how broad or narrow the problem. The issue is the existence
of an autonomous force—a self-governing union. This is what Solidarity
was and is seeking to get the state and the Party to swallow.

What, then, did Solidarity mean by agreeing to acknowledge the leading role of the Party? Were its leaders acting in bad faith? Neither the
members nor the leaders of Solidarity were overwhelmingly happy with
the formulation. They saw what it meant—that the Party still could and
would push for legal and political domination. Solidarity sought to interpret the phrase as providing for the leading role of the Party *in the state*,
thinking that such a formulation left greater latitude for the activities of
autonomous bodies in society. In any case the question of bad faith is
beside the point. The Gdansk Accord was a political compromise with a
face-saving formula. It would be left to the future to decide how and
whether the state, the Party, and Solidarity could truly bridge the un-
bridged chasm that gaped beneath the rhetoric of the accord. It would be
a trial of strength and also of the willingness on both sides to negotiate a
series of moves leading toward a settlement. Seen in this light, Gdansk
was a first step in such a series of possible moves. And as an initial trial of

strength it was a victory for the workers. Also, in this light it was clear that the government would want to limit and circumscribe that victory as much as possible and that the workers would want to emphasize its implications and so expand on their triumph. Both tendencies came into play almost at once.

But both tendencies were exaggerated in the course of events. The government became more and more defensive, at times disastrously so, as in the gratuitous beating of several Solidarity leaders at Bydgoszcz in March, 1981. The Party was bitterly divided among the hard-liners, the so-called moderates, and the increasingly numerous Horizontalists (those pushing for substantive, grass-roots reform of the Party). But the latter were frozen out before and during the Party conference in July, 1981—largely at the demand of the Kremlin—and left the Party by the hundreds of thousands. Thus, the victory of the moderates at that critical Party conference, and the procedural reforms undertaken there (such as an open election for Party secretary), proved a pyrrhic victory for the moderates. The people of Poland, including whole sections of the Party, saw through the seeming turn of the Party toward moderation and chalked it up as just one more subterfuge in a long line of pseudoreforms stretching back to 1956. They lost faith in the very capacity of the Party to lead.

Ironically, it was this evisceration of the Party, brought on as much by its own mistakes and the myopia of the Kremlin as by the growing appeal of Solidarity, that became an overwhelming and in the end insoluble problem for Solidarity. In the beginning, Solidarity emphasized the apparent assumptions of the Gdansk Accord. Its members first had to fight for the legal recognition that had been promised them at Gdansk. This should have been a normal and nomimal process, since it involved only implementation of what the government had already agreed to. But the government backpedaled, much in the style of its reneging on reforms after the worker rebellions in 1956, 1970, and 1976, so that, far from keeping Solidarity within the limits of Gdansk, the government seemed to be trying to roll back those limits. Although legalization was eventually achieved in November, 1980, this pattern of government backpedaling continued. [3] The fight for legalization was followed by repeated refusals of the government to treat Solidarity as a bona fide negotiating partner on industrial problems and policy. At the same time, Solidarity mushroomed in membership by the thousands and then the millions. Eventually it embraced most working people in all occupations.

Because of this overwhelming popular success, Solidarity's members had to rethink the situation again and again. They saw that to realize the promise of self-governing unions, other changes would be necessary. Chief among these was direct access to the state-controlled media. This point had apparently been won as part of the Gdansk Accord, but the issue developed into a bitter dispute between Solidarity and the government that was never resolved. The government and the Party were determined to preserve their monopoly on political information, news, and analysis. They saw Solidarity's demand as a clear signal of the union's intention to compete with the Party for control. Solidarity saw the demand as a natural outgrowth of union autonomy—and as a growing necessity in a changing situation. It grew impatient with the government's backpedaling. Furthermore, the people of the nation were beginning to look to Solidarity for leadership, both on particular grievances and on general policy.

This led Solidarity to issue its *Theses for Discussion* in April, 1981, which identified "the system" as the basic problem. The situation also led the union to respond to the growing self-management movement and eventually to incorporate the quest for effective self-management into its program. Solidarity also felt pushed to broaden its explicit goals even more to include the notions of the self-governing republic and of the need for a new nationwide institution, a Social Council of National Economy, that would be representative of self-governing bodies, perhaps functioning as a second house of the Sejm.[4] All this was an outgrowth of point 6 of the twenty-one demands, which had called for "enabling all social groups to participate in discussion of the reform programme" (see Appendix).

Was Solidarity becoming a competitor for power with the Party? Its members would not have put it that way. Yet they felt themselves thrust into a situation that increasingly demanded of them a political response. They felt the need for an overall negotiated settlement that would redefine and restabilize an increasingly chaotic political and economic situation. It should be a settlement that would institutionalize Solidarity within a renewed state and that would institutionalize a process of social and economic policy making by such means as the addition of a second chamber to the Sejm. This settlement would then also lead the way to the airing of opposing and alternative viewpoints in the official media.

But with whom could they negotiate? This was Solidarity's immense dilemma. The evisceration of the Party was in one sense a feather in Solidarity's cap. The Polish people, the community of the Polish nation, clearly identified with Solidarity and held the Party in contempt. But was the nation looking to Solidarity to lead it out of the wilderness? And if so, was this a good thing? Was Solidarity being pushed into a role of "national savior" that it did not really want, that it was not ready for in any case, and that would split the movement prematurely into factions and perhaps bring on Russian intervention?

The role of a new, and renewing, element within the Communist system of power that would substantially modify that system was a role that Solidarity could perform without falling short of itself, without falling apart, and, probably, without engendering Russian intervention. But to undertake the task of essentially running the country would put this alliance of unions lately become a national movement for change beyond its depth. Yet, after the highly touted but politically ineffectual Party conference of July, 1981, Poland experienced a paralyzing vacuum of authority and leadership. The Party, which till then had had the authority and had provided the leadership, was increasingly impotent. The government, which nominally had the authority and continued of necessity to act as if it had it in fact, was rudderless. The state was nearing the brink of nongovernance.

So, with whom could Solidarity negotiate? The real answer was no one. Where there had once been political substance, a vacuum now existed. If the Party had been stronger, if it had experienced renewal, if the Horizontalists had been successful, and if a renewed Party had continued to find favor, however grudging, with the Kremlin, then there would have been a political force with which Solidarity could have reached a modest but substantial compromise and effected a positive change in the political structure of the state. But what Solidarity faced was a government grown intensely defensive from habit and necessity, hiding from itself the knowledge of its own stupendous weakness, and trying vainly to act as if a vacuum did not exist.

In October, 1981, the ruling circles replaced Stanislaw Kania with Jaruzelski as Party chief. He was given this new position in addition to his already leading roles in the army and in the government (he had been prime minister since February). But this change did not, could not, restore the capacity of the state to govern. It was a change at the top, which to succeed would have needed a widespread and protracted process of consensus-building at the bottom and middle echelons, both Party and non-Party. As it was, Solidarity had the respect and represented the feelings of the people—their desire for a political change. Jaruzelski had the power of the state. Neither had authority in the name of which to govern. In these circumstances efforts at negotiation, such as that by the big three—Jaruzelski, Walesa, and Cardinal Glemp (head of the Catholic church in Poland)—in early November, 1983, foundered and slipped away.

Each side was under enormous pressure to act for itself to fill the vacuum—Jaruzelski from the entrenched remnant of the Party and the Kremlin, Solidarity from the growing impatience of its members and the deepening anxiety and political exhaustion of the people at large. Given this deadlock, and given the growing impotence of the Party, Jaruzelski had nothing with which to reassure the Kremlin should he continue a posture of attempted negotiation. Jaruzelski therefore struck with force of arms.

What he struck down by this action, and by his actions since then, was not only the supposed threat by Solidarity to replace the Party as the central political force in the country but also the early and abiding demand of Solidarity for respect for its subjectivity and for the subjectivity of all the people of the Polish nation as citizens and workers. The flouting by Jaruzelski, and by the Kremlin, of this demand (as if granting it must necessarily lead to the destruction of the Party) is the great failure of the Jaruzelski solution and the tragedy not only of Solidarity but even more of the communist system of power. This tragedy is the system's incapacity to absorb evolutionary development. Admittedly it would require a fundamental shift in communist consciousness, communist doctrine, and communist political practice to accommodate the demand to respect a subjectivity other than that of the Party. Yet who is to say with certainty that the subject in history—the proletariat, according to Marx—can be expressed and interpreted only by a special external agency, the Party? Or that the Party must and can be organized only in accordance with a rigid code of centralized direction born out of circumstances of civil war in one country at a particular time (the Soviet Union from 1918 to 1921)? Solidarity directly challenged both these assumptions and raised a banner for the realization of a broader, deeper theory and practice of participation in communist systems—for a renewed and more direct understanding of historical subjectivity.

THE LARGER MEANING OF SOLIDARITY'S CHOICE

Solidarity, by its simple and uncomplicated demand for self-governing unions, fused the defense of economic and social rights—on which communist regimes somewhat justifiably pride themselves as having made significant advances—with the demand for civil and political liberties. The latter constitute a necessary dimension of human rights that these same regimes have consistently ignored and defiled. The communist critique of Western patterns of participation—that they are restricted to a state sphere that is itself restricted—comes back to haunt the critics. The structure of their "real existing socialism" has unified the spheres of state and economy. In addition, the rhetoric of communist defense of their "nonbourgeois democracy" rings with appeals to all workers—indeed all citizens—to involve themselves in building socialism.

For communism a major irony of Solidarity is that the Polish workers took its ringing appeals and acted as if they were, or ought to be, true—not only in economic matters but in all spheres. Simply by acting, not as a working class overthrowing their masters (an historically irrelevant and distorting image in a communist context), but as workers defending and interpreting their rights, Solidarity reached a new level of political sophistication and opened up a new route in the possible evolution of a communist regime.

Solidarity's intention is *not* to reconstruct society, to start over in the manner of, say, a Leninist revolution. The intention instead is a more Burkean one in its method: to defend rights, expressed in both modern and ancient Polish traditions, so as to achieve a modest but significant modification in an already established system of authoritarian socialism. The result would not be the capitulation of the East to the West, something for communists to condemn and capitalists to acclaim. It would instead structure the dynamics of genuine dialogue into an ailing and straitjacketed socialist system. By joining economic and social rights with civil and political rights, Solidarity and Poland would achieve a degree and mode of political participation that could well serve as a model of political evolution for both East and West.

Participation in this model would be "red," or Eastern, in its *breadth*, embracing the full range of state, civil society, and cultural activities. There would be no return to the arbitrary, capitalist, self-serving dichotomy between civil society and the state. Participation would also take place within the assumptions of gemeinshaft rather than gesellschaft. Group and community loyalties and the full panoply of social and economic responsibilities would be honored and given large scope.

On the other hand, participation would be "white," or Western, in its stress on *accountability*, in both a legal and a fully constitutional sense. A balance of rights and duties would be struck, and restruck again and again, between officeholder (in whatever realm) and person (in whatever role). Furthermore, the *degree* of participation would be judged against a standard of full subjectivity for all workers—organized dually in unions and in self-management councils. There would be no return to the Party's monopoly of leadership, no return to its claim to a special historical role as the sole representative or agent of the proletariat. The fate of the Communist party would depend on the further evolution of the communist system, its socialist political economy, and the manner in which the state, the Party, and Solidarity would together structure the relation between one or more political parties and the national, regional, and local assemblies.

Solidarity's quest is a powerful beacon light in a stormy, treacherous time. Solidarity is a broad-based, nonviolent citizens' movement for a new society through the evolution of established power structures, and this needs to be understood in academic circles and reflected in the media. In addition, if Solidarity were well understood among leaders in Warsaw, Washington, and Moscow, it would contribute to their self-extrication from a bitter and self-destructive impasse.

PART III

POLAND'S WAY FORWARD

7
The Polish Phoenix

Is there a way forward for Poland? The answer is yes. It is disclosed by the historic rise in the political consciousness of the Polish people and by their discovery through Solidarity of a nonviolent, non-ideological method of constitutional change within the communist system. The situation in Poland today offers the possibility of moving toward a society in which both the economic and the political rights of ordinary citizens—in the aggregate and as a society—are at last joined together. Such an integration of rights would be a historical first.

This historic rise is revealed by, and gains substance from, a variety of factors: the geopolitical balance of Poland's eastern and western borders as created and guaranteed by the Communist victory in 1945, a balance that gives all sides in Poland a stake in that guarantee; Jaruzelski's infamous institution of martial law by force in December, 1981, which may have prevented a fully Russian "solution" to Poland's "waywardness"; the capacity of Solidarity's leadership to recover from the shock of martial law and to reorganize both underground and above ground in response to changing circumstances and the shifting policies of the regime; the resistance to secularization of politics and of culture by a virtually universal national church; that same church's defense and affirmation of a national community and culture; an ecological crisis of such awesome proportions that the government, even in spite of itself, must begin to shift its priorities and economic organization to light industry, agriculture, local markets, and decentralized institutions; and finally, the pressure on Moscow and Washington (and all European capitals) continually to find strategic compromises for conflicts involving Eastern and Western Europe. Such compromises become absolutely crucial in order to avoid the supreme danger of slipping into military solutions that in turn may easily degenerate into the ultimate and universally unacceptable insanity of nuclear war. Such compromises are further mandated by the increasing pressures on both superpowers that stem from problems elsewhere in the world: Third World regional crises, terrorism, and nuclear proliferation.

These propositions, which will be explored in this third and last part of the book, defy and overcome the arguments that are normally adduced to prove that Poland's internal life and external situation predetermine a continuation of the present drift, toward either continued economic stagnation and political squalor or toward a massive explosion. Among the negative arguments usually made are these: that Polish romanticism is always on a collision course with Polish realism and therefore nothing can come of either to produce true national leadership; that Solidarity has no unified program and therefore cannot be expected to give direction to public policy even supposing the Party (and the Soviet Union) would relent; that Catholicism and communism cannot and will not mix; and that the Polish Communist Party-state consists of a thoroughly entrenched minority whose only aim is self-perpetuation in the power and privileges of office.

Furthermore, it is often maintained that the government's commitment to heavy industry and to traditional energy policy is so pronounced that only token steps can be imagined to be forthcoming from them to deal with the ecological mess; that Jaruzelski must kowtow to the Kremlin and cannot negotiate with Solidarity or with the Polish people, even if he might want to; that the Kremlin cannot and will not allow any latitude for Poles to define their own institutional brand of "real existing socialism"; and that, strategically speaking, Eastern and Western Europe belong to two different worlds and neither East nor West can permit any real change in the present alignment of nations on each side. It is also argued that private Western capitalism will continue its "apolitical" trucking with the Jaruzelski regime, providing just enough credits to keep it afloat but not enough either to make a difference or to direct it toward the liberation of markets or, equally critical, cleanup of the environment; and that the United States will continue to pursue policies of relative destabilization interspersed with limited cooperative engagements whose net effect in Poland will reinforce the perpetual drift and make-do.

One acknowledges these negative factors and respects them. Yet the discussion in this and the two succeeding chapters presents evidence and arguments to show that either they are not the monsters people often see in them or they, as part of the irony of history, point toward their own transcendence into something new and positive.

It must also be emphasized, however, that I do not claim anything to be "inevitable" as a result of this positive assessment of Poland's situation. To write, and to interpret reality, in that manner would be only to put an optimistic determinism in place of a pessimistic one. It is true that intellectuals seem to like to write books in the mode of one or the other of those determinisms. But one of the foremost epistemological assumptions of this work is that there is no evidence that systems are closed or that a given trend of events means they will always continue in that direction or, in short, that the future will "inevitably" be this way or that. Scholars elucidate factors, forces, and trends; they seek to illuminate the milieu in which action takes place. But they do well when they leave to men and women in the crucible of action their own autonomy, their own free encounter with the imponderables of life and death.

AN AWAKENED SOCIETY

Many people have been surprised at the tenacity shown by the Solidarity movement since it was forced underground. But when one considers not appearances but underlying realities, Solidarity's continuing strength is not so surprising. When in a given social context there is a combination of significant structural and psychological factors all tending in a similar direction, one should expect to find that a rebellion, once launched, will be a profound and long-term affair. Quashings of the type administered by the Jaruzelski government in December, 1981, may temporarily sidetrack the rebellion, in the same way as a makeshift dam may be thrown up in a rampaging flood to divert the waters. But just as the physical flood must ultimately have its way, so, too, must the social flood—if it is as strong as Solidarity. One may attempt to channel the waters in a certain direction, but it is naïve to expect that the flood can quickly be dammed up and somehow dispersed.

This image of physical floods and sweeping tides is most appropriate to Solidarity. Both Jaruzelski's government and backers, on one hand, and Western observers, bankers, papal diplomats, and political leaders, on the other, must take heed. Solidarity is not just a labor union in the Western sense; nor is it just a national social movement. It is both together, and it is deeper and more pervasive than either. In the words of the movement's program adopted at its national congress in the fall of 1981, Solidarity is "the most massive movement in the history of Poland. . . . It has engulfed all groups in the labor world: workers, peasants, the intelligentsia, craftsmen. . . . We are an organization combining the features of a trade union and of a great social movement."[1]

Solidarity is not just a feeling—a lingering though still palpable passion left over in people's hearts from the heady days of the above-ground movement but bound eventually to fade into just a glorious memory. On the contrary, Solidarity is an invisible web of institutional forces that are fed by, and in turn feed, a strong political consciousness.

This institutional web includes a vast network of clandestine unions and associations and of underground and above-ground communications centers and activities that breathe the air of political opposition. It includes the social and economic self-help activities of millions of Polish citizens who produce and exchange goods and services outside the bounds of the official economy. It includes the hundreds of seminars and lectures on Polish culture and history that regularly take place in the sanctuary of the churches. Indeed the church is itself such an institutional force. The network also includes a flourishing underground system of education organized through lectures and courses in churches and homes all over Poland. One of the most interesting reflections of this educational effort is found in the publications of the Krakow youth group known as Promienisci. These high school students issue books and serial writings for their own use, and for the use of others in their age group, on subjects banned from the official curriculum.[2] The invisible web is also evident in the ingenious capacity of the movement to create functioning infrastructures under the very noses of the authorities, for example, in its success in mounting a formidable election-monitoring network throughout the country during the national parliamentary elections October, 1985.[3]

Finally, the web includes an invisible above-ground opposition that operates every day throughout established official society. There is an unspoken conspiracy (an honorable word in Poland) of noncooperation with what officialdom wants. It is seen in the people's general readiness to cooperate with acts of defiance and in their equal readiness to find alternative and unofficial ways to do things. Above-ground acts of. noncooperation by so many make it possible for active oppositionists not only to survive but to function with a fair degree of effectiveness. Their cover is the people. Mao Zedong, in the days of his opposition activities, once observed, "We swim in the sea of the peasants and cannot therefore easily be detected." Similarly, those in active opposition in Poland swim in the sea of the people and are often spontaneously protected by them.

As part of an effort to boycott the national parliamentary elections in October, 1985, an activist was setting up loudspeakers on the roof of a café in Warsaw when he was accosted by the police. According to the New York *Times*, he "slipped out of the grasp of two security officers and escaped in a passing car. Scuffles broke out as onlookers crowded around the car and prevented the plainclothes policemen from giving chase. A crowd of several hundred people gathered in the square."[4] Examples of similar incidents are legion.

A popular joke in Poland says that a man was apprehended for distributing leaflets and taken to the local police station. The police suddenly noticed that the leaflets were blank. They asked the man, "Why are these leaflets blank?" He replied, "Everyone knows what they would say."

In August, 1985, *Tygodnik Mazowsze*, a leading independent (underground) newspaper, featured statements by well-known personalities in response to the question of what they considered to be the most important development in the five years since the Gdansk Accord. Lech Walesa said it was simply the existence of Solidarity, and he traced its stages of evolution from its leading the people in their rebellion against forty years of oppression to its formulation of a detailed program during the congress in the fall of 1981 to its present and future implementation of that program.

Zbigniew Bujak, chair of the Warsaw Regional Board of Solidarity during its legal existence, and then for more than four years, until his capture in the spring of 1986, its leading figure in the underground, saw the imposition of martial law as the crucial event and coupled it with what he said was the equally important meeting of the first national congress of Solidarity. The congress was, he said, the first assembly of democratically elected representatives of over one-third of Polish society. Klemens Szaniawski, a professor of philosophy who was elected rector of Warsaw University in 1984 only to have his election vetoed by the minister for higher education, said that a lot of "irreversible changes have occurred . . . changes within our consciousness. We have matured and we face both the reality and the future of our country without illusions . . . and without fear. Now we know where we stand. And we try not to be passive in dealing with our world."

Jacek Kuron, a founder of KOR and one of the best-known dissidents, said:

> I think the outcomes of the August victory are more permanent than "Solidarity" itself. Something extraordinary happened in the life of the nation. . . . Our historical consciousness had been dominated by a series of defeats. This time we experienced a great victory. . . . Now we have an organized society within a communist regime—something that has not happened anywhere else. . . . We no longer depend only upon an intellectual elite whose first and foremost task is to preserve national consciousness—we now depend on workers, farmers, taxi-drivers and the like. Today, those actively participating in our movement constitute 25% of society.

Among eight points that Janusz Patubicki, a Solidarity leader from Poznan, cited, two related ones are especially interesting and ironic: "Delegalized Solidarity has nevertheless remained a peaceful movement [and] the government turned out to be an 'enlightened terrorist.'"

Henryk Wujec, a member of KOR and of Solidarity's national commission, said that "communism has died in social consciousness . . . but there is also a feeling of growing pessimism that arises from the realization of how limited we are to deal with the situation. . . . It is impossible to return to the August '80 agreements. . . . There is a need for permanent political solutions which would guarantee the right to determine our own future." Henry Somsonowicz, professor of history and former rector of Warsaw University, believed that "a very significant democratisation of social life has occurred. Above all, a social consciousness has undergone changes that foster a much better formulation of social demands. As a historian I can say that for the last 400 years it has never been possible to reverse this kind of change."

Bronislaw Geremek, high in the councils of Solidarity and for that reason dismissed from the Institute of History of the Polish Academy of Science, stated: "It is impossible to erase the fact that there was a confrontation between Society on one side, and the authorities on the other. . . . For the first time there was a prospect of reaching a wise compromise; it was a great chance for both sides, for the country as a whole. . . . [The struggle] has awakened a new range of social aspirations. . . . Solidarity has arisen as a result of a re-evaluation of the true meaning of words, a re-consideration of basic moral values that were then embodied in a general programme. In this sense Solidarity withstands repression." For his part, Jan Litynski, a member of KOR and later in the underground, lamented the passivity of many of Solidarity's members after its delegalization but added:

> One thing seems to remain . . . a process one might call "the struggle of national consciousness". . . . The Poles have surpassed the limitations of their present political and historical reality. They have stood against the ill fortune of "here and now" and embarked on a difficult and dangerous way towards freedom. . . . The most important development of the last five years is the *return to national memory*. The return of this memory together with a sense of national unity and growing acceptance of pluralism of views en-ables us to hope that the Poles are still able to bring about this most impor-tant development they are driving towards. [5]

These statements by Poland's "other leadership" suggest the depth of experiences and growth of consciousness that have accompanied the Solidarity movement. They signal an awakening of Polish society to a re-newed sense of itself—a "return to national memory," as Litynski put it.

A teacher of English literature at a university in one of Poland's larger cities told me during my second visit to Poland in June, 1985, that of all the things the Solidarity period of ferment in 1980–1981 meant for the country, the most important was the feeling of restored relationship, of community, of caring about one another. She said it was as if Poles had made a great rediscovery—that people exist in and for one another. The resulting feeling was in marked contrast to the increasing sense of self-isolation and mistrust that had been building for years. She said that this new feeling was still vital and that there was still a potential for renewal in Poland. She also told me that in those days Poles had learned a secret of life summed up, perhaps not well but at least vividly, in the phrase "being what you want to be." "We got out of our political inertia or quietism," she said. "We came to see and feel that economic and political systems should be judged by how well or badly they supported 'being what you want to be.'"

That same month I had a similar conversation with two young people who were brother and sister. The young man recalled the sense of new life they experienced in 1980 and 1981. It was a physical sense as much as it was spiritual. "We didn't always have to be looking over our shoulder," he said. "In the student newspaper we created, we could say out loud what we felt and believed, and we could contest in public about real things. We had a sense that we were, at least to some degree, in command of our life." He and his sister had not only lived through those events but had been changed by them. They greeted, at first with incomprehension and then with mirth, my (baiting) statement that the suppression of Solidarity had essentially returned things to normal and the new generations of the young would soon forget those heady days and might even scorn them as the visions of their overly romantic forebears. They proceeded to cite instance after instance of persons their own age (they were in their middle twenties) or in their teens who, while seemingly bowing to the inevitable pressures of the government, are in fact thinking and often acting at great variance with their visible outward behavior.

These vignettes could be dismissed as windy talk (the first occurred in one of those monster high-rise building complexes that are often on the outskirts of Polish cities; the other, in a crowded restaurant). I could multiply them, however, and so could virtually anyone who travels about Poland or talks with Poles who are knowledgeable about their country's affairs. Even those who have chosen to stick with Jaruzelski and implement his policies do not dispute that the government confronts a problem in trying to "reach" the youth, the workers, the farmers, large sections of the intelligentsia, or the priests and the church hierarchy. In a frank and memorable speech in that same June of 1985, much quoted derisively the next day by Poles in my hearing, Jaruzelski chided the Polish people for their failure to get off the dime and go to work with a will. He said that though there are over eleven million people employed in the state sector, on any given day no more than seven million are at work. These are symptoms of a profound disjunction between the people and their government.

During the same visit in the summer of 1985, I became familiar, through conversations with W. W. Adamski, with the results of interviews of a cross-section of Polish society done by a well-regarded aboveground group of scholars. The results suggested that about 20 percent of the Polish people strongly oppose the regime and about an equal percentage strongly support it. The majority of the remainder leaned toward the active opposition. Jaruzelski's personal image fared better than might have been expected: When asked the question "Which public figures do you most respect?" about 50 percent of the respondents named Jaruzelski. Walesa's score was also about 50 percent. On a series of questions designed to establish respondents' attitudes toward the system as a whole, about two-thirds of them registered a decidedly negative opinion toward it.

At about the same time, a group of sociologists were interviewed by *Tygodnik Mazowsze* on the results of various polls they had done and other polls concerning the attitudes of young people.[6] The following excerpts from the interview reveal a complex picture—and one of profound change.

> The political system of Poland is no longer, as it used to be before August, something natural and inevitable. . . . In the '70s students still had positive associations with the word "socialism". They made slogans like: "Socialism—yes, distortions—no". In 1958 and 1979 two-thirds of respondents replied "yes" to the question: "Would you like the world to move towards some form of socialism?" In 1983 only 43% answered yes to the same question. . . .
>
> Among the features of a good political system only 10% of students pick nationalized industry (in 1979—34%), 55% mention equality of opportunity and only 10% equality of income (in 1979 respectively 82% and 30%). On the other hand those elements of socialist ideology which can be described as concrete democratic measures increased in significance. Examples here are: independence of specialists 31% (14% in 1979) and a wide range of self-government forms—25% (as against 14%). Thus it is not surprising that 25% of respondents, as an example of a socialist country, named a capitalist one (the majority in this category named Sweden) while 31% named countries of Comecon or Yugoslavia (in 1979 the figures were respectively 15% and 41%). . . .
>
> At the end of the '70s nearly one-third of respondents wanted the world to go in the direction "of the form of socialism which exists in Poland". Today only 3.6% want that. Moreover, young people believed then that the obstacles on the path of growth of the country lie in Poles' weaknesses: laziness, poor quality of work, alcoholism. Young people of the '80s put the blame on faulty organization of the economy, misuse of authority, suppressing of criticism, etc. They understood that it is not the people who are at fault but that the system is faulty, anachronistic and undemocratic.
>
> Indices of life-optimism have decreased only marginally compared with the '70s. . . . Yet young people do not see any chances for the country as a whole and very pessimistically evaluate the future of their generation. Is that optimism merely a form of defensive mechanism against the hopeless situa-

tion individually and nationally? Is it yet another in Polish history's incarnation of the dictum: "we will somehow manage"? If you ask about that "how" it soon turns out that for the great majority it means escape into privacy: I work somewhere for a pittance, try my hand at moonlighting, I have a family, meet my friends, go to football matches or read books—and I do not care about the rest. . . .

The need to be involved is felt by only 43%, that is, less than in 1958 (50%) and 1979 (57%). Yet to be involved then meant to complete your degree and then to work in your specialty attempting to improve something, fighting corruption, respecting the rules in spite of and against cliques in one's place of work, etc. And first and foremost it meant good work: as a doctor, engineer or manager.

Today, to be involved means to fight the system or engage in some form of opposition or church activity. The results of our studies show that there has been a striking change of attitudes towards—as it was described in the questionnaire—"independent social activity involving high individual risk". Such activity was accepted by 23% of students in 1979 and today it is accepted by 67%. Of course, it does not mean that all those who declare the need to be involved are present or future opposition activists. A potential reserve for "Solidarnosc" consists—I would have thought—of 17% of students who attach greater significance to socio-ideological values than to stabilisation in personal life. In that group 89% accepts illegal opposition activities. Ethos of fighting confronts here ethos of escaping.

Another indication of deep changes in basic political attitudes is shown in a comparison of young men's willingness to do mandated military service in the 1960s and 1970s on one hand and in the 1980s on the other. According to official sources, opinion polls carried out in 1960 showed that 64.7 percent of young men aged sixteen to nineteen were happy to do their national service. In 1965 over 90 percent of all young men approved of serving in the army, an attitude also prevalent in 1974. Surveys carried out in 1984 showed, however, that only 47 percent of young men displayed a positive attitude to doing the national service, and every fourth schoolboy declared that he was decidedly unhappy about the prospect of being called up to serve in the army.[7] These conservative 1984 figures strongly confirm the decided impressions that my family and I received during our five-month stay in 1983. One should also note that the formation of the Freedom and Peace movement shortly after we left was rooted in opposition to military service and is gradually gathering strength throughout Polish society.

One can interpret these statistics and sociological findings in a variety of ways, some pointing toward a deepening of the confrontation between society and state and some suggesting that the people are lying low in the face of the monopoly of force enjoyed by the regime, backed up as it is by the proximity of the Great Bear. But one cannot misinterpret the great stirring that has shaken the people to the core of their being and now makes them a potent political force. Along with a social consciousness, a fresh sense of human possibilities, a renewed sense of themselves as a community, and the recovery of a sense of their national history, the people of Poland are capable of thinking of politics not simply as a matter of personalities and symbols, of the clash of interests, or of the venting of particular grievances. The statements above by Poland's "other leadership" and the evidence from the various polls strongly suggest that the Polish people now see politics as also very much a matter of structures of power. They are able to see and judge systems. Not many peoples in the world give evidence of being able to do this.

Michael T. Kaufman's account of his father's visit to Poland in the summer of 1985 dramatizes, in a direct and personal way, this Polish ability to perceive political structures. Kaufman was New York *Times* correspondent in Poland. His father, Adam Kaufman, an eighty-two-year-old retired economist, escaped from Pilsudski's Poland to the United States in 1935 after spending nine of the previous ten years in jail for his efforts as a young Communist to organize the workers. Fifty years later he returned to Poland for the first time.

A Polish friend of the son's asks the father about his first impressions. The younger Kaufman wrote of his father's reply:

> He told her there were many, but that one struck him as particularly ironic. He said that when he was a young Communist organizer in the 1920's, people in Poland had many ways to explain and account for their unhappiness and dissatisfaction. "There was a pluralism of blame," he said. "A worker might blame the factory owner, some anti-Semites blamed wealthy Jews, Jews said the problem lay with anti-Semites, and the peasants resented wholesale merchants. Others pointed to Germans or Ukrainians as the source of trouble. Meanwhile, we Communists, a small group, ran around saying, no, it's not a question of individual grievances, it is the system that is to blame.
>
> "Now, after 50 years, I come back and what do I see? The whole nation knows perfectly well that the problem lies with the system and only the leaders are saying, no, the difficulties are the fault of individuals, former

leaders, mistaken politicians, or, as during the anti-Semitic purges of 1968, the Jews."[8]

It is as if the people of Poland had learned well the portion of communist doctrine that the young intellectual Adam Kaufman had imbibed most deeply and that teaches one to ask questions about the system. Being apt students, the Poles have naturally applied this approach, often thought to be merely for intellectuals, to their daily lives under communism. They have pierced that veil of mystification—the scourge of the common man—which is the tendency to blame only particulars. They now readily connect their particular grievances to a system—the communist system. They have learned what they would probably never have learned from a bourgeois, capitalist culture, which is steeped in a particularist, nominalist understanding of life in which the blame is almost always first and last on the individual. So the Poles have actually grown up intellectually and politically, and the Communists have had a big hand in enabling them to do it.

But that is also saying too much. For though they imbibed a consciousness of systems from the Communists, the Poles did not imbibe the latter's dogmatic, abstract way of thinking about systems. Poles today make a direct connection between the particular grievances of daily life and the dynamics of the system. They perceive the workings of the system within the fabric, within the concrete realities, of daily living. There is a real juxtaposition between the particular and the systemic in their daily sense of things. To them, the system is not just an intellectual construct, an intellectual's perception. There is a natural governor of their perceptions, and that governor is sensuous, concrete existence and experience. Otherwise their comments on the system, and their actions toward it, might be just flights of theorizing, and abstract action based on such theorizing.

A split between personal life and political life characterizes many modern societies, both East and West. Movements to transcend this polarity, such as the Greens, are springing up in Western Europe and, more recently, in the United States, Latin America, and Japan. Their insistence on a more holistic politics, their effort to overcome the split between the personal and the political, is of a piece with what has been happening in Poland, and the Greens have reason to be encouraged by events there.

This split is muted and to a remarkable degree transcended—or just absent—in the contemporary Polish revolutionary experience. Absent, as well, is the related reification of revolutionary experience typical of the doctrine-oriented vanguard movements of the twentieth century. The latter have often become embroiled in sectarian disputes in which individuals and factions nitpick at each other's politics over hair-splitting distinctions of doctrine or the meaning of the party line. Adam Kaufman, for example, suffered terribly from this disease of the left. After bravely leading his fellow conspirators in their testimony at the bar of Pilsudski's courts in Lvov (then a part of Poland) and being sentenced to a miserable jail cell, he was subject to scathing attacks by his fellow Communist party members, indeed expelled. His "crime" was that at the trial he was said to have spoken in such a manner that implied "Polish patriotic aberrations." He was also condemned for favorably mentioning two "bourgeois" authors and for addressing the court in Polish, which the resolution condemning him described as "the language of the oppressor," instead of in Ukrainian, "the language of the oppressed."[9]

Such dogmatic and puritanical fruits of thinking in terms of system do not characterize Solidarity. Indeed the latter's posture and spirit are directly opposed to cruel and self-destructive practices of that kind. Its members have known too much of that, having for forty years had their minds held captive by just that kind of scholastic and casuistic overlay of real existence.

Nevertheless, the Poles do have a consciousness that is markedly aware of systems. On one hand the system is an immediate reality that must be understood (and in some cases withstood), and on the other it must be judged in terms of its capacity to achieve differentiation and diversity— the subjectivity of persons, groups, and the nation.

Furthermore, it has hitherto been a given among those who think about change and revolution—and among many who act in social movements—that consciousness of system must go hand in hand with ideology.[10] Thus, many observers, from both within and outside Poland, who have looked at Solidarity and not found ideology have despaired of the movement or put it down as immature, incompetent, or both. They have professed to find no program, believing that without a guiding ideology there can be no program. What is in front of their noses, that is, Solidarity's extant programs of 1981 and 1985, are dismissed as lacking in serious systemic thought.[11] These documents are considered to be merely statements of what to be for or against, statements that lack the inner unity of coherent thought and the logic of historical analysis. Thus, the ground for action is also lacking, it is thought.

The authors of such criticism are unaware of the limitations of their own cerebral concept of unity, which implies that unity must be produced or constructed and must be given some kind of verbal meaning in order to exist. This line of criticism is inherently rooted in an intellectually heroic view of the nature of social change that assumes that unity must be instilled, and instilled from the top. It has much in common with a Leninist conception. It has much in common with what the late philosopher Eric Voegelin called the Gnostic approach to man's relation to nature and history.[12]

Solidarity sets itself against this ideological notion. It affirms a constitutional notion and strives to limit power rather than assert it. It strives for balance of conflicting forces through negotiation rather than for hegemony. This is the real center of its historic meaning. The people of Solidarity are wiser than the Leninists: they do not want to reinvent the wheel—the wheel of hegemony claiming power in the name of just another new version of historic truth.

It is in this profounder light that one can understand Solidarity's rejection of both violence and ideology. The two are linked. Acceptance of ideology as the way of change invites the use of force. The disposition to use force invites the brandishing of ideology.[13] Solidarity, in choosing nonviolence, must have recourse to constitutional notions of change. Solidarity, in choosing to fight for Poland's ancient rights of person, group, and nation, puts the burden of proof on the regime to show that it is constitutional, is acting legally, and is not an arbitrary, tyrannical imposter ruling by force of arms alone. The movement's constitutional, nonviolent approach determines its strategy, which is to prod, coax, cajole, and embarrass the regime to make room for the people, for their subjectivity. Solidarity does not threaten the regime with destruction of the system or with the death or even effacement of its leaders. The union's members merely ask the regime to make room, plenty of room, within the system for the people's subjectivity. If that means that the system will change substantially, and in a way that cannot now even be guessed at, then that is all to the good, according to Solidarity, because the people and the government will have found that new way together.

What, then, is the character of Solidarity's unity? It is not an ideological one, a strategic one, or a programmatic one. It is a deeply spiritual one—nonmechanical, nonintellectualized, nonconstructed. It is organic knowledge rising from the experience of—and the resulting demand for political self-determination by—the great majority of Polish citizens together. From this quest, from this demand, there arise program, strategy, and even ideological statements. But the order of their meaning is that these latter come "afterward" and could not even exist were it not for the galvanizing of the spirit, the renewal of society expressed in the people's newly found demand for political self-determination.

It is crucial to note and appreciate this dimension of the spirit. For otherwise the anti-ideological stance of Solidarity could readily be translated into notions such as "the end of ideology" that were put forward in the West in the 1950s and 1960s.[14] But this would entirely distort Solidarity's meaning in another direction: into something materialistic, merely pragmatic, merely programmatic. In reaction to ideology, and in reaction to the Soviet Union, Western thinkers have retreated to the vulgarity of the merely practical and have consequently enshrined an apolitical status quo as the new "ideology" of the West. Solidarity is very far from this; indeed it is quite opposed to such antiphilosophical and antivisionary politics.

Sabina is an artist and an émigré in Milan Kundera's *The Unbearable Lightness of Being*. In the novel she escapes from Czechoslovakia during the halcyon and terrible events of 1968 when Soviet troops and tanks put an abrupt end to her country's and her own hopes for a renewed existence.

> A year or two after emigrating, she happened to be in Paris on the anniversary of the Russian invasion of her country. A protest march had been scheduled and she felt driven to take part. Fists raised high, the young Frenchmen shouted out slogans condemning Soviet imperialism. She liked the slogans, but to her surprise she found herself unable to shout along with them. She lasted no more than a few minutes in the parade.
> When she told her French friends about it, they were amazed. "You

mean you don't want to fight the occupation of your country?" She would
have liked to tell them that behind communism, fascism, behind all occupations and invasions lurks a more basic, pervasive evil and that the image of
that evil was a parade of people marching by with raised fists and shouting
identical syllables in unison. But she knew she would never be able to make
them understand. Embarrassed, she changed the subject.[15]

I believe that Sabina's impulse is Solidarity's impulse, that Sabina's
wisdom is Solidarity's wisdom. Lech Walesa would understand, Adam
Michnik would understand, and so would the martyred Father
Popieluszko. Each in his own way, and so many others, have already
traveled a long route. It has taken them through, and past, the myth of
violence and the equally empty myth of ideology. They strike for, and
strive after, a deeper sense of human bonding and individual dignity. And
that makes them far more practical, far more true to life, than the vaunted
wielders of force and ideology, whether East or West.

8

The Flight of the Polish Phoenix

Solidarity, the Polish phoenix, is the source of Poland's renewal. Its flight is manifested in several important forces that are at work in Polish society. Three are especially potent: the forging of responsible leadership in the ranks of the political opposition; the paradox of a political church that is not political; and an ecological time bomb that must push both government and society into new paths of economic development and organization.

THE FORGING OF LEADERSHIP

Lech Walesa, electrician, carpenter's son, worker among workers, and leader of Solidarity, has had many opportunities in the years of wracking struggle to lose his and Solidarity's way. He has had to know when to be quick in action, even impetuous, as in his scaling of the Lenin Shipyards' fence in August, 1980, at a decisive moment in the birth of Solidarity. Conversely, he has had to know when to be cautious and feel his way forward, as in his successful efforts to temper the crowds in the wake of the news of Father Popieluszko's murder by police agents in November, 1984.[1] He has had to deal with a regime that is ultrasophisticated in the cleverer arts of personal harassment without losing his temper. He has had to deal with the twists and turns of Cardinal Glemp's and the pope's attitudes toward Solidarity, and toward himself, without losing his sense of humor or his faith. He has had to deal with the dubious gift of freedom from prison without falling into a paralysis of guilt and self-pity while so many of his fellow activists were and in many cases still are in jail suffering deprivations and often torture.

Walesa has had to deal with the government's persistent efforts to belittle and vilify him, and has had to do so without falling into the temptation, into which many politicians fall, of defending endlessly his reputation and ego. Without becoming shrill in his speech or actions, he has had to deal with the maddening refusal of the government to consider any degree or form of dialogue with him or his representatives. Without losing his basic optimism or his faith, he has had to deal with a measure of papal realpolitik, which seemed at one point in 1983 to be ready to bypass him and Solidarity. He has had to deal with leaders in the Solidarity underground (especially the TKK, or Provisional Coordinating Committee), whose outlook does not and cannot always gibe with his own, without succumbing to competitive and factional politics and, an opposite danger, without deferring so much to the underground as to blunt his own above-ground sense of the matters at stake. He has had to sustain, learn from, and surmount the suspicion, and often the ideological opposition, of a myriad of underground protopolitical groups without either turning away in impatience and anger or allowing them to distort his own sense of the path he must pursue. And when most oppositionists were released from jail in September, 1986, he had to adapt to their understandable desires, if not demands, for leadership opportunities and status.

Perhaps most difficult of all, since the outlawing of Solidarity, he has had to deal with the frustration and feeling of doom that follows the apparent collapse of a movement—and with the consequent skepticism of many supporters in Poland and abroad who have been so ready to write "finis" to Solidarity. The mood this generates can soften the will and pressure a leader—especially one so exposed as Welesa is—into alternating bouts of paranoia and foolish hope. At one moment the government may appear to be a totally hostile and monolithic adversary; at another its promises and seemingly reformist behavior may easily lure one into laying down the intolerable burden of resistance.

Walesa has avoided these pitfalls. What has kept him steady? Surely his religious faith has been a continuing source of spiritual balance and courage for him. His intimate connection with his parish church and its priest, Henryk Jankowski, his closest friend, sustains him daily. His family—his wife, Danuta, and their seven children—has given him immense support and the abiding sense of an even keel in life. The community in which he lives surrounds him with respect and even affection, and this sense of the community's (usually unspoken) support extends in concentric circles out to the farthest corners of Poland. He is an ordinary person greatly respected by the ordinary people of his society. He is in tune with them. Although Walesa has an ego (and it has sometimes gotten him into trouble), it is not as an ego that he is grounded in his society or his time. He is not a "charismatic figure" in the style of an ego-oriented, self-glorifying cult hero, as America's mass media have often sought to make him. He is not that, partly because of his own good sense in the face of the adulation he has received, but mostly because the Polish people do not regard him that way. They do not let him become such a figure. He is first of all an ordinary person, one of them, with the same faults and virtues as their own.

Walesa has thus avoided the pretentiousness of leadership. His essential modesty, a considerable moral virtue, extends into his intellectual posture and into his politics. Both reveal a similar and instinctive sense of balance. This sense of balance is a continuing source, and a secret, of his power.

A further strength is his own shrewd political intelligence and political imagination. He has a fine appreciation of his anomalous position. In some ways the epithet that government spokesman Jerzy Urban likes to use to describe Walesa—"the former head of a former union"—is quite accurate. Urban means to belittle Walesa, but nobody is impressed. It only brings into sharper relief the anomaly that has been created by the government. This former head of a former union, this electrician at the Lenin Shipyards, is so important that the chief spokesperson for the government has to keep insisting that he is unimportant. Friedrich Kramer of Austrian radio interviewed Walesa in August, 1985, in Gdansk at the parsonage of St. Brigida's (Father Jankowski's home).[2] Kramer asked him whether he still felt himself to be chairman of Solidarity. Walesa replied: "At present I am working in four places. First, as you have noticed, I have been working at the shipyard—since 5 A.M. I am just coming from work and have not had lunch. Second, I am the only breadwinner in a family of seven children. My third job: I am trying to lead a Solidarity that does not exist, and fourth I am trying to lead a Solidarity that does exist. That is what I do." Walesa is very alive to the irony of his situation and his role in it. He has few if any illusions about its limits—or about its possibilities. He is aware that the government has given him a kind of freedom: far from eliminating him physically, they have even let him out of jail. They cannot or will not truck with him, and yet they watch intently his every move.

So Walesa has some space—not much, but some. And he has the shrewdness to try as carefully as he can to use that space to alter the situation and the structure of power in his country. It is a bafflingly difficult role.

He must have received an intimation of just how difficult as early as the time of his release from custody in the fall of 1982. There had been much prodding of the government by Catholic church officials and others to secure his release. Walesa was eventually persuaded to write a letter to Jaruzelski requesting his release. There was a tacit understanding that if he did so, the government would let him go, which did in fact happen. But Walesa's real difficulty was how to sign his letter to Jaruzelski. To sign it as chair of Solidarity would be to come on too strong, since the government would point out that such a position does not legally exist. To sign it simply with his name, as a private citizen, would signify that he, Walesa, acceded to the new situation and accepted "normalization." So he did neither, but with an impish and doubtless sardonic flourish (especially given the stark military nature of the new regime) he signed his letter "Corporal Lech Walesa."[3] Thus does irony serve one well if one knows how to use it.

Walesa meets with foreign correspondents. He meets with antigovernment activists both above-ground and underground. He participates in gatherings at the monument of the crosses near the shipyard in memory of the fallen workers of 1970. He makes statements and speeches, to audiences at home and abroad, that identify a line of march. He issues calls for action, and for nonaction. He travels to different parts of the country to participate in ceremonies, usually of a religious kind. He and his many advisers work steadily at the development of a program. It is as if a shadow cabinet is at work in the shadows, monitoring and criticizing the official program and calling for more effective politics. He acts and behaves like a leader.

Walesa is careful not to give the government too much cause to figure that it is safer to have him in jail and risk the consequences of putting him there than to leave him loose to do what he is doing. The pressures are enormous, and it is always possible that, since he errs on the side of action rather than of caution, the regime will find a way legally to "throw the book at him" and make that action seem completely plausible. It will be hard for the government to do this given the overwhelming skepticism of the people at the way it has conducted trials of activists in the past several years. But government leaders may find an issue that will work for them. They cannot be faulted for not trying.

Walesa is repeatedly told by the government to curb his activities. They became especially exercised at the time of the parliamentary elections in October, 1985, when the monitoring network put together by Solidarity throughout the country proved so effective. Walesa was much involved in the process. He made a series of public statements during and right after the election that gave figures of turnout for the election considerably lower than those provided by Jerzy Urban, the government spokesman. In the days that followed, Urban was forced to outdo himself in the number of press conferences he gave. Urban was not amused, and immediately after the election the government started criminal proceedings against Walesa for alleging official falsification of the election results. Urban called it slander against the state.[4]

The much-publicized trial of Walesa for slander finally took place on February 11, 1986, in the provincial court in Gdansk. Outside the courtroom before the trial Walesa said that he was feeling fine. He wore a sweater emblazoned with the words GOD AND THE HOMELAND. Pinned on it was a Solidarity badge and another of Our Lady of Czestochowa. His friend Father Jankowski was allowed to attend the trial, but all foreign observers were excluded. All twelve plaintiffs who said Walesa slandered them were judges. During the trial Walesa spent a good part of the time doing crossword puzzles.

After a late start and several recesses the judge asked whether either side saw any chance of setting the dispute without going any further. The public prosecutor then told Walesa that if he could make a statement that would render satisfaction to the plaintiffs, it could lead to the charges being dropped. Walesa said: "My intention was not to slander anyone. I did not intend to demean anyone." The court again went into recess for half an hour. On reappearing the prosecutor asked Walesa whether the court was to understand that he wanted by his statement to give satisfaction to the plaintiffs. Walesa replied that he was sticking to what he had already said. Another recess was declared. After four hours the court reconvened. The prosecutor announced that he was withdrawing the charges because he believed that the plaintiffs could feel satisfied with what Walesa had said. Walesa's comment after the trial was that he hoped that that day's way of dealing with things could in the future prevail in public life. A compromise between government and the opposition, which would include representatives of Solidarity, had been possible for a long time, he stated. [5]

The scene largely speaks for itself. The government by inches backs away; Walesa goes so far but no farther, playing his role with humor, agility, and sharp awareness of what is going on. Walesa is also at pains to turn the immediate matter at hand back to the central issue: the need for the government to negotiate with the opposition and find a settlement. Walesa's entire posture and performance can be seen as itself a model of how this can be done, or at least begun: essentially by finding that angle in the situation that permits bargaining to take place, which pushes back or precludes an either-or confrontation and which preserves the amour propre of each side. And above all, his posture is a model of how a citizen can stand up to presumed authority, refuse to be cowed by it, assert his or her own right to self-determination, and at the same time be flexible enough to invite the forces of that presumed authority to look for settlements of issues, including the vital issue of power itself. Of course, Walesa has a lot going for him that other Polish citizens do not—the close attention of the world's press, for example. But then he has more pressures on him, too.

He is constantly being warned, constantly being interrogated (often for hours at a time), constantly under surveillance and under the threat of multitudinous little harassments invented by a security apparatus increasingly adept in such matters. In June, 1986, for example, Walesa was subject to questioning for three hours about his contacts with the arrested underground leader Zbigniew Bujak and with Stephen Mull, the American diplomat who was accused of being a spy. Walesa said afterward that he refused to answer any of the police's questions and that he would continue to meet with foreign diplomats. The government, in retaliation to such defiance about foreign contacts, has repeatedly refused to give him a passport to respond to invitations from abroad, such as to go to San Francisco, where a street has been named in his honor, or to Italy to attend a peace conference. Yet his firm and flexible stance clearly influences the government to be flexible, though also firm. The government did not intervene to prevent him from having an extensive four-hour meeting with John Whitehead, the United States deputy secretary of state, during Whitehead's high-level and critical talks with government officials in January, 1987. These talks led to the lifting of the United States sanctions that had been in force since 1981–1982. Whitehead's meeting with Jaruzelski, the highest-level contact between Poland and the United States for more than five years, came the day after Whitehead's visit with Walesa and other Solidarity leaders. At his weekly press conference for foreign journalists, Urban was of course pressed about this anomaly. With gorgeous irony Urban said that Whitehead's meeting with Walesa was "a private contact of an informal character" beyond the range of the government's interests.[6]

These scenarios were repeated during the visit of Vice-President George Bush to Poland in September, 1987. On Sunday, September 27, Jaruzelski and Bush conferred for two hours. That same evening the authorities permitted Walesa and other Solidarity leaders to visit the vice-president at the United States residence in Warsaw. Even so, there ensued the usual harassment. Walesa's car was stopped about a hundred yards from the residence by police officers who asked for his identity papers and pretended not to know who he was. Bush was apprised of the delay by Bronislaw Geremek and eventually the meeting took place.[7]

The slander trial illustrates the opportunities the regime has to pick and choose an issue that they feel can intimidate Walesa or perhaps even provide them with a chance to "legally" put him away with a minimum of public fuss. But they are wary of crossing that line, and Walesa knows that. His undoubted success over the years since 1982 in treading very close to the line became even more important following the surprising clearing of the jails of almost all political prisoners in September, 1986. His style is a precedent on how to oppose the powers of the state above-ground. He became a model for each of the many leaders of Solidarity who suddenly found themselves outside the prison walls—and a precedent for all of them together. Walesa and these other leaders took immediate steps to develop a new type of above-ground organization (to parallel their underground organizations) capable of dickering with the government should the latter ever be so inclined. They followed up this organizational change with yet another in the fall of 1987. Jaruzelski's proposals for a renewed effort at economic reform and for greater political consultation with the nation spurred Solidarity to make its own internal decision-making process more efficient and timely. Its leaders abolished both the underground and above-ground executive committees and formed a new body, an eleven-person National Executive Commission, headed by Walesa.[8]

Yet, of all the elements that have kept Walesa steady, I believe that the most important is his clear sense of Solidarity's demand for independent, self-governing unions coupled with his equally clear sense of its strategic commitment to nonviolent communication with the government. His clarity about both the end and the means, and the natural fit each has with the other, has been a major and critical factor in helping Solidarity to find and renew itself again and again in these difficult years. The danger of descent into fear and hopelessness is always near, along with the correlative danger that the movement will balkanize into a multitude of isolated groups. But actually, Solidarity is helped in this regard by the fact that it has always been a do-it-yourself, pluralistic movement. Thus it is able to bear these shocks of enforced fragmentation with greater resilience than could a tightly organized and centralized movement. Walesa's own pluralistic outlook adapts nicely to this situation.

At the same time, his firmness about the end and the means is an intangible but effective glue that maintains a consistent line of march for the entire movement. One result has been to discourage the formation, within the overall opposition, of powerful opposing factions, each with its own ideological positions and "favorite son." Four themes seem to constitute the core of Solidarity's and Walesa's program: the self-governing nation; the self-governing union or association (and its self-management); the self-governing local territory; and the self-governing person, both as worker and citizen. Walesa, in the foreword to Solidarity's 1985 statement of its program, "Poland Five Years After August," writes: "We say our programme is the one adopted by the First Congress of Solidarity, the programme of a self-governing Republic: a say for the citizen; non-fictitious worker's and territorial self-government; work that makes human sense."[9] All these themes are joined together and have not come unstuck in the travail and paradox of Poland's long struggle for renewal. Combined with the commitment to nonviolence, they become a comprehensive program that thereby preempts potential balkanization of the overall movement and resists those seemingly inevitable tendencies of excluded activists to adopt an exclusivistic either-or, all-or-nothing attitude toward the oppressive authorities.

Yet, side by side with Solidarity there have emerged many tendencies and political formations in the underground that do not share this comprehensive and dialogic approach. One moderate but clear example is the voice of the underground journal *Polytyka Polska*, in whose pages have appeared the writings of an articulate leader, Aleksander Hall. Hall has ties to underground Solidarity but withdrew from active involvement with it, because he differs both with its strategy and to some degree with its ideas. He hits hard on the theme of self-government for the nation and seems to intend by this more than national autonomy: he stresses full independence and sovereignty. He also has a strong belief in the church's role and a commitment to political democracy.[10] Thus, at least some of the themes of Solidarity's program are Hall's concerns, too. But there is less emphasis on forms of worker democracy and the fundamentally egalitarian impulse of Solidarity's and Walesa's program. This is not an insignificant difference.

Furthermore, Hall downplays Solidarity's strategy of pushing for serious negotiation with the regime on behalf of self-governing institutions. He favors less confrontation, maintaining that it is better to ignore the regime as much as possible. In a word, the opposition should not expect anything from the regime. In the meantime it should put all its energy into the nurturing of Polish society's "internal sovereignty" and into "the defence and development of the national community in the context of a non-sovereign, alien state." This approach, he says, is not new but "has already been elaborated by Primate Wyszynski" during his long struggle with the Communist state.[11] The building of an alternative "sovereign" society should be done as much as possible above-ground, he argues.

Having said this much, Hall then comes back some distance toward Solidarity by saying that his approach does "not imply abandoning the attempts to influence the government. One of the most important tasks ahead for the society is to apply pressure upon the state, and, in this way, to compel it to retreat and evolve." Then he adds, "We have to tolerate the Communist state—we have no other choice." A few paragraphs later, he observes: "In exchange for the abandonment of the attempts on the part of society to transform People's Poland into a state of the nation, the Communists might accept the autonomy of national life, and, above all, the existence of institutions and social organization independent of the government. Such a compromise could be a realistic programme for a 'new August.'" This is very close to what Solidarity and Walesa are promulgating. But does Hall mean only church autonomy and related organizations, or does he also include in "social organization" the full spectrum of independent, self-governing unions? And then, again, he quickly iterates that "at present this is not feasible" and concludes by insisting that "just a 'new August' is not the ultimate aim of Polish politics. Its final goal is an independent statehood." There is more than a hint of nineteenth-century nationalism in Hall's posture, and also a strong dose of anti-Russianism and thus also of settled prima facie opposition to the Jaruzelski regime as being merely a Soviet puppet with which it is unwise and impossible to negotiate. Yet, at the same time, and presumably with one part of himself, he thinks that such negotiation might eventually be feasible. It is not a clear position. But much of it does overlap with the ideas of Solidarity, and that part may be said to be a variation on the union's basic themes.

A similar variation is found in the Committees for Social Resistance (KOS), which began in Warsaw immediately upon the imposition of martial law. They put major stress on the nurturing and development of alternative self-help institutions, above-ground if possible, underground if necessary. They continue the spirit and actions of KOR. They are not, however, sanguine about pushing for negotiations with the authorities, and they seem in this regard almost apolitical, somewhat along the lines of cultural revolutionaries in the West. It should be pointed out that Solidarity not only does not oppose, but strongly encourages, the building of an alternative society. For example, the "Draft Manifesto" of Solidarity's Interim Coordinating Committee in July, 1982, recommended that union members should ignore the regime and construct their own alternative information networks and educational system, organize support for the victims of martial law, and set up workshops and cooperatives. [12]

One important difference between Solidarity and such small groups as KOS and the Young Poland movement is that the former combines organic cultural and social work with a strategic political readiness to find a structural settlement with the regime that includes both society and the government. The small groups are dubious about such a strategy or do not perceive it clearly.

Fighting Solidarity (Solidarnosc Walczaca) is even more militant. It

was formed in mid-1982 in Wroclaw when a number of Solidarity activists came to the conclusion that Solidarity's policy of, as they called it,
"forcing authorities to concessions" would not and could not work. Their
aim therefore is to fight for Poland's independence by overthrowing the
Communists. As for what they wish to see in place of the current regime,
they advocate parliamentary democracy, a free-market economy (with
the exclusion of large-scale private ownership), workers' self-government, local self-government, human rights, and an independent
workers' union that would unite—on a voluntary basis—people of all
professions. It is clear that there is much overlap with Solidarity, but the
sticking point is the strategic posture vis-à-vis the Communist state (and
to some degree the question of the ownership of the means of production). And it is not clear that the group is committed to nonviolence,
though for the time being they are stressing information and propaganda
as tools of resistance.[13] They are organized in many places in Poland, but
mainly in the Wroclaw and Poznan regions. Its underground leader is
Kornel Morawiecki.

Writing under the pseudonym Sejan, a Polish analyst in early 1984
attempted to formulate a political geography of Poland's opposition
groups.[14] In addition to those mentioned above, Sejan identified several
other groups that reject even more of Solidarity's means and ends. The
Underground Word group, for example, advocates a liberal economy, a
multiparty political system, and the breakup of the Soviet Union into a
number of independent states. Sejan also mentions the Independence
organization, which stresses the paramount need for an independent
Poland. Its members also want to see society and the economy organized
on the basis of the principles they say are practiced in modern democratic
capitalist states, i.e., respect for individual freedoms, the limitation of
state interference in people's lives, the decentralization of power, and a
free-market economy.[15] This group also stresses the need to achieve
cooperation among the nations of Central Europe "enslaved" to the
Soviet Union. On November 11, 1984, the Independence group formed
themselves into a political party.[16]

There are many other groups and voices, some closer to, and some
farther from, Solidarity's overall line of march. They take various positions on various issues. The dominant tendency of several is to do even
more starkly what Aleksander Hall has done—elevate the absolute sov-

ereignty of Poland above all other considerations and reject all strategic compromise with Jaruzelski's regime.

These other groups bring into sharp relief the program and politics advocated and practiced by Solidarity and its leadership. Their existence also raises the question of how Solidarity's leadership can best deal with them. A good illustration of the leadership's approach and attitude is offered by the remarks of Zbigniew Janas, an industrial worker, chairman of Solidarity in the Warsaw Ursus Works and member of Solidarity's National Commission. After being underground for three years, he re-emerged into the open in December, 1984, by agreement with the TKK. In an interview quoted in the *Uncensored Poland News Bulletin*, he was asked his attitude toward Fighting Solidarity. His answer could also be applied to most of the other groups. He extended his best wishes to the leader of Fighting Solidarity and observed that the group obviously had its followers and seemed to be efficient. He added that they seemed to pursue the same general aims as Solidarity, though they wanted to achieve them by other methods. Then he said: "And this is just as well—on two conditions: that they consistently renounce violence, and that they do have a number of followers and are efficient."[17] It is clear that the emphasis on nonviolence—and on efficiency—was crucial for Janas.

Therefore, the effect of the existence and the often intense activity of these small groups is paradoxical. On the one hand it gives some credibility to the government's insistence that the opposition is counter-revolutionary, that it will not be satisfied with structural compromise but wants to overthrow the system. Indeed, it feeds the government's paranoia and gives it an excuse to go to extremes in a hard-line direction and write off the entire opposition as a bunch of unrealistic provocateurs. On the other hand, the existence of these other groups reveals dramatically, by contrast, the essence of Solidarity's realism: the firmness of its constitutional commitment to a restructured system, its equal firmness concerning national autonomy, and its continuing determination to bring the government to the negotiating table and to do so without violence. None of the other groups can match Solidarity's union of comprehensive program and strategic compromise.

Thus, the effect of the other groups on Solidarity is paradoxical and ironic. But one must look at the reality that is the ground of the irony and not only at appearances. The reality is that Solidarity is not what the regime in its paranoia and political game-playing is eager to make it appear, but is in fact a possible and plausible partner in the restoration of vigor to Poland. Will the regime recognize and acknowledge this reality in time for it to make a difference?

Zbigniew Bujak was the foremost underground Solidarity leader until his arrest on May 31, 1986, prior to which he had eluded the police for four and a half years. He shared in the amnesty later that year. It is commonly acknowledged that his political stature in the movement is second only to that of Walesa. Looking back to Gdansk from his vantage point in the underground, he had second thoughts. He said, in an interview with *Newsweek* at a clandestine location in September, 1985, that "the Gdansk Agreement was not a good idea for us and did not solve anything." The whole experience, he said, had been very dangerous. He answered that way partly because he felt that the sudden disintegration that occurred in the aftermath of the Gdansk Accord had brought incredible tragedies. But his answer was also due to the fact that the government, though it spoke in the Gdansk Accord in language of strategic, structural compromise, did not understand or believe in it. He likewise implied that Solidarity itself did not altogether comprehend its real position and has had some learning to do. The point is, he argued, to continue pushing the government to make a genuine, workable structural compromise and for Solidarity's leaders not to let themselves be party to it until they can be sure it is genuine. That, said Bujak, will probably happen within the next ten to fifteen years.[18]

Only thirty-three years old in 1987, Bujak was born on a farm in the village of Lopuszno. His father, a soldier in the Home Army during the Second World War, moved to Warsaw because of severe financial hardship. Zbyszek, by which name he is now known far and wide, had to work from an early age, first at a pharmaceutical works near Warsaw, a plant highly hazardous to health, and then at the Ursus tractor works, where he eventually made his mark. He attended evening technical college, graduating with a diploma that certified him a "technician" (skilled worker). He did his two years of military service as a parachutist from 1974 to 1976. He joined the official trade union in 1978 but soon lost interest. He became familiar with KOR-inspired activity and read opposition literature, soon becoming an important distributor of *Robotnik* (The Worker), a new opposition publication. During August, 1980, he took a leading role in the formation of a workers' Solidarity committee at Ursus and then helped set up a Solidarity founding committee in the Mazovia (Warsaw) region. He was its chairman and therefore also became part of Solidarity's National Commission. On December 12, 1981, he was in Gdansk for a meeting of Solidarity leaders. He was one of the few top leaders who escaped and managed to avoid detention when martial law struck the next day. He became a founder-member of the TKK, Solidarity's underground organization, on April 22, 1982. During the succeeding four years, until his arrest, he grew to be a national figure, even a national hero. He, perhaps more than anyone else, represented the continuity of Solidarity's existence. He continued to be extremely active in union matters. He was also accessible. He appeared at press conferences, gave many interviews, and was even available to be filmed by Western camera crews—all this while still underground, a fact that testifies to the existence of a vast network of people willing to risk their own freedom. Yet, it was to some extent Bujak who, by his energy, commitment, and charisma, evoked such daring and determination in people. At the same time, he is no adventurist, but consistently argues for a nonviolent and steady pressure on the authorities to settle issues, especially the issue of power.

After his release in September, 1986, and after he, Walesa, and others formed the new, above-ground Provisional Council of Solidarity, Bujak gave an interview that appeared in the underground publication *Wola* on October 13, 1986. He was particularly impressive in a response he made to one of the interviewer's best questions: "What do you think are the limits of the authorities' quiet consent for the expansion of Solidarity?" Bujak replied:

> There are different points of view. Some say that the authorities will never allow us to act under the name of Solidarity. In my opinion they will. Others still maintain that we have to transform into a different shape, to abstain from the activity adopted so far. They say that now the time has come to start working in various councils. I disagree with that. We can stick to our present organization and structure and they will accept it, too. Political practice in our country does not necessarily need rational arguments. The present situation has arisen dynamically—both sides carry on with their policy and at some point a boundary has to be found. It is up to us now how far the boundary can reach. [19]

What is perhaps most striking about Solidarity's leadership is its sense of time. "There are many people, particularly young people, who want victory at this very moment, by any methods," said Walesa on Austrian radio in August, 1985. "But those who care for the country with more responsibility want to know what the solutions will look like. They do not call for victories now, because these would be no gain for us. Therefore, the whole thing has to last a bit longer, and a climate must emerge in which these solutions can be realized. At present such a climate does not exist, as we can see. So, we are not in such a hurry, even though we are working very hard."[20]

This sense of not being in "such a hurry" is part of Solidarity's innate constitutionalism and demand for partnership. Its members consequently bear no big ideological load on their shoulders that makes them feel as if they must create the world anew. Their demands are practical, historical, and decisive. "Of course," said Walesa in the same interview, "it is not our objective to take over power or to fight against it. Our objective is to change Polish reality—in such a way that the system becomes more efficient and we have a better life. And we are above all for structural security—and we will not swerve from this issue." The telling phrase is "structural security." By now the reader must be aware what it means and does not mean. It means independent, self-governing unions (and by extension all professional associations) with adequate support systems in civil and political rights; a decentralized economy with self-management as its touchstone; and autonomy for the Polish state. It does not mean the overturning of the system, the destruction of the ruling party or the government, enmity toward the Soviet Union, or readiness to resort to violence. Adds Lech Walesa, "It is impossible for us not to win."[21]

In a carefully crafted speech of November 11, 1985, to the Oxford Union Society in Britain, one that he was unable for obvious reasons to deliver himself and that was given for him by Frank Chapple, the former president of the British Electricians' Union, Walesa said:

It has to be said emphatically that the future of the independent trade union movement in Poland depends in large measure on whether the government creates the psychological, legal and political conditions for its coming into the open. It has to be stressed that it is the government which is in the position to initiate such moves, which is why we expect the first move from the government. Such a gesture would have to be accompanied by a vision of how the government's relations with the trade unions should be conducted in the future, so that the possibility of social tensions, which could wreck the new agreement, is minimalized. In other words, what is needed are solid guarantees for both parties. This new agreement, which I consider to be the most important aim of our activities, should not only create a new political and legal climate but also change the mood of the whole of the society and create conditions for progress in Poland. Is this possible? My answer is: It won't be easy, but it is not impossible. It will, of course, depend to some extent on the international situation and on the condition of our social movement. Both of them can enhance or weaken the atmosphere of dialogue.[22]

There is a reach of understanding here, of political wisdom, that should be listened to by everyone concerned, East and West, and within Poland by both the government and the underground. On the occasion of the ceremonies surrounding the commemoration of the fifth anniversary of the Gdansk Accord, Walesa said, "This is our country, our homeland, and there is no other way to solve the crisis but through dialogue."[23]

We witness within the overall Solidarity movement the forging of a leadership that is nonideological and yet firmly rooted in fundamental principles. The leadership takes a clear constitutional approach. It has grown in perception, in understanding of what is at stake, and in political maturity. I have focused on Walesa and on Bujak, both industrial workers. But many other voices in the leadership of the movement are equally revealing of insight, judgment, and a correlative wariness of ideological posturing. Furthermore, Solidarity's leadership is rooted firmly both in the industrial workers and the intelligentsia and has close ties to the church and to the farming population. It is this union of diverse social elements, a union lacking in other communist countries (and lacking also to varying degrees in the political opposition in Western capitalist countries), that makes Solidarity so much a power in Poland. Its leadership, though so very diverse, speaks basically a common language wrought from both hard thinking and hard experience. An example of the hard thinking is found in a statement by Bronislaw Geremek, a leading adviser to Solidarity and the church, and an instance of the hard experience is found in a brief account of torture in Poland's jails.

In April, 1985, Geremek made the following statement.

I was astonished, leaving prison, how broad the resistance is to the new policies—not resistance in the underground which is necessarily an elite and divided movement, but embodied in people's aspirations toward a better society. . . . The problem for the society is a choice of action and attitude. In the young generation, there is a view that the whole system is structurally ill and cannot be improved. At a church meeting, I met a young man who said: "You're looking how to improve the system, and we're looking how to destroy it." . . . Though the government would like to see youth with an attitude of enrichissez vous, amusez-vous with film, video, discos and porno, I feel this young generation is very rich in national and social values. But how to employ this energy in a good sense, in the interests of the country? I can't answer them right now.

I think a social contract is still possible. The government, pressured by the economic crisis, could accept it—I'm not saying they will—and society could accept the same terms as in August 1980, recognizing the monopoly of the party but attaining more independence for themselves, if not actual political independence. Thousands and thousands are waiting for Solidarity's program, for a word from Walesa: what to do, how to do it. They're waiting for Walesa, with the Red government, to make a deal. [24]

An example of Solidarity's hard experience comes from a letter that was smuggled out of prison by a young man who, along with a leading Solidarity activist, Seweryn Jaworski, was convicted in May, 1986, of planning to incite public unrest before the parliamentary elections in October, 1985. At the trial the young man was given an eighteen-month jail sentence. The letter is in part a sickening and deeply disturbing account of his arrest. It is far from the most gruesome story available, but it seems especially significant because what happened to this young man can so easily happen to anyone in today's Poland. Such occurrences constitute part of that "threshold of fear" by which the government seeks to keep its people in thrall and that nevertheless has again and again been faced and overcome by Poland's "other leadership." Wladyslaw Frasyniuk, for example, was brutally beaten four times in prison, but in spite and because of it he has played an important role in Solidarity's core leadership. In this case the young man's "crime" was that he placed a speaker on a shop roof in Warsaw's main shopping precinct in connection with the efforts of Solidarity to persuade the Polish people to boycott the elections in October, 1985.

On the day of my arrest I was interrogated in the Warsaw police headquarters by five plainclothed men who took turns during the questioning. I was nervous and told them that I would write down my account of events but as I finished writing one of them grabbed the piece of paper and threw it away saying that this was not the kind of deposition he had in mind. They began to beat me. I was kicked in the groin and I fell, whereupon they continued kicking me as I lay on the floor. When I sat up again at the desk they kept beating me about the head and face. Later I was told to stand still in the corner without leaning against the walls. Following that they made me walk there and back to the adjoining room without any support. Afterwards, when sitting at the desk, I was ordered to get up every so often and each time I was up, one of them kept punching me hard in the stomach. As I was sitting they kept kicking me, albeit not too hard, at the soles of my feet. The interrogation lasted some 4 or 5 hours and only afterwards was I taken to a clinic where both my fractured legs and my left arm were put into plaster. [25]

There is more, but the excerpt suggests the intensity and brutality of the struggle in which and through which the opposition in Poland has been formed and from which they have emerged as a political force for social change.

A POLITICAL CHURCH

The church in Poland is deeply political in many senses of the word, but it is also not political in important ways. As with so many aspects of Polish life, the situation of the church is a case study in historic irony, and in the irony one discerns a force that because of itself and in spite of itself vitally supports, indeed helps to express, the Polish phoenix.

Communism in Poland has had a major impact on the church's social teachings and on its outlook toward the ordinary person. Before World War II the church was a reactionary institution steeped in the concepts and practice of hierarchy, rooted in the modes and values of a class system that excluded two-thirds of the people from education and opportunity for a better life, and deeply tainted by anti-Semitism. Under the powerful and often vicious blows of Communist force this system toppled. The church, in order not to be shoved aside by this social revolution, did an about-face. It increasingly adapted its teachings and its outlook to the socioeconomic needs and progress of the ordinary man and woman. It did so in order to compete with communism, in order not to lose credibility with the people of Poland in their striving for modernization and a better material and social life.

At the same moment, it sought, under Cardinal Wyszynski, to blunt the atheism and doctrinaire relativism of the new ruling ideology and to reaffirm the grounding of morality in the human being's God-given (and

therefore natural) rights. Thus, in this struggle over values the church
was forced to abandon its pre–World War II hypocritical acceptance of,
even connivance in, the suppression of human rights by the old reactionary regime in order more effectively to use the argument of human rights
to resist the communization and growing Party domination of Polish
culture. In so doing, it struck a profound chord in the psyches and values
of the ordinary men and women of Polish society. In addition, the
church could point to and sustain its long-term historic role as defender
of the Polish nation. In this role it could always outbid for loyalty the
ruling Polish United Workers party, given the latter's much-too-umbili-
cal relationship to the Kremlin. All of this also meant that, as the decades
went by, the church was able to attract thousands of young men and
women to its service; they were some of the most creative, dedicated, and
idealistic people in Polish society.

By purging itself, by adapting its outlook on social and economic
issues, by affirming human rights in the face of arbitrary rule, by insisting
on the autonomy of the nation, and by thus appealing to generation after
generation of Polish youth, the church has re-created itself in Poland as a
moral and spiritual force for change. The elevation of a Pole to the
papacy and his visit soon thereafter to Poland in the summer of 1979,
when he through symbol and preachment proclaimed a dynamic, concerned church, provided a climax for the success of Wyszynski's new
posture for the church and a prelude to the people's rebellion against an
ossified communism the following year.

Yet, precisely because of this rebellion and because the church has
always itself been on shaky and guarded terms with the regime, the
church is now faced with a fairly difficult if not dangerous situation,
dangerous to itself, that is.

The Polish church has five vital interests: liturgical, pastoral, national,
international, and missionary (or hegemonical). First and perhaps foremost is its own continued institutional existence. It perforce depends on
the regime to allow it to keep the churches open and functioning, to keep
them maintained, and to build new ones. This might be called its liturgical interest, which is the one the regime would like to see it limited to.
Second, the church considers it vital that it have the opportunity to
preserve and sustain the Catholic religious life of its parishioners. This
pastoral interest goes beyond mere preservation of liturgy to the oppor-

tunity to do in-depth parish work: spiritual education; provision of religious symbols in the home, school, and hospital; involvement in the
birth, marriage, and death of its parishioners; and so on. This second
interest readily spills over into opposition to the secularization of life and
into the closely related effort to reinvigorate social and cultural life with
religious values.

These first two interests would of themselves be sufficient to involve
the church in a degree of politics, given the nature of the Communist
regime, which preaches and tries to practice the totality of the cultural
and social mission of the Party, and given the fact that over 90 percent of
the people are Roman Catholic. But the church has three further interests that decisively catapult it into politics. It feels itself to be, and to have
always been, the special guardian of the Polish nation. Intertwined with
this national interest, therewith, however, is the fact that the Polish
church hierarchy serves the international church centered in Rome, and
the latter has worldwide concerns that may or may not gibe in particular
times and circumstances with what the Polish church wants, especially
on so sensitive an issue as nationhood. So these two interests sometimes
cancel each other out, or one wins out over the other. Jan Szezepanski,
Polish sociologist and former member of the Council of State, wrote in
Odra in 1980: "It must be remembered that [the church] is a Catholic or
global Church and that its interests do not *completely* coincide with those
of the Polish nation, that in spite of the involvement in Polish affairs it
must consider its own interests which result from its universality and its
involvement in many continents, lands and political systems." Bogdan
Szajkowski demurs from this view, arguing that for the Polish church,
Poland is, next to God, its highest loyalty.[26] His argument is persuasive,
but in addition to this special national feeling there is another interest,
often embraced by and lost to view in the national churchly ardor: the
enthusiasm for missionary expansion, the hegemonical impulse. Thus,
there is an additional complication, a fifth interest—"Ostpolitik." In a
profound sense the church in Poland and the papacy (regardless of who is
pope) consider Poland pivotal to the historic destiny of the Roman Catholic church. This perception antedates communism. Poland is and has
been the critical outpost, the border land, beyond which Roman Catholicism has not extended. Poland is the defense line of the Roman religion,
but it is also a frontier and thus a base for its further development east-

ward. With the coming of communism, the stakes have been raised even higher, and in the church's terms the struggle for the soul of Poland is, at the base line, the struggle for the church's overall survival. It is thus also an opportunity to turn the tables on communism and move Roman Catholicism farther east.

A telling example of that sentiment is found in a farewell message by Cardnal Wyszynski to his fellow bishops six days before his death in May, 1981. It is an affecting document in which he delivered his last words of advice and gratitude to the leaders of the Polish church. "Our greatest worth is found in the faith of our people," he declared, "their ties with the Church, their bond with the Church in Christ and His Mother, in your faith, in your burning love and in your own uncommon apostolic fervour. I can expect no more. The Church must remain where it is. For without exaggeration, it is the bulwark of Christianity. From here, the Church goes East." A bit further along he said, "I am so indebted to you all," and addressed in turn several bishops whose responsibilities lay in various parts of Poland: "To you, my dear Bishop of Przemysl [Ignacy Tokarczuk], and not only of Przemysl, but of all the rich land opening out to the south and to the east of Poland, will fall a heavy responsibility for the extension of the Church in Poland, towards those horizons." Those horizons, one should realize, include within their Communist setting the religions of the "other" Catholicism, the Greek and Russian Orthodox churches. Toward the end of his remarks the primate exhorts them all:

> I fall with all humility as Primate of Poland at your bishops' feet and embrace them. Remember, that the very traditions of Polishness are linked by the primacy of Gniezno, despite anyone's brooding or intentions to the contrary. Poland became strong through this, when Baltic lands and Baltic people felt the conscious proximity of the primacy to their dioceses. It was then that their power grew. And this territorial strategy must be respected as a cornerstone of the building up of the Church in Poland. Poland in the south will be forever strong, unswerving, Poland in the north and west will constantly require the spiritual fortification of those who through historic acts of greatness have been made to endure the incursions of Swedes, Teutonic Knights and Germans. Of the east I will say nothing, because the east is open in its entirety, to be won by the Church in Poland.[27]

He does not mince words. "Of the east I will say nothing"! Yet he has said everything, the decisive thing. Although he presents the Eastern

policy as the assumption of a missionary burden, only one who is igno-
rant of the history of Christianity, Catholic or Protestant, could miss the
hegemonical message within that assumption.

One must also note the mixture of nationalism and missionary zeal in
Wyszynski's utterances. His zeal is both Polish and expansive. Is it Poland that he loves, or is it the defense and progressive expansion of the
Catholic church? Would he be willing to use Poland and the Polish
faithful as shock troops for an Eastern crusade? His is not a clear position.
Consequently the politics that emanates from such a blurred position
must also be unclear and open to the suspicion of deviousness. One
might argue Wyszynski's zeal died with him, but that is unlikely. This
fifth interest, the missionary interest, whether defensively or offensively
understood, remains a fundamental churchly motivation, even though
the particular emphasis or coloration given to it by the aged cardinal has
been muted.

Into the cluster of these five interests of the church in Poland and into a
political situation in which the church was the cardinal focus of opposition to communism and its Polish regime, there burst the rebellion of
Solidarity. How this must have upset the church's plans! Solidarity is a
counterloyalty, a counterfocus of opposition for people to rally around.
In addition, it provides a program that calls for economic and political
rights for ordinary people in institutions and associations of their own
making. But economic and political democracy for Poles was not among
the cluster of the church's interests. To be sure, the "nation" was one of
those interests, but economic, social, and political rights for the masses?
The masses could become much too volatile and unpredictable. They
were an unstable force. And furthermore, the program of Solidarity based
itself partly on the assumption of making a strategic compromise with the
Communist regime. Although its nonviolent posture recommended itself to the church, the policy of the church had always been one of
tactical compromise. The church put up with the regime and made deals
with it, because it had no other choice. But a strategic compromise
suggested the possibility of a renewed Poland within the general am-
bience of a Communist system. What would be the role of the church
then? What about its pastoral opportunities, its guardianship of the nation, its *Ostpolitik?* The fact that answers to these questions are unknown

suggests how much these unspoken questions loom large in the church hierarchy's assessment of the new situation created by Solidarity.

But of course there were and are significant overlaps. Solidarity's demand for independent, self-governing unions parallels, and thus supports, the continuing efforts of the church since 1947 to carve out a sphere of autonomy for itself. Solidarity's demand for a relative end to censorship would also assist the church's pastoral activity. Furthermore, the very existence of Solidarity is useful to the church in that it constitutes a prod to the government and by so much helps the short-term interests of the church in its own particular struggles with the regime.

Consequently, the church's response to the Solidarity phenomenon has not been clear. It is an ally, sometimes a powerful one, sometimes a disappointing one. It is a competitor, usually a covert one, obnoxious for that reason. And it is a go-between, often an effective one. But overall it must be admitted that the activity of the church has been far more supportive of Solidarity than one might have thought likely. The reason is not hard to find: it is lodged deeply in the phoenix-like character of Solidarity.

The church, whether it likes it or not, is confronted by a politically aroused membership comprising the vast majority of the people. The church is therefore irresistibly drawn to provide advice and varying degrees of protection and support to its members who are engaged in the struggle for national, union, local, and personal rights. It must do this to some measurable degree, or it will lose credibility.

In addition, a large though indeterminate number of priests and nuns themselves share—as Polish citizens—these same political aspirations. Some of them, such as Father Popieluszko, clearly see it as their duty publicly to criticize what they regard as an oppressive, unconstitutional, and arbitrary exercise of authority in the state, even when the particular actions they object to do not directly threaten or concern the liturgical or pastoral limits of their priestly work. They see it as part of their duty to give comfort and support to activists who struggle against oppression. This posture is not unlike many priests presently in Latin America who, whether they espouse the controversial Liberation Theology or not, think and act in terms of its basic principles.

Indeed, there is so much support, from those high and low in the church hierarchy, that many Westerners (and some elements in the Jaruzelski government) are convinced that it is churchly power that arms the people, implying as well that it is the church that thus leads the opposition to the regime. But this is a misreading of the church's ironical situation: the struggle of the opposition is not based primarily upon a churchly agenda, though it is influenced by it. Nor is the struggle led by church officials. The church perforce aligns itself with the struggle to a degree, especially on issues that overlap with its interests. The church gets drawn deeper into issues of less immediate concern to itself, because it is committed to Poland, because its own priests at the grass roots get drawn far into the struggle, and because if it did not respond, it would lose the credibility it needs to preserve itself, to say nothing of the credibility it needs to play the role of mediator between the opposition and the regime.

A further angle in this complex pattern, one that Westerners have difficulty comprehending properly, is the relatively unsecularized culture of Polish society. Jan Jerschina, a sociologist at Jagiellonian University in Krakow, formerly active in the PUWP on behalf of basic reforms, and an acute observer of the values of Polish culture, points out that though modernization worldwide has generally been accompanied by secularization, loss of faith, and the progressive rationalization of life, Poland is somewhat exceptional in this regard. [28] Poland is the twelfth-largest industrial society, but its values are family- and church-centered; its culture is organically connected to the cycles of birth, coming of age, marriage, and death, and—in spite of pervasive bureaucracy—Poles are committed to those personal qualities that stress the importance of relationships and the importance of what Western sociology weakly calls affective values.

To put this in different language, it is as if the world of spirit and the world of matter had not become disjoined. There is and remains a continuity among the spheres of life that has long since evaporated or gone into subterranean channels in most other industrial societies. The church has contributed to this defense of organic culture, but it would be a mistake to associate this development wholly with the church. The relation between church and society or between church and state is not identical to the relation between spirit and matter. A milieu of the unity of spirit and matter continues to persist in Polish life; this unity manifests itself in all spheres to varying degrees and in various configurations.

Thus, the people of Poland do not find it as strange as Westerners might to affirm spiritual values in the realms of economy, education, and the state, often in the guise of religious morality and ritual, and likewise to affirm political aspirations in the realm of religion. Nor do they find it all that strange to see the church express material and political concerns or to see the state express itself, albeit in nontheistic language, on spiritual and religious issues. The realms are separable, but there is not that wall of separation that is—or is supposed to be—the rule in Western societies. This makes the roles of church and state more ambiguous, more open to contestation over boundaries of legitimate jurisdiction. Since Solidarity also makes claims in spiritual terms, the potential for dispute is endemic. But the other side of this paradox is the fact that the common concern of all three for morality and spiritual enlightenment offers a basis among these institutions for dialogue and compromise. But of course they have not reached that point yet.

In the twenty-eight months between the pope's visit to Poland in June, 1983, and the elections to the Sejm in October, 1985, there occurred a series of events and interactions that suggests the kind of jostling and wrestling for definition and space that presently characterizes the three-way tug-of-war. The events in this period illustrate the pressures on the church (from the state, from the people, and even from itself) and the zigzag course it tends to pursue.

In the immediate aftermath of Pope John Paul's euphoric visit in June, 1983, it seemed as if the church were backing away from Solidarity and from Lech Walesa. There was more than a hint that the church saw itself moving into the gap created by the presumed demise of Solidarity. It would itself negotiate with the regime for an end to martial law and a guarded return to normalization of life, a primary goal of the regime and one that included the minimal restoration of civil liberties. The pope had presumably received assurances from Jaruzelski that political prisoners would be released.

The pope had also tried out on the Polish leader an interesting new idea: the establishment of an agricultural fund in the billions of dollars for assistance to Poland's small, private farmers. The notion was that the funds would be forthcoming from the West, from both private and public sources, and would be spent under the guidance of a foundation in which the church would participate as a partner.[29] This left Solidarity out of the

picture—even Rural Solidarity. Doubtless, the regime would categorically refuse any such project if Solidarity had been involved, but the point
was that the church was going ahead enthusiastically with the project
without considering that it shut Solidarity out and in effect would put
the church in the role of a social, even an economic, agency. Was the
church angling to replace Solidarity? At the same time, in Rome the
semiofficial Vatican newspaper L'Asservatore Romano stated that Walesa
should now take a back seat and perhaps find some role to play other than
leader of Solidarity.[30] The author, Father Vergilio Levi, was forced to
resign, but the incident gave grist to the mill of the rumor-mongers, who
claimed that the church was losing interest in Solidarity.

Indeed, it now seemed that the church would no longer allow itself to
become embroiled in defense of Solidarity's demands for a democratic
realignment of power in society and state. True enough, the pope had
used the word *solidarity* often in his several sermons to millions of Poles,
though in lowercase, and had even spoken feelingly of the need by the
state to acknowledge the subjectivity of nation and worker.[31] But, in
the aftermath, these could be seen as rhetorical flourishes expressed in
the heat of a great Polish passion play.

So the church seemed to have a new posture, one that must have been
disheartening for Walesa. Yet some incidents offset this impression.
Henryk Gulbinowitz, a bishop imbued with the spirit of opposition,
boldly asserted in Rome in early July that "Solidarity is not finished." In
late July the church strongly opposed some of the more stringent laws
being pushed through the Sejm that would in effect "normalize" the
arbitrary powers enjoyed by the regime under martial law. In September
the Primate Glemp got angry—on behalf of Walesa and others—at
Deputy Prime Minister Rakowski's visit to the Lenin Shipyards in which,
according to the story filed by New York *Times* reporter Michael Kauf-
mann, for five and a half hours Mieczyslaw Rakowski harangued, and
put down intellectually, the shipyard workers. In mid-November,
Glemp revealed to his fellow bishops that the government had in a letter
told him to silence sixty-nine antisocialist priests. Government
spokesperson Jerzy Urban characteristically denied this in early December. On December 20 Glemp told priests not to deal in politics, and in
early January, 1984, he met with Jaruzelski for five hours. Church
sources said Glemp agreed to try to curb outspoken priests. The same

sources also said that he had told Jaruzelski that such priests did not surface of their own accord but as a result of errors and injustices committed by the authorities.[32]

In late January, there were indications that Glemp might visit the Soviet Union. There was renewed talk of opening diplomatic relations between Poland and the papacy in Rome. In late January after a two-day conference presided over by Glemp, there was a statement by the bishops that walked a fine line. It said: "Social tension has not disappeared. Many working people feel embittered. Some of them are in prison despite the fact they believe they served a just cause. Many have been dismissed from work or discriminated against. The Church has not reduced its efforts to eliminate these harmful phenomena, because this is part of its mission. But the Church also teaches that people should protect the good of society, which the state represents."[33] In mid-February, Glemp transferred an activist priest, Mieczyslaw Nowak, from his worker parish in Ursus. The latter is the site of a sprawling tractor factory that is one of Poland's largest industries and a Solidarity stronghold. This move produced a storm of protest and considerable maneuvering in the church hierarchy, but Glemp held firm.[34]

During this time "the War of the Crosses" erupted in Garwolin. Children, backed by their parents, fiercely resisted the order by the local Communist authorities to remove crucifixes from the walls of the school. Since crucifixes appear everywhere in Poland, not only in schools but in hospitals and most other public places, this promised to be a thorny and divisive issue between Glemp and Jaruzelski. However, "meeting for the eighth time since 1981," the two leaders managed a tactical compromise: the crucifixes would be removed from the wall, but the students could have them on their desks.[35] The New York Times correspondent observed that it seemed hard for the two leaders to quell the passions of the people.

In March, Cardinal Glemp was quoted in a São Paulo, Brazil, newspaper as saying that Lech Walesa had been "manipulated" and had "lost control" of Solidarity and that the union no longer defended "the working class." It was claimed that he also said that half of the members of Solidarity "belong to the Communist Party which means that its ideals are not the same as the church." Later, in the storied month of August, which was replete with memories of Solidarity's triumph, Glemp pointedly avoided criticism of the state in a sermon to over 160,000 at Czestochowa; the following week he supported the government's position on Germany, something he had refused to do the previous year. Jaruzelski, in an address on July 22, 1984, marking the fortieth anniversary of Communist rule in Poland, had cited what he called the increasing militarism in West Germany and the revanchist and anti-Polish claims of some West Germans who have insisted that German ethnic minorities in Poland have been culturally deprived. Glemp in his Czestochawa sermon emphatically chided the German Catholics by saying there were no culturally deprived or genuine Germans in Poland. However, he also briefly met with Walesa and reassured him about the tenor of his remarks in Brazil: they were not true, he averred. In July the government had proclaimed and followed through with a general amnesty for virtually all political prisoners. Walesa cautioned against protests in August. Andrzej Gwiazda, newly released from prison, said, "We are in a state of negative calm." The church seemed to back off more and more from Solidarity. A church leader at Czestochowa chided the workers who made the pilgrimage to the Black Madonna in September. What were all these Solidarity flags doing there? he asked. At about this time, in late August, Walesa acknowledged that the hierarchy of the Catholic church was not fully in support of the Solidarity movement.[36]

Thus, it seems that there was in effect a steady policy by the church hierarchy to make a tactical peace with the regime, to keep Solidarity at a distance, and to hope in this way to both help bring Poland to a better place economically and politically and assure for itself a prime place as a moving force in Polish society and politics. The government of Jaruzelski must have been pleased by these developments, must have even congratulated itself on its success in dividing Solidarity and the church, and must have looked forward to gradual and successful normalization. There may even have been some private rejoicing among the more liberally inclined members of the government that normalization might also make possible the permanent incorporation of some of the reforms brought about by the Solidarity rebellion.

But then came a searing event: the murder of Father Jerzy Popieluszko by three security police officers. The event chilled relations between church and state officials. It deeply stirred the people of Poland, simultaneously as church members and as Solidarity supporters, making them

even more defiant of government authorities; it intensified their commitment to Solidarity's goals and gave the entire opposition a renewed sense
of determination to realize their goals. Jaruzelski suffered a setback in his
apparent policy of limited accommodation to those goals via negotiations
with the church, a pathway that for him excluded negotiations with a
renewed Solidarity trade union.

It seems reasonable to conclude that Father Popieluszko's murder was
engineered by hard-line elements in the regime who took advantage of
their entrenched power in the security apparatus of the Ministry of the
Interior. These elements were uneasy and unhappy at the policy of
limited accommodation with the opposition via the church. Father
Popieluszko was a natural target in some senses, since he was an outspoken critic of the regime for its policies of repression toward Solidarity.
He conducted a "Mass for the Homeland" at his St. Stanislaw church in
Warsaw on the last Sunday of every month. This mass was always attended by thousands. He took those opportunities to preach opposition
and nonviolence to the gathering, and through those present he preached
to all of Poland. His power was such that for months before his murder,
Jaruzelski's officials had been cautioning Glemp to put a rein on this man
and had attacked him in the press. (An especially strong attack on
Popieluszko was written in September, 1984, by Jerzy Urban, the government spokesman, writing under an assumed name, Jan Rem, in
Polityka.[37]) Partly as a result of this pressure, according to the pseudony-
mous underground writer Dawid Warszawski, the church authorities,
with the approval or perhaps the command of the pope himself, were
planning to reassign Father Popieluszko to the Vatican. Cardinal Glemp
later denied that he had taken the initiative to get Popieluszko reassigned
to Rome. "It was not me who suggested it," Glemp said. "Some of his
friends, fearing for his safety, came to me to tell me it would be a good
idea if he went to Rome and stayed there for some time. I was asked to
convey this to him. I did so, leaving him the freedom to decide. Fr.
Popieluszko replied that he would leave Poland under obedience, if
ordered to do so by his bishop. This I could not do."[38]

But in another sense the murderers and their backers overshot their
mark in making Popieluszko their target. He was deeply and widely
respected not only for his outspokenness but even more for the depth and
purity of his Catholic convictions. He was a kind of saint, and his

qualities of saintliness were manifest to many. His death, therefore, electrified Poland. The outpouring of grief and anger exceeded all expectations and threatened to exceed all bounds. Walesa made considerable exertions to caution the marchers in Gdansk, for example, and 250,000 attended Popieluszko's funeral in Warsaw—as many if not more than for the funeral of Cardinal Wyszynsky in 1981.

So the Jaruzelski government was forced to act. More to the point, perhaps, it now had the opportunity to act with some decisiveness toward those who had perpetrated the deed and toward the hard-line elements they represented. The deed therefore came back upon the heads of those who had planned and done it. If their effort was to embarrass Jaruzelski or to provoke the opposition, they failed. However, if their effort was to deflect Jaruzelski's attempt to find an accommodation with the church, which would isolate Solidarity, they succeeded. Solidarity gained greater strength from this event and became bolder in action during 1985, though it did not succumb to any temptation to "go for broke," as the hard-liners might have hoped.

Jaruzelski and his "moderate" cohorts also gained strength within the government. On the other hand, with politic wisdom, and some courage, Jaruzelski and his supporters brought the murderers to public trial. It was an action that brought widely favorable comment from the Western press and political leaders and no criticism from the Kremlin. Poland's opposition was also impressed. Adam Michnik, one of Poland's best known and most often jailed dissidents, stated: "I simply cannot understand it. It is remarkable and nothing like it has happened in the history of Communism since 1919." Four members of the security police were convicted and sentenced to long prison terms, though some in Poland felt that the key figure, Grzegorz Piotrowski, should have been given the death sentence, which could then have been commuted. Instead he was sentenced to twenty-five years in prison.[39]

The newly resolved government embarked on a different course from that pursued before Father Popieluszko's murder. It was a course that combined their continued firmness against any negotiation with the opposition with a far more aloof and critical attitude toward the church and with a stronger effort than hitherto to create openings toward the Polish middle ground (the 50 to 60 percent of the people who are neither activists for the opposition nor loyal to the Party-state).

The church, in the aftermath of the murder and the trial, took a harder stand against the government and a correspondingly stronger stand in support of Solidarity. The brutal killing of one of their own, however imprudent he might have seemed to Glemp and others, was not a matter they could take lightly. Thousands of priests and nuns felt the sting, and the pride, of Popieluszko's martyrdom. Millions of the faithful shared their feelings. The church had no alternative but to bend to this powerful sentiment. And since so much of the emerging Popieluszko mystique was interwoven with the myth and the goals of Solidarity, the church by extension had also to accommodate itself to a reaffirmation of Solidarity's mission and program.

At Father Popieluszko's church in Warsaw, his colleagues in the clergy continued the Mass for the Homeland on the last Sunday of each month. I attended the one in June, 1985. It was a beautiful and powerful event. It took the presiding priest, Father Przekazinski, over half an hour to read the names of the delegations present from every corner of Poland, many of them openly flourishing the name of Solidarity. These were the ordinary people of Poland, spreading out from the church, at least twenty thousand of them, listening, worshiping, and singing. For the length of each of four of the songs with particular national content, the vast congregation lifted their hands high to form the forbidden V sign. There was present a strong sense of political community, one at odds with the ruling authorities, and at the same time, the gathering seemed like a great revival meeting. Once again I was experiencing directly the interwoven texture of the Polish people's religious and political life.

Father Przekazinski's sermon was a graceful blend of spiritual and political concerns. He spoke about the meaning of culture and the importance of autonomy for artists and writers. He defended the church for giving numbers of them opportunity to practice their art, and at several points, to massive applause, he chided the authorities for failure to provide a state in which such autonomy was assured. No one could mistake this outpouring as people seeking solace in the promise of the life hereafter. I was shoulder to shoulder with people resolute in their will for a better system here and now. The repeated evocation of Father Popieluszko's life and spirit is an incalculable and vital force in the depth and determination of that will.

After the service I lingered at the church, which has become a national shrine. One million people had already visited the church between Father Popieluszko's death and June 30, 1985. The church is filled with memorabilia, pictorial biography, and a small chapel dedicated to him. The church courtyard contains his grave and is festooned with Solidarity banners and mementos.

Events up to the national elections in October, 1985, showed the altered situation in the aftermath of Popieluszko's death. In April, 1985, the pope appointed as cardinal the archbishop of Wroclaw, Henryk Roman Gulbinowitz, known to be a strong Solidarity advocate. On May Day opposition activists stormed official parades. Their numbers in Warsaw and Gdansk were the largest since Solidarity was declared illegal in 1981. Also in May the government admitted that the number of antigovernment priests had risen markedly since Popieluszko's murder. In June, Glemp preached to seventy thousand people and declared that basic justice was being denied in Poland.[40] His statements were generally interpreted as a hard criticism of the government for the fact and the manner of its trial of Adam Michnik, Bogdan Lis, and Wladyslaw Frasyniuk, the three opposition leaders who were about to be sentenced to prison for advocating a half-hour work stoppage that never took place. In September, at the annual pilgrimage of many thousands of working-men and -women to Czestochowa, Polish prelates praised Solidarity and Walesa, who was present. The *Uncensored Poland News Bulletin*'s daily calendarium for Sunday, September 15, 1985, read in part:

> 50 to 70 thousand workers attend a pilgrimage . . . popularly known as "the Solidarity pilgrimage". Cardinal Gulbinowitz concelebrates mass with more than 50 priests. Just below the altar on a special platform are Solidarity leaders including Lech Walesa. The congregation carries many Solidarity banners. . . . The Cardinal leads a prayer for social justice and invites the congregation to another pilgramage next year (last year the Church was reluctant to call the Occasion "a pilgrimage"—Ed.). . . . The abbot of Jasna Gora in Czestochowa, Father Rufin Abramek, greets the pilgrims and pointing to Walesa says "among the pilgrams let me name at least one ordinary citizen". There is an ovation.[41]

This scene was a marked contrast with that of the previous year, when at a similar pilgrimage an officiating member of the clergy chided the pilgrims for their Solidarity banners. Later in September, Glemp went to Gdansk for a meeting with Walesa. That same month Glemp disputed a government statement to the effect that the church's silence on the election boycott implied support for the elections. Earlier, on August 28, the Polish bishops' conference, in a pastoral letter, pointedly did not mention the election. Glemp and several bishops found it convenient to be in Rome on the day of the election, October 13. It was reported that of more than eighty Polish bishops, only three voted.[42]

Yet, on the day after the election, at ceremonies on the first anniversary of Father Popieluszko's death held at his church in Warsaw, and with Walesa present, Glemp rebuked the silent congregation of five thousand. He said the church had become too much of a political attraction and that the regular parishioners were receiving far too little attention.[43] Was this a signal for yet a new turn in overall church policy vis-à-vis Solidarity and the opposition?

Whatever the answer, the general record is clear. The church plays its own independent role, sometimes closer to Solidarity, sometimes more interested in making deals with the state. It hovers, it zigzags, between the two. But in the main it continues to be a bulwark for the opposition. The major reason is the continuing strength and vitality of Solidarity, the Polish phoenix. Father Popieluszko was, and is, part of the phoenix. That is why in the longer run his martyrdom belongs to Solidarity, which is what Lech Walesa meant in his remarks at the martyred priest's funeral. Said Walesa: "Solidarity lives because he shed his blood for it."[44]

Pope John Paul II, son of Poland and son and supreme leader of his church, has now visited his native land three times as pope—in 1979, 1983, and 1987. He has been and continues to be an enormously important catalyst for the emergence and sustaining of a self-confident political consciousness in Poland and also for a restraining of actions stemming from that aroused consciousness.

His visit in June, 1987, revealed both emphases. Again he met with Jaruzelski; again he addressed millions—at the village of Tarnow in the countryside, for example, speaking to two million people at once; and again he spoke with Walesa, this time in Gdansk itself. At one level he vigorously stirred the people to keep faith with the goals of human rights and of gaining a stronger voice in decision making for ordinary people. At another level he conducted what he hopes is a political balancing act between dangerously conflicting forces; at yet another he sought to enhance the influence, power, and growth of the Catholic church. In this

he was much drawn into Solidarity's trajectory as he advanced the fortunes of the church. But he could not avoid advancing to some degree the
legitimacy of Jaruzelski's regime.

Of special note, as suggested by accounts of the visit in the New York
Times and the *Uncensored Poland News Bulletin,* was the pope's vigorous
appeal to breathe life into the agreements that the government concluded
in 1981 with the farmers' union, Rural Solidarity. There was also his
persistent invocation of the name and example of Father Popieluszko.
He thereby identified with the liberal elements in the church, tacitly
criticizing Cardinal Glemp and other conservative church leaders and
fostering hope and commitment among priests sympathetic to Solidarity's goals. Furthermore, his meeting with Walesa in Gdansk was
symbolically dramatic and meaningful. Walesa and other opposition
leaders had been afraid that the pope would fall short, would fall into the
trap of "normalization" so assiduously pursued by the authorities. Walesa
had written a note to the Pope reflecting his fear. Consequently, he and
other opposition leaders were relieved and greatly encouraged by the
pope's performance. It seems clear that the pope deliberately "leaned to
one side" in order to help produce and sustain a situation in which a
genuine accommodation between the authorities and the opposition
can, in time, proceed. Jaruzelski was nettled by what he perceived as the
pope's excesses. Yet it is probable that Jaruzelski's own stature and his
moderate realist politics were not dimmed by the pope's 1987 visit but
were actually shored up and further legitimated.

NEITHER CAN COMMUNISM IGNORE NATURE

Ecologically, Poland is in an extremely vulnerable place. Its water and air
and soil are being assaulted by rising levels of industrial pollution. The
health of the people and the self-renewing power of their natural eco-
systems are as much under siege as are the basic rights of the people by the
government, perhaps even more so.

Solidarity expressed concern about the growing ecological crisis in its
original program. Its new program statement, "Poland Five Years After
August," published in August, 1985, reveals even more concern, but that
concern is not yet commensurate with the actual dimensions of the crisis
nor with its interesting political implications.[45]

The government has for over a decade modestly affirmed the need to limit pollution, but the political will and administrative energy to act have not matched even these modest pronouncements. Already in 1973, the government prepared a document entitled "Programme for the Protection and Shaping of the Environment in Poland." This program was accepted in 1975 by the Politburo of the Communist party and adopted by the government for implementation. But it was never carried out. In 1982 the government's planning commission took up again the problem of environmental protection in the "Theses on the Goals and Strategy of Economic Policies," which recommended government programs to deal with what was correctly seen as the interdependence of three issues strategically vital to the life of the nation: food production, housing, and the restoration of ecological equilibrium. But again there was no serious effort to follow through.

The catastrophic decline of Poland's economy after 1979 virtually shut the minds of government officials to all thoughts of alleviating pollution, much less actively regenerating the environment. They saw only the desperate need to increase production, of coal and sulphur especially and of heavy industry generally. The planners, managers, and bureaucrats, much like their counterparts in the West when faced with a crisis, went back to what they knew best: industrial production spurred by fossil fuels, and rising growth rates measured in quantitative GNP. Their conventional wisdom precluded any "postindustrial" outlook that might have led them to question the economic feasibility of abusing the health of the people and the environment. Even if they had such thoughts, they were too immersed in narrow and short-term calculations to give them much shrift. They were faced with an "impossible" Western debt of nearly $30 billion and with shortages of every kind, including of the Western components and spare parts needed to complete over a thousand projects begun in the Gierek years and now languishing unproductively in city and countryside. They were faced with the absence of substantial Russian assistance, which had been given to Hungary and Czechoslovakia in their moments of desperate crisis. Russian assistance could have helped to soften the blow of the severe Western sanctions that were imposed in the wake of martial law.

Coal was all they could think of—to fuel their own economy and to sell East and West for credits. They saw "ecology" in only negative terms, as a set of yet additional constraints that would inhibit production and cause the economy to sputter even more. They were very far from seeing the positive side to ecology: the opportunity to shift to a diverse energy base utilizing alternative forms of renewable energies; the correlative opportunity to diversify and decentralize economic activity; the further opportunity to achieve greater local and regional self-reliance in production through emphasis on light industry and local market economies; and the opportunity to tap the enormous potential of Poland's farmland through decentralized, regenerative, and scientific agricultural projects.

But of course the government was also blinded by its own felt political needs. Heavy industry was safe. The Russians were comfortable with it. Most planners, managers, and bureaucrats were comfortable with it. Heavy industry went hand in hand with centralized technologies and administration and planning, which they were used to. The kind of real economic experimentation and reform that a "postindustrial" ecological approach anticipates implies as well an uncertainty about control and political predictability. In the face of Solidarity's and the church's demands for autonomy, the ecological way might have all sorts of hidden political traps tending in a similar direction.

Thus, whether consciously or not, the government leadership, especially the higher middle ranks, could not for economic and political reasons shift their thinking or their action in an ecological direction. In addition, the people as a whole were only sluggishly feeling their way toward greater awareness of ecology and pollution.

However, such insouciance cannot last forever. The ferment of the early Solidarity years erupted also in the realm of ecology, and since then a steadily growing concern and criticism has been expressed both aboveground and underground, in both official and unofficial circles alike. The Polish Ecology Club was formed and by 1985 claimed seventy chapters and three thousand members.[46] During my visit to Poland in June, 1985, I met several members in different parts of the country.

In August of that year a curious event occurred, a harbinger of things to come. The official daily *Zycie Warszawy* published on August 30, 1985, an article by Bozena Kastory summing up a report on the environment that had been undertaken by the Polish Chemical Society at the urging of the Polish Academy of Sciences' committee on the chemical sciences. It was condemned the next day in a news conference by government spokesperson Jerzy Urban. But an unrepentant *Zycie Warszawy* in an unusual move came back tartly the next day to defend the report and the need to address the problems it was raising. [47]

In her article Kastory quotes the report as saying that "the degree of damage to the environment in Poland is much bigger than could have been expected judged solely by the standard of the technological development of the country." She also points to a report of 1983 by the European Environment Commission that declared that Poland occupies first place in Europe in terms of environmental pollution. Kastory went on to say, "The situation in the Upper Silesian Industrial basin, the Glogow-Legnica Copper Basin along the Gulf of Gdansk, and in the vicinity of Krakow must be termed an ecological disaster." She cited some of the 1985 report's findings:

> Poland leads Europe in atmospheric pollution. The main reason is the heavy reliance . . . on burning coal without treating the fuel beforehand or filtering the resulting exhaust gases, the development of energy-intensive industries, the development of motor transport without concern for the environmental quality of auto engines and the growing use of chemicals in farming. . . . Out of 1,066 factories whose discharges have been classified as environmentally harmful, only half have fixed maximum permissible emission levels while 304 of the worst polluters observe no limits at all. . . .
>
> The volume of motor exhaust fumes is disproportionately high compared to the number of cars, buses and lorries on the road. They burn almost twice as much petrol for every kilometer they travel as the average consumption in the world. . . . Poland has the highest proportion of smokers in the world in its population; not only do many people smoke, but they smoke heavily and the cigarette quality is low.
>
> . . . Spending on the environment was less and less over the years. It had been planned to spend slightly more than 1% of the national income a year between 1975 and 1990. In reality, in 1979, only 0.37% of the national income was spent on these goals, a ratio ten times lower than in other developed countries. . . ."
>
> Food is mainly contaminated by heavy metals, radioactive elements (a byproduct of burning coal and the production of phosphorous fertilizers), harmful substances such as plastifiers, stabilizers, pigments, dyes and components of plastics, construction materials, etc. Poisoning with such substances is responsible for most contemporary non-contagious diseases, especially the so-called civilizational diseases, and circulatory disorders, cancer, psychiatric diseases, or allergies. . . . The report gives the average and maximum concentrations of lead, cadmium, mercury, nitrites and other

dangerous pollutants in vegetables, milk, pate, cottage cheese, etc. For example, the maximum concentration of lead in lettuce grown near the Boleslaw and Miasteczko Slaskie metallurgical works was found to reach 230 milligrams per kilo whereas the largest permissible dose is 3 milligrams of lead per person per week.

Urban, in his press conference the day after Kastory's article appeared, attacked the scientists' report for its "alarmist and exaggerated formulations," which after all, he said, merely expressed the views of individual contributors. But the next day *Zycie Warszawy* in an editorial said with controlled irony that it was pleased at the attention the government spokesman devoted to the question of pollution. It went on to say that *Zycie Warszawy* had been devoting space to the ecological issue for years, and it was thanks to its "frequently alarming" coverage that the public awareness of the ecological threat had increased. The editorial pointed to the Sejm report on the environment the previous June by the head of the Office of Environmental Protection and noted that it had "presented the prevailing situation without beating about the bush and without hiding the serious dangers arising in some areas of the country."

This public debate on the environment is instructive. Such debates seldom occur on any issue. That it should occur on the issue of the environment indicates the gravity of the problem and the sensitivity of the government to the growing internal and international criticism. Urban had ignored an earlier dramatic statement by the main party paper, *Trybuna Ludu*, which on August 1, 1985, had said that "35% of our country's population live in exceptionally bad environmental conditions." Neglect of environmental protection was enormous, and it would take at least twenty-five years to recover ecological balance, the paper said. [48]

Some months prior to Urban's debate with *Zycie Warszawy* a group of independent ecologists began a systematic publication of ecological problems in a specialized journal—*Biuletyn Informacyjny o Srodowisku* (Ecology Information Bulletin). One of their early issues dealt with water pollution. One article noted:

> According to data from the Senate Inspectorate for the Protection of the Environment (SANEPID), the purity of river waters underwent a marked deterioration in the years 1967–79. . . . Waters exceeding the pollution limit include 100% of the river Bug, 98% of the Bzura . . . 63% of the Oder,

56% of the Vistula, and 51% of the Warta. . . . 120 cities are seriously threatened by epidemics due to the bad quality of the drinking water. Already in 1980, SANEPID condemned 45% of public wells in cities and 51% in villages. . . . Out of 804 towns, only 357 have treatment plants (and these are mostly outdated). Out of 3,800 industrial enterprises producing the greatest amount of effluent, 1,800 discharge directly into the water and almost 20% of these have no treatment plants. [49]

Thus, many scientists who may have tended to a noncommittal posture on the issues raised by Solidarity are now raising their voices on the mortal environmental threat to the Polish nation. No matter how much the governmental and Party leadership backpedal on the issue or publicly deny the true proportions of the problem, the fact is that the problem worsens daily and that there is a growing consciousness—among experts and among the people as a whole—that something serious must be done.

The Chernobyl disaster in April, 1986, thrust itself into this context of mounting anxiety. The government reacted quickly by distributing an iodine preparation called Lugol to eleven million children under sixteen (the Poles soon developed their own name for it—"Russian Coca-cola"). The government took other actions, such as a restriction on the sale of milk. Partly to protect themselves and partly as a gesture to Russian sentiment, they also presented numbers of government scientists on radio and television to reassure the people that radiation had not reached levels of significant danger anywhere in the country. [50]

Despite such reassurances, there was a general uneasiness. An old joke got a sudden new application: In a Warsaw barbershop a customer asks a barber whether she had been frightened by "the cloud" (a term widely used). The barber replies, "At first I was frightened, but now that I have heard all the explanations, I am still frightened." In the eastern city of Bialystok, three thousand people signed a petition calling for the suspension of plans to build Poland's first nuclear plant at Zarnowiec. Freedom and Peace, a group known mostly for draft resistance, staged a sit-down demonstration on May 2 in Warsaw to protest the building of the plant. Solidarity publications, such as *Tygodnik Masowsze*, expressed outrage at the withholding of information by the Soviet Union and demanded a clearer, more resolute environmental policy by the government. In so doing, Solidarity hoped to shape the amorphous anger widespread throughout Poland into coherent political action.

In the general Polish response, there seems to be more anger at the Russians—which brought a corresponding governmental effort to keep that anger within bounds—than a deeper awareness of the ecological threat and of the need for immediate action by Poland. Thus, awareness of the ecological threat and its immense ramifications for livelihood and health—may still be insufficiently deep, but shocks such as Chernobyl do leave an additional residue in public consciousness. They may contribute to a growing disposition both in the government and the opposition to make it a focal point for sustained public action.

Seen from one angle, the situation appears hopeless. Poland does not seem to be able to allocate the capital and other resources necessary to tackle the problem effectively. Actions taken are too little and will probably be too late. The ecological crisis is part of the overall crisis afflicting Poland: the obdurate barrier, the bitter standoff, between the opposition and the government. Only weak responses to the impending ecological disaster can be expected from the government under these circumstances. Neither Jaruzelski nor the opposition seems able to break the deadlock.

Yet the ecological crisis is also in effect a made-to-order conjuncture of forces. It offers the government, the opposition, and the church an opportunity to work together to restore Poland or, to put it with the strength of language the crisis demands, to save Poland. They all have an immediate stake in such a venture.

The government needs to broaden Poland's economic oportunities, to get out from under the burden of an overcentralized and skewed economy that is much too narrowly dependent on fossil fuels and concentrations of heavy industry. It has an objective interest in creating a more diversified and integrated economy, which means moving toward light industry, retail and service industries (including postindustrial "high tech" development), and, especially, a new agriculture. Such moves in the economy would galvanize latent forces of progress and change and would shift people's attention to the common betterment of themselves and their country. Many in the top leadership long for this to happen but are allowing themselves to be dominated by an entrenched heavy-industry and, consequently, by old-line policies that rivet them to a strait-jacketed existence and that structure them and their country into deadly ecological impasse. The new policies, by contrast, would bend the economy not only toward reduced pollution but also toward a set of structures in which the air, water, and soil of the nation and the health of the people would be regenerated.

The church's stake in a new ecological policy is the opportunity it gives to keep alive and develop even further the hope for agricultural renewal. The agricultural foundation the Pope proposed to Jaruzelski in June, 1983, would be a clear step in the direction of greater investment in small, privately run agriculture and in greater local autonomy, both of which have long been part of the church's goals for Poland. Although the project had a rocky road with the government and was bitterly called off by Glemp in September, 1986, the idea is still strong. Furthermore, other, similar projects involving foreign investment for agriculture have been discussed by the government, including those brought up in talks between the Rockefeller Foundation and Jaruzelski in his trip to the United Nations in New York in September, 1985.[51]

Such projects still do not embrace fully their own ecological implications. Yet, I believe the realization is dawning in Poland that the nation's greatest resource, one that can pull Poland out of the doldrums, is its land: especially the 73 percent of it that is farmed "privately" by three million families. A policy of controlled investment in technical training, in appropriate technology, in credits to small farmers, in nontoxic fertilizers, and in ecological methods of cultivation would trigger a renaissance in Polish agriculture. Nor would this be a radical shift for the government. In 1982 the Sejm passed an amendment to the Polish constitution guaranteeing the small farmers their land, a move to reassure the farmers and court their favor for the Jaruzelski regime. Earlier the government had introduced a plan to persuade elderly people to give land to the state in exchange for a pension, the hope being that in this way land now held in supposedly inefficient small plots would find its way into the state's farm sector. But more recently, this plan has been modified so that such land can be sold on the market to people who wish to buy a farm of their own or add acreage to their existing private farm. The stipulation is that the buyer must have had agricultural training and must be able to show commitment to agriculture. There remains in place the legal caveat that no private farm is to exceed 125 acres.[52]

The significance of such policy is that the way is being prepared, though still too slowly, for a revival of Polish agriculture. Such a revival would avoid two pitfalls that on historical grounds seem to be equally antisocial and antiecological: the two are state farms (the 21 percent of land now in state farms—mostly in the northern and western regions of the country—would presumably remain stable) and capitalist enterprise (the legal limit of 125 acres is designed to prevent the latter).

An ecologically grounded agriculture, accomplished in terms of training, new tools, and structure, would in turn encourge impulses in Poland for the revival of local autonomy, both for the country and for the towns and cities. These impulses are at present not inconsiderable, both in and out of government. An interesting example is provided by a ten-page document presented in April, 1983, to the Sejm's committee working on a new local government bill and entitled "Proposals to Reconstitute Local Government in Poland." The document argues that independent representation of local interests is a necessary condition for the success of economic reforms and for national accord. Local government should not serve merely as a direct extension of the state administration, it maintains, and local authorities should have their own executive organs, their own sources of income, and the right to manage their own property. It acknowledges that in certain instances local government should be subject to control and intervention by the central authorities, but such instances should be clearly defined and should not restrict or replace local initiative.[53] Such bold words, unfortunately, are lost to view in the process of implementation; yet they indicate the kind of thinking and potential action that lies beneath the surface of events.

Another interesting example is an ambitious practical research project called Local Poland, funded by the Ministry of Education and part of the new five-year plan for 1986–1991. This is an interdisciplinary ecological research and development project that draws together experts in the physical and social sciences.[54] Its aim is to develop a conceptual and practical model that can be applied to a given locale. The model, with modifications, could then be applied more widely to various regions in Poland that are especially in a bad way ecologically. The interrelated themes of region or locale, ecological balance, economy, and effective government are all brought within the parameters of the project. Such thinking and research bode well for the future of Poland—if they can gain momentum.

Solidarity's stake in a new ecological policy is also clear.[55] In addition,

Solidarity's goals have always included local self-government. It embraced the goals of Rural Solidarity for a better deal for private farmers. And an overall ecological approach to Poland's problems would provide much greater scope for an overall and genuine adjustment of the mutual needs of ordinary people and the government. In a practical, immediate sense Solidarity could find in such an approach a focus for its program that, though not directly in line with its major demands (for self-governing unions and reduction of censorship), would nevertheless direct people's energies and lead in the direction of those goals.

So it is to the interest of all three—government, church, and opposition—to join together on such an ecological project. Each would risk something, too. The government would risk creating a vigorous and politically autonomous periphery, both urban and rural; the church would risk losing its relative monopoly on the loyalty of farmers; and Solidarity would risk diluting its concentration on the major goal of independent, self-governing unions. Yet, the project promises economic revival and diversification, relief from environmental terror, the possibility of finding political settlements through ecological cooperation, and a release from the present straitjacket of fixed, unworkable policies, and fixed positions.

Whether anything like this could happen without something also happening in the world outside Poland is highly questionable. Contemporary Poland's position in the international realm is the final aspect of the country's way forward that must be explored.

9

Defeating the Deadlock

Adam Michnik, sentenced once again to prison in June, 1985, smuggled a letter dated "Barczewo Prison, August 1985" to Bishop Tutu in South Africa. The text reads in part: "From a Polish prison I am extending to you my great admiration for and unreserved solidarity with the struggle of your countrymen against the system of apartheid and for a democratic order and human dignity. . . . Your efforts to find peaceful means give hope and encouragement to all those who carry on a fight against discrimination and violence. We shall never be deprived of this hope by decisions taken by dictatorships which have replaced the power of arguments by arguments of power."[1]

Michnik, in the long years of struggle, has found a voice that is not only brave but clear. There is no muddle in it, and no ideology. He speaks in the voice that most characterizes the stance of Solidarity: a constitutional voice, a voice beyond violence, beyond the Gnostic temptation to reconstruct the world, and beyond the foolishness of a politics-as-usual that denies and yet practices the one-sidedness of discriminatory power. It is a voice that affirms that the human being per se has dignity. No one, no government, no system has to confer it on anyone, or has the right to do so. Michnik's is a voice that demands that state power acknowledge this already-existing human dignity. And it is a voice demanding of those who seek social change, even and especially those who justifiably seek fundamental alteration in the structure of power, that they seek it through peaceful means.

Yet Poland, South Africa, and much of the world are embedded in seemingly intractable conflict. The web of relationships in each case is tangled, and though one might speak with the tongues of angels, it is moot that a voice, however clear and firm and brave, can be heard. Yet the stance of nonviolent persuasion that doggedly affirms one's own dignity and with equal persistence invites the sides in conflict to serious, strategic negotiations would seem to be the only real hope for Poland, for South Africa, and for the world.

Yet, again, a question obtrudes: Is there any basis for thinking that in a situation such as the one in Poland there is room for the power of arguments to offset the arguments of power? In a word, is communication even possible? Or is the world between the warring sides so immersed in shadows that it quickly makes a pessimist out of the most incorrigible optimist?

In this final chapter I explore these shadows and invite the reader to join me straining to look into the twilight that marks relationships between hostile forces inside and outside Poland. It is profoundly important to realize that the outlook is not totally dark. Of course, the question may justifiably be raised as to whether the situation is one of fading points of light in a gathering darkness or a dusk that is actually the anticipation of dawn. I am not sure it is necessary to state categorically that it is one or the other, or whether it is even possible to do so. What is more important is to show that twilight, not a definitive darkness, exists and to leave it to human political imagination and action to nurture those seeming points of light in the darkness or to dissolve the dark mists that hide the imminent brightness, so that no matter what the present prognosis, a new day will surely come. A good place to begin is with the paradox of public speech in Poland, which both is and is not communication, and then take a look at the looming shadows of the international, geopolitical landscape.

THE POLITICS OF DISTORTED COMMUNICATION

To the question of whether dialogue exists in Poland between the government and the opposition, the immediate and emphatic answer would seem to be "Of course not!" In a literal sense that is probably true. There are no meetings, certainly not public ones, between Lech Walesa and the underground Provisional Coordinating Committee of Solidarity on one side and the government on the other. Nor are there meetings, as of this writing, between Jaruzelski's new consultative council and the (aboveground) Provisional Council of Solidarity, which was formed by the movement's leadership following the amnesty of September, 1986. Walesa once intimated that there were exploratory and inconclusive secret talks between one or more of his advisers and certain government officials.[2] It is entirely possible that there are and will continue to be informal conversations between members of the government and of the opposition. However, such contacts are so clandestine and mercurial. They do little to affect the basic pattern of mutual and seemingly mute standoff.

I have vivid memories of days in Poland conversing with government people in the morning and with Solidarity supporters the same afternoon. One experiences a kind of schizophrenia. One believes oneself to be in two separate regions of the world. Yet, turning it over for a moment, one also then realizes with a shock that both the morning and the afternoon conversations took place in the same country and concerned the same country. Furthermore, much of their talk presupposes, or takes its point of departure from, the existence of "the other." It is like a bad marriage in which no separation is possible.

By so much one already recognizes a strange and palpable phenomenon: each side's consciousness is formed partly in reaction to the existence of the other. It is as if each is a reluctant, deeply unwilling partner in a macabre dance, a dance that must go on. One conjures up an amusing but tortured image of two people dancing gingerly together, each holding his or her nose as they stride and hop and pirouette across a dismal landscape. Or perhaps one thinks of Jean-Paul Sartre's *Huis Clos* (No Exit), in which several people who hate one another are stuck together in hell for all time.

This strange dance need not, and probably cannot, continue unchanged. It could suddenly degenerate into brutal violence, or it could gradually turn into a dialogue. Dialogue is a possibility because even in the present form of the dance, there exists a broken, awkward, distorted, angry, but nevertheless nonviolent exchange of messages between the two parties.

Fully to appreciate this point, one might hypothesize as follows: Suppose a Stalin in command of the system. Surely Stalin would sweep away the likes of Walesa. He would be long dead by now. Zbigniew Bujak would never have been able to elude discovery for four and a half years, and this underground chieftain would have suffered the same fate as Walesa. Adam Michnik would also have perished, and so would Jacek Kuron, Bronislaw Geremek, Tadeusz Mazowiecki, Bogdan Lis, and many, many others, whether radical or moderate. Furthermore, Stalin would push the church literally to the wall and muzzle it so tightly it would have trouble breathing. To round the scene out, Stalin would treat

society, awakened or not, with the stiff boot of force. He would so squash
the population that they would resemble the totally abject and prostrate
"proles" depicted by George Orwell in 1984.

But one should stop and think for a moment. Stalin did try something
like this, and he failed. It was he who said, with an effort at levity and
scorn but also with deep chagrin, that "trying to bring Communism to
Poland is like trying to put a saddle on a cow." So it is, too, with the so-
called hard-liners in the Party and the government—Stefan Olszowski,
Tadeusz Grabski, Stanislaw Kociolik, and others: Were they to try something on the order of Stalinist repression, they would also fail, and they
know it. Indeed, it is doubtful if they would ever try, since they, too, are
Poles. Poles are not likely to cooperate in the total destruction and en-
slavement of their own country.

There is a further, and far more important, point: Jaruzelski is neither a
Stalin nor an Olszowski, and he is in the driver's seat. He is himself, sui
generis, a Pole, a man in charge of an "impossible" situation who nevertheless is determined to "mind the store" and somehow muddle
through. He, together with the moderate and less antiliberal elements
that remain in the ruling network of Party-government-army-police, is
trying to keep Poland afloat as a nation and as an economy, yet without
altering the inherited communist system of power. This of course puts
the ruling network at loggerheads with an aroused opposition, which
by the government's own acknowledgment numbers at least 20 percent of
the population. The regime must also contend with a powerful church
and with a restive, skeptical, but grudgingly conforming middle group
numbering between 50 and 60 percent of the population.[3]

The government's posture of communication (or noncommunication)
toward each of these three elements differs somewhat in character. Jaruzelski and his cohorts have tried to develop what they consider to be
modes of consultation with those who are in the middling frame of mind,
who generally conform outwardly to what the authorities require, and
who are not entirely closed to modest initiatives taken by the government
to stimulate citizen response. Most of this middle group are very skeptical
and would prefer to follow Solidarity. But being realists and needing the
security that comes with at least passive obedience to authority, they are
vulnerable to government pressure and promises.

In the wake of the psychic disasters for the regime and the Party that came with the imposition of martial law, the government created a new organization, PRON (Patriotic Movement for National Survival). PRON was touted as a new beginning for relations between the Party and society. Many organizations were included in this "framework" of organizations, this umbrella, whose purpose was to provide channels of communication between the people and the Party and to assure a flow of information and ideas back and forth. The notion was to increase the sense of consultation, so that though the Party would retain "the leading role" (and would do so in PRON as well), it would be more open to pressure and initiatives from the people.

PRON has been especially active in the electoral field. There were local elections in June, 1984, and a critical national election for the parliament (the prestigious Sejm) in October, 1985. The government set considerable store by these elections, especially the one for the Sejm. Party leaders initiated an ambitious program of consultation with a variety of groups (all approved, meaning that they had been set up at one time or another with the advice and consent of the Party). As one official told a group of American scholars in June, 1985, whereas the old method was simply to call up the leadership of a given group to more or less tell them which person would be selected to run for the parliament, now there were meetings, discussion, and some coming to terms with disagreements over whom the nominee should be.[4]

In addition, the election laws were changed. Instead of one candidate per seat, as is the usual practice in communist countries, now there were to be contests for 410 of the 460 seats in the Sejm. Of the two candidates for each of these seats, one was approved. The other, though in a sense a token candidate, could also campaign freely and vigorously. The 50 safe seats were reserved for the leaders of the government and the Party.

One may call this sham, and indeed many in and out of Poland did and still do. Yet such a judgment is not wholly warranted. The new election law is a minimal step that assures some degree of political input from society at large. The form of that input seems to me to be best conveyed by the word *consultation*. It is not yet the participation by autonomous groups and individuals that Solidarity demands. But it is consultation, and it is real. Jaruzelski and his cohorts deserve not so much congratulations and credit for this change, since it is not all that much they are sharing, but they do deserve to have their actions called by the right name.

The opposition decided to boycott the elections. They had done so in June, 1984, with some success, and they decided to do it again in October, 1985, apparently for two reasons. One was that they want not just consultation but participation—a legitimate demand considering the broken and forgotten promises of past Polish Communist regimes. A second reason was that they, in their paranoia, did not and could not believe that this was even consultation. They dismissed it as sham, which is unfortunate. One can readily understand the paranoia, considering the record of broken promises. But the paranoia hid from them the fact that there was the substance of consultation within the sham. Of course, they might not have wished to cooperate anyway, since the entire process was far short of participation. Yet, perceiving the regime's effort as, though too little, at least genuine in its own terms, would make the opposition stronger, less shrill. But they chose to boycott.

The regime, one can tell, was furious, and also very nervous. They made it their aim to get a large turnout, setting a goal of 80 percent. The threatened boycott laid down the gauntlet: they now had to perform quantitatively. It was a matter of getting out the votes. Argument, debate, discussion, and exploration of issues were shoved aside. Perhaps the possibility of such debate was tiny in any case, given the limited terms in which the consultation process would be carried out. But the bitter fight over the size of the vote pinched off even the tiny possibility. The election became a referendum on Jaruzelski's legitimacy. It also became a contest over the accuracy of the election turnout figures. One perhaps should not ask for too much. There was communication in the campaign, or at least the shadow of communication.

In the event, the regime claimed a 79 percent turnout and construed this figure to mean a clear endorsement. They believed it would help them convince parts, perhaps even all, of the West henceforth to be more forthcoming diplomatically and financially. And they believed it shored up a measure of political support in Poland from society at large. Although a slender reed, it might be enough for the regime to continue its policy of going it alone, braving it through the crisis without Solidarity or the church. The church, of course, had deeply irritated the regime by its clever neutral posture on the boycott, by intimating in numbers of ways its support of the boycott, and by the absence at the voting booths of eighty of the eighty-three bishops.

Yet the regime must also be mindful of a few facts. They have committed themselves to a policy of minimal consultation. The PRON experiment must go on. It will not stand still. The government has embarked on a dynamic process. It declared the need for new channels, and the circumstances will require it to use them, and use them with some degree of genuine honesty. The overwhelming reason why this is the case is the twin existence of the middle group (the regime's slender reed), whose visible skepticism toward the government hides their unrequited love of Solidarity, and, behind this middle group, a powerful opposition. The government cannot escape the fact that the opposition was able to convince large numbers of people in a communist country not to vote. Voter turnout in such countries is regularly within a few percentage points of 100. Thus, even a figure of 78.87 percent is a decisive rebuke. In the previous election to the Sejm, the government had claimed 20 percent more. Actually, a true figure for 1985 would probably be considerably lower than 79 percent. Claims made by Solidarity put it somewhere in the neighborhood of 66 percent.[5]

The final report of the TKK, Solidarity's underground leadership, on the elections was signed by the mathematician Konrad Bielinski and published in the underground *Tygodnik Mazowsze*. Bielinski, formerly employed by the mathematics institute of the Polish Academy of Sciences, had the title of TKK plenipotentiary for monitoring the elections, and he was a key figure in a vast operation involving tens of thousands of Poles. Despite the government's secrecy on the matter of who was entitled to vote and despite the great personal danger for everyone involved in the sampling, in the continuous observation of the selected sites, and in making the random, five-minute checks, the care and discipline of the monitoring operation was remarkable. Bielinski said in an interview: "I think the greatest satisfaction was that we were so many. And the effort was not wasted. We have built up an efficient organization, so that out of the multitude of individual effort one great good has come. I mean, above all, our knowledge of reality. Our main aim was not just to show that the authorities lie when they announce the election results. This could have been done with much less effort. . . . We wanted something more—to break the monopoly of information about ourselves in the hands of the authorities. And this we have achieved."[6]

The final report states that "the countryside was for obvious reasons beyond the scope of a reasonably credible exercise of this kind. The final conclusion pertains only to cities and towns. It gives the total number of the electorate in this sector of the population as 15 million 800 thousand and the number of voters as 10 million 400 thousand which is 66%, with a possible error of 200,000 or 1.3%."[7]

The largest cities tended to have the lowest turnout. In the six cities with over 400,000 inhabitants—Warsaw, Lodz, Krakow-Nowa Huta, Wroclaw, Poznan and Gdansk—the percentages went from 64.9 in Poznan to 45.7 in Wroclaw. Since the final report indicates that in general the smaller towns showed a higher turnout, the implication of their results might be that in the countryside Jaruzelski fared better than 66 percent, which would push the overall nationwide result somewhat over that figure.

The TKK's statement of October 22, 1985, on the election includes the following assessment.

> The thesis of official propaganda claiming increased popular support for the Jaruzelski team has not been borne out by facts. On the other hand, expectations of those who thought that this year's boycott would show increased support for social resistance were not fulfilled either. In our opinion, the fact that a stable situation exists in which roughly one-third of society—not because of transient emotions, without naive illusions, but in full awareness of possible consequences—openly declares its will to continue to resist is of great political significance.[8]

In addition to showing its power in terms of quantity, the opposition also positively affected the integrity and quality of the election process itself. Because the opposition had a strong, functioning network monitoring the elections throughout the country, the regime had to make sure that the elections were as fair as possible. Noted Bielinski:

> This year there has been less gerrymandering at the level of ward committees in Warsaw. I think that the experience of last year—awareness that Solidarity is capable of producing highly credible estimates of results, the amounts of information we received from committee members, and law

suits on cases violating electoral law—all this has brought about a change of attitude. This time the election committees knew that the truth would be out anyway, so more members were opposing efforts to cheat. The falsifications were engineered at a higher level.

It was a strange election. The boycotters (the opposition) actually participated in the election, not as voters, but as clandestine overseers. The government, which pretends the opposition does not exist, nevertheless acted in a manner to demonstrate that it was well aware that the opposition exists and must be taken heavily into account. The election was essentially an undeclared but very real competition between government and opposition for the loyalty of the middle.

The competition was again in evidence two years later when the regime presented a referendum on November 29, 1987, to the nation asking the people to vote on two generally worded propositions:

> 1. Are you in favor of the full realization of the program presented to the Sejm on the radical recovery of the economy aiming at the clear improvement of the living conditions of society, knowing that this requires passing through a difficult two- or three-year-long period of rapid changes?
> 2. Are you in favor of the Polish model of profound democratization of political life aimed at strengthening self-government, broadening the rights of citizens and increasing the participation of citizens in the governing of the country?[9]

By employing this vague language, the regime hoped to get support for its economic policy without giving up Party control and power. Its aim may also have been to drive a sizable wedge between the middle group and the opposition. Included in the package of proposed reforms were items Solidarity had been pushing for, such as economic decentralization, more reliance on market mechanisms, and a second chamber of the Sejm to address economic issues. But the regime also wanted leeway to raise prices in order to stimulate investment, and it wanted the people to work harder. The government was careful to apprise the nation of the extent of the intended price rises should the people approve the referendum: basic foodstuffs would increase by 110 percent in 1988, amid a general price rise for consumer goods of 40 percent.[10]

The seemingly forthright posture of the government in seeking prior approval of these price increases and coupling this with advocacy of some long-sought goals of the opposition made Solidarity at first cautious in its response. The caution was also partly due to the decentralized character of Solidarity's leadership. The members of the movement needed time to assess their collective feelings and judgment. First they made a structural change, abolishing both the underground organization (TKK) and the above-ground Provisional Council, which had been formed in 1986 in the aftermath of the amnesty. They established in their place a single body, the National Executive Commission, composed of ten regional representatives and Lech Walesa as chair.

The new body immediately issued a statement critical of the referendum. It said in part:

> A package of genuine political, social and economic guarantees is needed. But have the authorities provided such guarantees in the questions announced for the referendum? The plain answer must be "no." The questions have been put in a vague way and do not concern any concrete proposals for democratic reforms. . . . This is why we must clearly say "NO" to the question whether to participate in the referendum. Society should not take part in the action which merely serves propaganda purposes. . . . What is left, therefore, is to continue our struggle for full civil liberties, for the implementation of political, economic and trade union pluralism.[11]

The results of the referendum startled the world, and startled many Poles. So many people, whether from inattention or doubt, had been influenced over the years by the Polish government's persistent efforts to portray the opposition as small and ineffective. But according to Jerzy Urban, only 67.32 percent of those eligible to do so voted, and of these only about two-thirds approved the referendum. By Polish law, a majority of all eligible voters must approve a referendum in order for it to pass. Only 44.28 percent of Poland's eligible 26.2 million voters supported the economic side of the referendum, while a slightly larger number, 46.29 percent, supported the political side. Therefore the government lost the referendum.[12]

Solidarity maintained its direct hold on the allegiance of fully one-third of the eligible voters. One recalls its leaders' claims that in the national elections of 1985, at least one-third of the eligible voters heeded Solidarity's call for a boycott, as compared with the government's insistence that 78 percent of the citizens had voted. Yet not only did Solidarity confirm and maintain that degree of allegiance, but it did so under circumstances that seemed to be very favorable to the government. For the government had taken a bold, well-advertised, new approach, especially on the economic side and also to a degree on the political side. But the Polish people seemed to be responding to the voice of the opposition, which warned them not to put too much stock in the government's proposed new reforms.

On the other hand, the referendum was by no means a complete rejection of the government: two-thirds of those who voted did after all approve the propositions. The government has preserved its flexibility. Its leaders can point to the referendum itself as evidence of their good faith in instituting greater democracy in Poland, thus mollifying Western critics who have withheld credits partly because of a lack of democracy there. At the same time, the government can point to its setback in the referendum as a justification for not raising prices as high as Western creditors and potential donors have been demanding. The situation thus offers the regime a chance both to obtain Western credits and to escape triggering the wholesale work stoppages that sharper price rises would probably incite.

So, as of this writing in mid-December, 1987, it seems that both sides have a right to claim a piece of the action and that both sides should more and more clearly perceive that this is the case. The government needs to go beyond its efforts at "great consultation," as Urban described the referendum, and once again begin dealing directly with the solid core of the opposition, namely Walesa, Bujak, and the other leaders.[13]

The rank-and-file opposition, for its part, needs both to hear and to accept the long-standing call of Solidarity's core leadership to adhere to the principles and assume the posture of genuine negotiation, and to find flexible strategies and tactics to deal effectively above-ground with the government. Jacek Kuron seemed to be pointing clearly in this direction just a few months before the referendum in a challenging and much-discussed article addressed to his fellow oppositionists entitled "Landscape After the Battle." He reaffirmed the fundamental strategy of social self-help and of building up autonomous groupings and linked it with an analysis showing the divisions within the government between standpatters and reformists. This division can only increase, he argued. He urged that members of the opposition stop lumping together everyone in the government as a single "enemy" and that they seek shrewdly to find and select ways to deal with the reformists.[14]

Jaruzelski's government also had the middle group primarily in mind when it created a Consultative Council shortly after it surprised the world with the sweeping amnesty of September, 1986. The regime's goal in setting up this council is to institute fairly high-level consultation, between elections, with "moderate" voices (*moderate* being defined by the government). Yet the dividing line between moderate voices and members of the opposition is not always easy to draw. The tendency of the government is to turn to prestigious Catholic intellectuals. Yet such intellectuals often have close communication with opposition leaders, and—more important, actually—with opposition *thinking*.

Jaruzelski and the Party went a step further in the fall of 1987 by calling for the formation of consultative councils at the local level and coupling this proposal with the proposal to establish a second chamber of the Sejm to consider economic questions. In appearances, the government was putting into effect an earlier demand that Solidarity had originated. This move has the advantage for Jaruzelski of bolstering still further his image as a moderate (in the eyes of both the middle group and the West) and of confusing some members of the determined opposition. He may therefore gain support for his efforts to strengthen the economy through price increases and harder work. He, and the Party, must feel that they can adequately control the consultative councils and the second chamber of the Sejm through the normal processes of nomenklatura, just as they do the present Sejm.

But there is a risk, one that Jaruzelski is doubtless not unaware of. The risk is that these new bodies, together with the present Sejm, may become effective vehicles of substantial opposition. The interesting, ironical question is: At what point, both structurally and psychologically, does consultation become participation? At what point, in other words, does power begin to slip from the Party and lodge, to some degree, in other institutions. The Sejm will be stronger as a result of the new reform. Its very name evokes memories of genuine debate and serious confrontation stretching far back into Poland's constitutional past. If, at the same time, the opposition continues its independent course, its members acting from without and also, when chance affords, from within these new channels created by the reform, then the opposition's campaign for independent, self-governing unions and associations will be reinforced and the way will be open for an evolution toward constitutional government.

The second major force the government "communicates" with is the church. The government maintains many official contacts with the church. Jaruzelski and Cardinal Glemp meet periodically on a variety of issues. Their talks are a kind of dialogue, but it is of the sort one associates with diplomatic encounters between severe, and severely correct, strangers. As is the case between representatives of nations, their diplomatic exchanges are not fully political in the sense of discourse among citizens of a common and commonly acknowledged polity.[15] A necessary wariness and caution is always present in their encounters: much is tactical, and much less is strategic.

So the diplomatic pattern of communication does not suggest a breakthrough to a new set of closer relationships, but an exchange based on the maintenance of an existing, largely tacitly understood set of mutual interests. Yet the pattern is a step up from force and violence, and it proceeds via actual, physical acts of common meetings and verbal communication. The pattern is thus open to strategic breakthroughs that may occur simply because the pattern exists. Given small changes in circumstances in or out of the country (which of themselves would lead nowhere), the existence of the pattern may lead, at some point, to its own transcendence into direct political dialogue. In sum, we see here, too, a kind of shadow of communication, in which there is not yet the mutual exchange of real partners. We see the not unfriendly talk, and doubletalk, of two wary strangers trying to figure out, in a piecemeal, crisis-management way, how to solve extant problems. By so much they do communicate and affect each other's outlook and policies on a range of issues.

But what about the government and the opposition? Here communication is especially awkward and convoluted—but it exists. If the government's communication with the turned-off middle group may be described as an attempt at consultation (however specious some may say it is), and if the government's communication with the church is in the style of diplomacy, how should one describe its affair with the opposition? There are four motifs in the "communication" between the regime and the opposition. One is outright repression. Another is a pretense that "the other" does not exist. A third is indirect, convoluted public speech. And a fourth is the underground publishing network.

The first motif, repression, is a steady disposition to use force and forcible restraint. At this level there is no dialogue, no communication. The regime acts upon the opposition as if it were some hostile object that needs to be contained if not indeed eliminated. But there are other motifs, engendered by the fact that the repression stops short of total warfare.

A second motif, therefore, is the pretense that the opposition does not really exist. Lech Walesa is a private citizen, the "former head of a former union," Jerzy Urban, the government spokesperson, likes to say. Solidarity is likewise treated as if it were a phenomenon of the past. There may be remnants of the movement scattered about, the regime suggests, but there is a new situation now, a "normalized" one, and Solidarity does not figure in it at all. This pretense is comic, yet it is one of the ways the government deals with something they would otherwise have to destroy. It is a rhetorical device. If one cannot or will not use total force and the hated object does not go away, then he or she can ignore it and pretend as cleverly as possible that it does not exist. There are many social situations in everyday life, in the East and in the West, in which this device is used, and often with great effect. In this regard, the realm of government is no different from other social realms of existence, though often the stakes are higher.

Still, force and the rhetoric of denial are not sufficient to deal with so weighty and persistent an object as the Solidarity opposition. Another motif, therefore, that the government and the opposition each employ may be called indirect or garbled communication. This practice is based on a simple fact, a fact so obvious that its significance is ignored by most people who appraise the Polish situation. Walesa, the de facto leader of Solidarity, is above-ground. He carries on a wide range of activities: he works at the Lenin Shipyards in Gdansk; he goes on trips to Warsaw, where he meets with above-ground and underground Solidarity leaders; he meets highly placed Western officials on state visits to Poland, at their request; he travels to Czestochowa to participate in mass religious ceremonies that in the Polish manner are charged with deep political feelings; he regularly lays wreaths fraught with political symbolism at the great workers' monument outside the gates of the Lenin Shipyards; he leads, and sometimes follows in, public marches of protest; he constantly comments on the events of the day in Poland; he publishes programmatic statements; he issues calls for action and calls for caution and inaction;

and, in addition to coverage in the underground network, he receives guaranteed media coverage throughout Poland through the agency of foreign correspondents, who often interview him, frequently surreptitiously. They publish what he says in the West. West German, English, and French broadcasts are available to Poles, who listen in great numbers, as they do to Radio Free Europe and the Voice of America. According to a New York *Times* story of 1983, about 11.5 million Poles listen to the Voice of America on a given day. This is about 43 percent of the adult population. Before martial law in December, 1981, VOA did two hours and twenty minutes of broadcasting in the Polish language per day; since martial law it has done seven hours per day.[16] Foreign correspondents then ask Urban at the latter's press conferences questions that probe for his reactions to Walesa's or other opposition leaders' statements or actions. From Urban's deliberate nonresponse or elliptical response, the Polish people glean something of the views and thinking of the government. Walesa may pick up on Urban's comments at the next interview with foreign correspondents, and the cycle starts again. This same cycle has applied to other figures in the opposition as well, especially since the mass release of political prisoners in September, 1986.

Michael Kaufman of the New York *Times* has described this process and noted the crucial role of Jerzy Urban. Officially, the latter is "simply the spokesman for the government," he notes.

> But in fact, Mr. Urban . . . shapes policies and seeks to mold internal and external public opinion on all aspects of public life. By his own account, he sits in on meetings of the Council of Ministers and offers opinions but does not vote. . . . As a consequence, a certain news cycle has developed around Mr. Urban and his office. Western correspondents often report information gleaned from opposition and clandestine sources. Foreign radio stations like the BBC, Radio Free Europe, and the Voice of America then often broadcast these reports in their widely heard Polish language programs. Mr. Urban in turn comments on or criticizes these reports at the weekly news conferences, which are then transcribed or reported in the government press. The process, tacitly and paradoxically, provides at least a pale approximation of the pluralistic journalism that the Solidarity movement had actively sought.[17]

Kaufman quotes Urban as saying, "In a real sense my job was created by Solidarity." It was not only created, but, I would add, it is sustained by the continued presence and action of Solidarity, so that in Jerzy Urban—in his role and how he performs in it—we see a new institution in the communist state. He is a surrogate communications officer, a surrogate for the real thing, but nevertheless a medium through whom—and in whom—debate takes place. The attentive public in Poland (or at least the 43 percent who listen to the VOA and the higher percentage who listen to BBC) are exposed to both what opposition leaders say and what the government says. Not only that, but the government and the opposition carry on a kind of communication, convoluted though it usually is, with each other.

An especially bemusing example of this convoluted method of communication occurred in December, 1983, around the time Walesa received the Nobel Prize for Peace. His address accepting the award was read in Oslo by a former Solidarity leader, Bogdan Ciwinski. Walesa indirectly repeated an appeal he had made the week before when he urged the West to drop the economic sanctions against Poland. On that same day, ironically, a government official condemned Walesa for supporting sanctions.[18] This was doubly ironic because not only was the substance of the criticism no longer valid but the government, by criticizing this "private" citizen, once again acknowledged that he is after all a public figure with whom they find it necessary to contend publicly.

In addition to the lifting of trade sanctions, Walesa also strongly urged the West to follow up with a bold program of financial credits to Poland (in the billions of dollars) in return for the government's agreement to negotiate outstanding differences with the opposition. President Reagan responded the next day, saying that he would give the appeal by Walesa earnest consideration. The following day the government said it would study Reagan's promise to consider lifting trade sanctions.[19]

In January, 1984, Reagan lifted some sanctions. Poland would regain fishing rights in American waters and would be able to land eighty-eight Polish charter flights in the United States per year. But remaining in effect would be a freeze on new credits and loans, suspensions of tariff concessions, and the cancellation of all regularly scheduled flights of the Polish state-owned airline, LOT, to the United States. Also still banned would be food shipments except for humanitarian reasons and scientific exchanges. The government was clearly disappointed: "These partial moves," it said, "can in no way be considered proper, since they are only illusory actions constituting a dodge in the face of the obvious need to depart from the policy of restrictions."[20]

Walesa professed himself to be pleased by Reagan's response. "It was my initiative," he said. "It seems to go in the direction I wanted, so of course I am satisfied." But whether he could have been very satisfied is open to doubt. In the New York *Times* he was quoted as saying, "I was in favor of lifting all the sanctions."[21] Reagan responded to only the first part of the proposal, the lifting of sanctions, and to that tepidly, and was silent about the proposal for a bold economic program. Yet Walesa's proposal itself was statesmanlike. It jarred the powers that be into public speech with one another on an extremely sensitive issue, and it spurred what must have been considerable behind-the-scenes debate and discussion within their respective orbits. It illustrates the importance of the Polish opposition and Walesa's shrewd use of the limited powers he has, and it illustrates that a communication of sorts is conducted back and forth between forces in Poland that often seem hopelessly deaf to each other. Eventually, these moves culminated in the lifting of all sanctions in February, 1987. Walesa's initiative bore fruit for Jaruzelski and for Poland. It may also in time bear fruit for Solidarity.

Another example of this communication of sorts occurred near the date of the elections to the Sejm in October, 1985. As noted above, the government set great store on getting a large turnout: 80 percent was its goal. In a speech at the United Nations in late September, Jaruzelski indicated that if the electoral turnout was in the neighborhood of 80 percent, the government would consider a new amnesty.[22] Polish jails accumulate political prisoners at a regular and disturbing rate, so that previous amnesties of 1983 and 1984, though they largely cleared the jails, nevertheless gave only temporary relief from this chronic and depressing disease in the body politic. At the time Jaruzelski spoke to the UN, the number of political prisoners had risen to over 390.[23]

The offer of amnesty by Jaruzelski was made with all three of the opposition audiences in mind: the church, the middle group of doubters and conformists, and the activist opposition. He also angled his remarks to the West and the world at large, of course. The government hoped that such an offer would induce more people to vote and undermine the determined efforts of the active oppositionists to persuade people to boycott the election. The activists condemned Jaruzelski for trying to "bribe" the people and the opposition leaders. Seven opposition leaders in prison said his action was "unprecedented blackmail."[24] The elections came and went, the regime put a positive face on the event by claiming a 79 percent turnout, and Jaruzelski, through the new Sejm, made good, to a degree, on his promises. The Sejm passed legislation that instituted a complicated set of procedures and qualifications for the repatriation of selected political prisoners. This was not the virtually blanket amnesty of 1984; nor did it seem to match what Jaruzelski had promised before the election. Walesa said, "You cannot call it an amnesty." But he added, "Any step in the direction of observing rights is positive, and a few people who were innocently imprisoned will come out of prison."[25] Thus there was some action that fall to follow through on Jaruzelski's promise, and a year later there was near total fulfillment of it.

The release of political prisoners in September, 1986, and the prompt formation by Solidarity of an above-ground Provisional Council produced new expectations of dialogue and negotiations, and there followed redoubled efforts by the government to sidestep the appearance either of dialogue or of condoning the creation of anything so independent as Solidarity's new council. When asked at a press conference in early October, 1986, what the government thought about such open public meetings as Solidarity's large press conference in Gdansk on September 30, 1986, to discuss the formation of the Provisional Council, Urban replied that of course "social gatherings" go on all the time in Poland.[26] In other words the government chose not to accord those meetings the status of "political" and in that way blinked at what was indeed a very political gathering. But Urban warned that resuming union activity would be punishable.

At his press conference on October 7, when asked whether he could imagine the participation of Bujak or Walesa in the Consultative Council, Urban flatly replied that he could not. At the following week's press conference he was asked how the authorities evaluated Walesa's declaration that he strives for national agreement. Urban shot back that Walesa, together with Bujak, was trying "to create a new illegal structure and has manifested his unity with political extremists." He then made a long but interesting "if . . . then statement."

> If Walesa distanced himself from such aims, if he pledged to observe the law instead of establishing illegal organizations, if he sincerely and publicly drew conclusions from mistakes of the union which he had led, if he became unambiguous in his declaration of a will to agreement, if he re-

spected the constitutional principles of Poland's political system and did not hide up his sleeve slogans of so-called pluralism and other political aims hitting out at our political system, if he did not ally openly with Western forces hostile to Poland—then, maybe, the principle of "it is not important where one comes from, what matters is his present stand" could apply also to Lech Walesa, the man whom many once believed.

The rhetorical putdown is still manifest, the barely concealed anger is there, but also there is a note of expostulation and of a need to defend the government's refusal to talk by mounting up "all the arguments."[27] And there may be a covert message that the government is willing to talk—under certain conditions. That they are conditions that Walesa cannot accept, and will not, must not blind the observer to the fact that a certain sparring is going on.

The sparring was again much in evidence in the fall of 1987, when the government announced what it termed radical reforms affecting both the economy and political structures. There seemed less unwillingness on the part of the government to consider asking oppositionists to join the local and national consultative bodies. On the other hand, the opposition continued to be wary of accepting a merely consultative role. The core of its leadership steadfastly insisted that independent, self-governing unions and associations must be acknowledged by the Party if social peace and renewal were to succeed.

One cannot call this sort of communication a model of political dialogue. But then neither is it force; nor can it be called mere propaganda and rhetorical flourish. There was an attempt to "get through," to "deal." Although officially the government pretends the opposition does not exist, it will make a disguised appeal to this "nonexistent" movement when it seems necessary or useful. This distorted effort to "talk" fits the motif of indirect, garbled, convoluted communication.

A final motif in the political posture of government and opposition toward one another is the flourishing existence of a vast underground literature. Several hundred publications, many printed on what must be above-ground presses, are turned out regularly and read avidly by millions of Poles. It appears that in numbers of publications the illicit press rivals and may exceed the state-run publishing houses.[28] Persons are regularly caught and put away for engaging in this illegal activity. Yet it simmers and persists. The government spends an incalculable amount of time perusing this material, much of which is of great political interest to itself. It can always point to an Independent (underground) article or journal for every fresh evidence of what it calls counterrevolution and antisocialist cant. It is a club the regime can hold over the heads of Walesa, Michnik, Geremek, and others who do not subscribe to much of what is expressed. The government also tolerates the outpouring of weeklies, books, and periodicals no doubt as a kind of safety valve. In the regime's view it may deflect people from taking harsher, more direct, even violent action. It gives "those 20 percent" something to do. An example of the government's toleration, and yet also its prickly sensitivity, is seen in a story told to me. The government let it be known to the editors of an underground weekly that a certain article should not be published. The editors published it anyway. They were fined, but what is stunning, if one thinks about it, is the fact that the government dickered with the editors to begin with.

Government leaders tolerate the continued publication of the famous Catholic weekly in Krakow, *Tygodnik Powszechny*. They could shut it down, but have not. The editor, Jerzy Turowicz, is subjected to considerable pressure, if not harassment, but he remains in charge and continues to be a voice of opposition. He publishes eighty thousand copies per issue. Thirty Catholic publications in Poland have an overall circulation of about 1.2 million. Similarly, the government continues to permit the existence of the Catholic University in Lublin (KUL), a small but leading intellectual center, the only one of its kind in a communist country. It is true that the government in 1985 moved to further restrict university autonomy throughout Poland, including that of KUL. It would be harder than ever for Polish intellectuals and university administrators to adhere to even minimal standards of scientific and philosophic integrity. Yet that tradition persists in Poland, and it is doubtful if even the government wants to suppress it altogether.

Do these four motifs add up to communication between the regime and the opposition? Yes and no. Yet there is enough to suggest that bridgeheads exist between these two uneasy "partners," which could under certain circumstances be exploited to yield a positive dialogue.

Such bridgeheads may be widening. A good example lies in the public disagreement that surfaced briefly in the official press concerning the severity of Poland's ecological predicament. In addition, in late May, 1987, a three-paragraph item appeared in the official press containing the gist of a condemnation of Jerzy Urban. Four scholars, all with close ties to

Solidarity, were filing slander charges in civil court against Urban, asserting he had caused them injury when he told a news conference that they had all met on different occasions with Albert Mueller, an American diplomat. Mueller had been allowed to leave Warsaw after he was filmed giving materials to a man the government described as his Polish contact. Although Urban was given space for a three-thousand-word reply to the three-paragraph condemnation, nevertheless the exchange caught the attention of many who said they could not recall such another instance since the halcyon days of Solidarity's above-ground existence in 1980–1981.

Are events such as these still only mere flashes in the pan, or are they a harbinger of greater public debate between the government and the opposition? In either caes, they indicate some movement, however grudging, toward more direct communication.

What takes place in Poland today, then, is the politics of distorted communication. It has analogues everywhere that human beings who are in conflict with one another, and who will not or cannot fight or take flight, fumble toward each other to exchange meaningful messages somehow. What occurs in Poland is not a difference in kind but in degree. It is more starkly evident there, mostly because of the fact that the opposition has abjured violence and yet has not abjured hard, tough objection to its own exclusion from power. A complicated relationship thus develops, illustrated by motifs ranging from chronic and sporadic use of force by the physically stronger partner to stutterings and garbled cries of communication by both sides in the direction of the other. The ace in the hole for the physically weaker partner is its steady commitment to its own subjectivity coupled with its unyielding stance of nonviolence, which becomes in this context more and more a core value for the movement, not just a tactic. Insofar as nonviolence is persisted in, the opportunity remains open and the possibility is enhanced that negotiation will take place and a way forward will show itself for both together.

THE GEOPOLITICAL GLOOM: LEARNING
TO ADJUST ONE'S EYES

It has often been said that Poland is in a double bind geopolitically and that this fact is really the source of all, or almost all, of the country's problems. Jaruzelski desperately needs the people to work with a will, but they cannot and will not. They cannot, because the economy is top-heavy and inefficient. They will not, because, having arrived at a deep sense of their own historic subjectivity, they demand that the regime make a basic change in the structure of power. But Jaruzelski cannot push through the necessary economic reforms or meet the demand of the people for real participation. He cannot, because the Soviet Union stands in the way and because the entrenched middle echelons of his own regime block both economic and political reform. He will not, because he fears the hard-liners and their backers in the Kremlin; because he fears the chaos that he thinks would follow a relaxation of control; because he fears for his own career, perhaps for his life, should he deviate more than the Russians could bear; and because he himself is a devoted Communist, a convinced supporter of the Warsaw Pact and of Poland's need to remain firmly allied, indeed adhesively attached, to the Soviet Union.

The Russians, in this scenario, cannot and will not give Poland any scope. They cannot, because such a change as is implied in self-governing unions, workers' councils, and market socialism means too great a variation in the pattern of communist rule and thus threatens the internal power of the Soviet ruling group. Furthermore, they cannot, because such a shift risks the emergence of a too-independent Poland, and like it or not, a dependent Poland is a vital, geopolitical necessity in the face of a possibly resurgent Germany, general West European hostility, and a determined superantagonist across the Atlantic whose missiles and armies are poised in Western Europe with first-strike capabilities and presumed intention. The USSR will not allow Poland scope, because Soviet leaders enjoy the exercise of imperial power that their position of dominance in Eastern Europe gives them. Furthermore, they are ambitious and may wish to extend their influence, if not their domination, westward.

The United States cannot and will not be deflected from its long-standing policy of containing communism and the Soviet Union through reliance on overwhelming military force and the selective use of economic power, thereby also touting its own power and way of life in the world. Poland and the rest of Eastern Europe are always points of concern to the United States, since they abut Western Europe and are, especially in the case of Poland, substantially represented in the population of the

United States. Nevertheless these countries are clearly on the other side of the curtain. They are part of the Communist bloc, part of the USSR's sphere of influence. Thus, even though in American rhetoric there seems an inclination to regard them as separate, or separable, from the bloc, they can receive only secondary, if not tertiary, consideration in actual policy. They become important only in relation to their impact on Western Europe—especially West Germany—and in relation to their impact on the USSR. Their internal problems help unsettle "the evil empire" and destabilize it, though of course too much turmoil risks the kind of crisis that could embroil Western Europe and the world in nuclear war.

As part of this script, one should also note the opportunity Eastern Europe offers Western business. Eastern Europe's internal political climate becomes a concern of the policy makers in corporate and government bureaus. For example, a disconsolate or "spoiled" work force worries the bankers.

But on the whole, American policy makers in government perceive that they must treat Poland, and Eastern Europe generally, in the context of the East-West conflict. Thus, it is unrealistic, even unfair, to the East Europeans to pretend otherwise. Thus, the United States cannot do much about or for Poland in any substantial way; in addition, it will not do much, for to try to would simply compound an already tragic situation. Such a policy posture then, of course, reacts in turn upon Poland. The Polish people, and the government as well, feel the positive identification of the United States with Polish aspirations for self-governing institutions and a more open economy. This stimulates the people to thoughts of support from the United States and prods the Polish government into a steady irritation and stubborn anger at the United States. It also serves the interest of the hard-liners in the Kremlin and in Warsaw.

Yet, at the same time, both the people's hopes and the government's anger are blunted by the ultimate "hands-off" policy that is in actual fact pursued by the American State Department. The situation has, then, the effect of helping to harden the lines of the cleavage in Poland. And so we are back to our point of departure: the fundamental and seemingly intractable standoff between Jaruzelski and the people.

All the forces in this scenario seem to be in lockstep with one another. It is like a closed circle, a long metal chain, each piece wedged into place.

And within this hard circle Poland merely plays its appointed role: that of a tragic figure with the eternal smile of hope upon its worn, once elegant face. The moral is that Poland, though virtually a Western country trapped in the East, must learn ultimately to accept its fate.

But how true is this picture? How permanent, how securely placed, are those fetters in the metal chain that seem so tightly wedged together to produce standoff and stagnation? Each link in the chain is worth examining.

Within Poland, experience has shown that Solidarity is committed to the defense of ordinary people's subjectivity and on that fundamental basis is determined to achieve dialogue and compromise with the Communist regime. Its posture of nonviolence has meant that there has been no terrorism in Poland, even though similar conditions in many places of the earth have given rise to this new and dreaded international disease. The spirit and energy of renewal represented in Solidarity is a crucial, perhaps the only crucial, element in the dissolution of the iron chain that binds Poland.

Another important internal element working for a modus vivendi is the common commitment of both sides to what for lack of a better word may be called a workers' society. Unfortunately, the government's commitment is often merely rhetorical—a repetition of slogans from the past. Unfortunately, as well, the church's commitment seems more to nationalism than to a worker-oriented society. However, its concept of nation is rooted in peaceful patriotic values and in notions of gemeinschaft (organic community) rather than gesellschaft (aggregated association). This allows for, indeed encourages, overlap with concepts of worker solidarity. So the major thrust of the opposition is noncapitalistic. It insists on the fulfillment of the socialist promise, arguing for workers' rights and for workers' participation in economy and polity. Jaruzelski and his center-moderate wing of the Party could cheerfully live with this and could find ways to accommodate it by bending present structures. That is, they could more readily do so if they once understood that this is what the opposition wants. Whether this is what they see and hear is problematic. They may be prisoners of exaggerated fears and of the easy temptation to associate the opposition solely with the inevitably shrill and extreme voices of some in the underground together with their Western supporters.

It is my belief that Jaruzelski is and remains a Pole. He is not a puppet. He has made efforts, roundabout as they may be, to bend in the direction of the opposition—not ever to the point of according political status to them, but to the point of often listening to their criticism and even conforming in appearance and to some degree in substance to their demands.

Jaruzelski has granted four amnesties since 1983. He has pushed the Party's new creation, PRON, toward at least a posture of consultation in elections. He seized the opportunity to conduct a public trial of four security policemen involved in the killing of Father Popieluszko, an unheard-of event in a communist country. After the national elections in October, 1985, he dropped leading hard-liners from government and from the Party's Politburo. Stefan Olszowski was removed as foreign minister and Stanislaw Kociolek as ambassador to Moscow. He has thus distanced himself from the more extreme repressive measures advocated by the Party's hard-liners. He continues to use careful but steady diplomacy in his dealings with the church. Following the amnesty of September, 1986, he established a consultative council attached to the Council of State giving a limited voice to moderates aligned with the Catholic church, who in turn have lines of communication with the opposition. He followed this with major proposals for economic and political reforms in the fall of 1987, including local consultative councils, a second chamber of the Sejm, and the debureaucratization of the economy. But he must be careful of what Moscow thinks and does, and he is a cautious man.

But is Moscow unalterable and monolithic? Does it, can it, give no room for maneuver? To ignore these questions is to be rigid and monolithic oneself and to deny that change is the stuff of life, even for Moscow. One should not overlook the actual record of Moscow's internal political and economic development, its relations with Eastern Europe, or its checkered, uneven stance toward the West.

First, there is the situation within the Soviet Union. The Russian Communist party has been characterized by a continuing tug-of-war between "conservatives" and "liberals," with smaller numbers of Stalinists on the right and of even smaller numbers of democracy-oriented Communists on the left.[29] Although intent on Party supremacy, and thus their own supremacy, the leading cohorts have not foreclosed new ways to make the Party a more efficient and responsive vehicle for aggregating sentiments and interests from the nonparty elites and the people. Styles of leadership have changed substantially from Stalin to Khrushchev to Brezhnev to Gorbachev.

Kosygin in the 1960s had already called for an economic reform program, including market discipline, profit criteria, and greater autonomy for the individual firm. Although soft-pedaled in the Brezhnev years, economic reform persisted as an idea and thus as a goad to internal Party debate. With the accession of Andropov and now especially with the triumph of Gorbachev, economic reform has again become a priority of public policy. How much and how far it can or will go is not yet clear. But Gorbachev's new team is keenly aware of the need to introduce some significant changes in a moribund, straitjacketed economy. Hungary's example has long been a point of considerable interest and concern to them, and China's extensive experiments with market techniques and private businesses (both individual and collective) are surely not lost on them. And they do not need to be excessively alarmed about any threat that these changes may have on the leading role of the Party in these countries. There is little evidence that economic reform is not compatible with strong Party rule.

A major problem facing Gorbachev and his team is the degree to which the Soviet economy is geared to war production (which takes up almost twice the percentage of GNP as in the United States). The 12 to 14 percent slice of the economic pie that goes for armaments, in the context of the highly inelastic economy characteristic of "real existing socialism," means that there is little room for the planners to experiment with significant economic reforms, such as nonadministrative, nonbureaucratic, and nonquantitative methods of stimulating production and consumption. This barrier, in tandem with the engrained habits and entrenched power of the Soviet bureaucratic elite, means that Gorbachev, like Khrushchev and Brezhnev before him, will find it extremely difficult to bring some light, levity, and spirit of enterprise into the Soviet economy. Economic reform, including production for consumer needs, is stymied and continually frustrated physically and structurally by the arms race and the nuclear stalemate. *Time* magazine's famous interview with Gorbachev some weeks before the Geneva summit ended with a pointed statement by the Russian leader, a statement that in the context of Soviet efforts at economic reform seems almost a lament and a dire warning: "I would like to end by just saying a few words that are important in understanding what we have been talking about all along. I don't remember who, but somebody said that foreign policy is a continuation of domestic policy. If that is so, then I ask you to ponder one thing: If we in the Soviet Union are setting ourselves such truly grandiose plans in the domestic sphere, then what are the external conditions that we need to be able to fulfill those domestic plans? I leave the answer to that question with you."[30]

During 1986 Gorbachev began what the New York *Times* described as a great push to revitalize the Russian economy, state, and Communist party and to arouse the Russian people to respond. Serge Schmenann wrote: "Gorbachev [on coming to power] immediately set about replacing the top level of the government and the party. He offered some new liberties to economic managers and legalized some private services. He declared war on the blight of drunkenness, demanded a new openness (glasnost) and turned a new diplomatic face to the world." In 1987 Gorbachev went further. Hundreds of political prisoners were released. At a Central Committee meeting he called on the Party to approve a series of reforms that could bring about significant changes in the Soviet system. As part of a campaign for restructuring (*perestroika*), he proposed that local, republic-level, and perhaps even national Communist party officials be chosen from slates of more than one candidate. He also said the leadership was considering giving Soviet voters at large a choice of candidates in general elections. He further suggested the election of factory managers by their workers. In addition, discussion of new economic policies is now encouraged more than ever before. For example, the work of a leading economist, Tatyana Zaslawskaya, whose calls for decentralization had been squelched for years, is now given prominence.[31]

Most of these changes, one may almost wryly note, had already been embarked upon by Jaruzelski's government. What do such changes in the Kremlin's modest but substantial approach to economy, culture, and political systems augur for the further evolution of Polish political institutions, economy, and culture? If the Polish past is any guide, and if the Polish phoenix maintains its power, one can hardly doubt that not only will there be more evolution in Poland but that it may go beyond "consultation" to a genuine structural shift on the part of the regime. Such a denouement is not a mere fancy.

The Soviet Union's posture toward Eastern Europe is a second ingredient in prospects for change in Poland. In Eastern Europe the Soviet Union has pursued a rather zigzag course. One perceives this in the geopolitical realm, in ideology, and in economics.

The USSR, not without great mortification, eventually acknowledged the independence of Yugoslavia and swallowed that country's turn to a system of political economy that represents a substantial modification of the Soviet model. Likewise, later, the Soviet Union put up with the intransigence of Albania. Romania has won a fair measure of autonomy in its foreign policy, though its internal political structure and repressive apparatus mirror the Soviet Union's politics from the top down.

Changes in the internal structure of power in Hungary (1956) and in Czechoslovakia (1968) were perceived as a double threat. To the Soviets these "deviations" were an unacceptable departure from the Soviet model and, largely because of that, a threat to Russian geopolitical interests. Deviation from the model implied a risk of too much national independence and also the frightening possibility that these countries would be sucked into the Western orbit. The nature of the rebellion in each country may have contributed to the Soviet fear: both were inspired and led by intellectual elites, not industrial workers.[32] Invasion and repression were the answers given by the Soviets. It proved costly to them each time, diplomatically and economically.

Poland has also consistently appeared to constitute a double threat to the USSR.[33] And since Poland is, of all the Eastern European countries, the largest and the most strategically located in terms of the Soviet Union's geopolitical interests, any deviation is a matter of intense concern to the Kremlin. Poland's political economy and overall structure of power, especially since 1956, has never conformed to the Soviet model. In addition, Polish nationalism has always seemed too vigorous a thing to be comfortably trusted. Polish agriculture has been, in form and to some degree in substance, an affair of private economy—unheard of in communist states. The spiritual qualities of life have consistently been protected and nurtured by a church that has won and maintained for itself a considerable autonomy—also unheard of in communist states. University life in Poland has also been more self-confident and more persistently, even doggedly, attached to intellectual standards that resist Party encroachment more than in most other Communist states. Even the Sejm, because of its historic roots deep in Poland's constitutional past, which stretches back many centuries, has more respect and more of a political role in the power structure than supreme soviets or people's congresses in other systems of "real existing socialism."[34] Thus, the Soviets have had to put up with a deviant Poland almost from the beginning of the communist experiment.

Solidarity's rise in 1980 deepened the sense of Poland's exceptionalism. In addition to strengthening the already quasi-autonomous sectors of society (church, agriculture, and higher education) the movement added a new dimension, namely independent, self-governing unions. Not only priests and farmers wanted autonomy, but industrial workers and their newfound intellectual and professional allies among the intelligentsia were pushing for it. One must, however, note that the cutting edge of the movement is the industrial workers. They give it its élan and its foundation in social democracy, without which it would be limited, as were the Czech and Hungarian rebellions, to the goals of national revival and increasing civil liberties. Because Solidarity is rooted in social democracy as well as in demands for civil liberties and national revival, it is therefore stronger than any other dissenting movement in communist Eastern Europe to date and would seem to be even more threatening to Polish and Soviet adherents of "real existing socialism." However, and this is ultimately the most interesting datum, Solidarity also therefore fits into Marxist and traditional Polish socialist goals, thus providing a bridge across which communists and noncommunists can walk together to reach a new blend of economic and political democracy. It is partly for this reason that the Polish government found it possible to negotiate and sign the Gdansk Accord in August, 1980. Government leaders knew they were not dealing with capitalists or alienated intellectuals longing for "Western freedom." Any assessment of the possibility of breaking the deadlock, of cheating "fate," of sidestepping the "inevitable" must take this interesting fact into account and know that if it happened once, it can happen again.

It is true, of course, that late in 1981, some elements within Solidarity were questioning the continued appropriateness of the Warsaw Pact. As a result, Soviet fears rose to an even greater pitch, and the Kremlin virtually ordered Jaruzelski to act or else. There was a definite threat of intervention, yet it did not take place. Nor had it taken place in the past, when, as in 1956, Khrushchev fretted and stormed at the effrontery of the Poles in bringing Gomulka back and almost ordered the army in. Thus, even in the circumstances of the iron circle there is much room for doubt that Poland is merely at the Kremlin's beck and call.

East Germany is another special case, with the presence of nineteen Soviet divisions proving to be a decisive factor. Because of this presence, there has been no opportunity to test the terms on which the USSR would or could live with "deviation" there. But that is not the whole story. The Soviet Union has had also to deal with a latent but deeply visceral force of change: German nationalism. The USSR has sought to use East German sentiment for a unified Germany as a lure to West Germany, so as to get the latter to turn away from pro-American policies; at the same time, it has sought to prevent that sentiment from pushing East German policy toward such ties with West Germany as might be too close or might seem to threaten Russian strategic interests. The USSR, and the regime in Warsaw, also continue to use the threat of German nationalism as a goad to keep Poland red.

What, then, is deviation, according to the Kremlin? What is the line between acceptable and unacceptable change in Eastern Europe? It is difficult to know it precisely or to know how and when it will be drawn. The bottom line seems to be the Kremlin's perception of its security and, correlatively, its continued opportunity to play the role of a superpower, together with some assurance of a degree of conformity with the Soviet model on the part of the countries of Eastern Europe.

The bottom line may demand invasion, or it may not. It may demand strict conformity with Soviet political economy, or it may not (and usually does not). It may demand Party dominance in everything, or it may not. It may demand ideological verisimilitude, or it may not. Sarah Terry's instructive essay on theories of socialist development in Soviet–Eastern European relations should disabuse anyone of the notion that the Soviet Union has pursued a single, monolithic set of doctrinal guidelines for itself or for Eastern European countries.[35] One may question whether *deviation* has a clear and consistent meaning for the Soviets themselves.

Finally, the bottom line demands some degree of economic linkage and coordination. Such linkage and coordination serve overall security and imperial needs, and they require some measure of consistency between the structures and methods of Soviet political economy and those of the Eastern European countries. Whether they also serve to benefit economically the Soviet system and its people is a moot point. Even if it could be shown that a secret reallocation of products and services of Eastern European resources and skills does take place and is considerable, these—when added to the net flow of trade between Eastern Europe and the Soviet Union—would not indicate such a substantial advantage to the USSR that the economic factor on its own could deeply influence Soviet policy. It is a factor, but separate from geopolitical and imperial concerns and concerns of institutional compatibility, its influence must be judged to be small.[36] One should also note that as the Eastern European economies age and as their pollution and ecological problems deepen, the region may lose even the limited economic attractiveness to the Soviet Union that it has hitherto enjoyed.

In early November, 1987, in a speech to foreign delegates attending the commemoration of the seventieth anniversary of the Bolshevik Revolution, Gorbachev made a major policy statement concerning his government's approach to its allies. He spoke of a new flexibility. He said: "We have satisified ourselves that unity does not mean identity and uniformity. We have also become convinced of there being no 'model' of socialism to be emulated by everyone." Gorbachev outlined five principles. These were, in his words, "unconditional and full equality, the ruling party's responsibility for the state of affairs in the country, concern for the common cause of socialism, respect for one another, and a strict observance of the principles of peaceful co-existence by all."

Gorbachev's remarks may mean that Poland and other countries of Eastern Europe will have greater and more consistent latitude to run their own affairs than heretofore. Nevertheless, the second and third principles are clear reminders of the Soviet Union's intention to keep such autonomy within bounds. The USSR will continue to insist that in each country the ruling party must maintain its "responsibility for the state of affairs," and it will of course continue to express "concern for the common cause of socialism" in the face of perceived deviation. Gorbachev's poilcy is no invitation for Poland to make an internal settlement that could, in the eyes of the Soviet Union, compromise the "responsibility" of the PUWP.

Yet at the same time, there is some leeway, both in terms of what constitutes the correct model of socialism to be followed by the ruling party and in terms of what percisely is the manner in which that party is to execute its "responsibility."[37]

What about the Soviet posture toward the West? It has changed and changed again since the halcyon days of the Revolution. Early revolutionary zeal led to a program of fomenting revolution in the West, an impulse partly dictated by the perceived need, given Russia's backwardness industrially, for capital assistance. Revolutions in industrially advanced countries, so Lenin and Trotsky argued, would install socialist governments there whose new and friendly policies would grant capital assistance and thus shore up and save the Russian Revolution from Thermidor, perhaps even from total failure.

But the revolutionary posture shaded off quickly under Stalin into a posture of "going it alone" and a policy of protection of the Socialist Fatherland against capitalist encirclement. This policy went hand in hand with Russian nationalism to the point where it became questionable whether it was the interests of a sovereign state or a penchant for exporting ideology that truly lay behind the motivations of the Kremlin's Communist masters. Khrushchev modified this posture even further with his talk of peaceful coexistence. He combined this notion with heady anticipation of successful economic competition with the West. His posture may have been induced by a growing awareness of a nuclear standoff between the superpowers. Such an awareness deepened in the 1960s as the USSR strove for parity in numbers of nuclear weapons. Under Brezhnev in the late 1960s and 1970s overall parity and even superiority in some categories of nuclear weapons was achieved, and the Soviet Union paraded a posture of détente. This posture was partly a cover for gaining nuclear parity or even an edge. But it may also have been an ever deeper, though reluctant, acknowledgment of a growing double bind: not only was there the danger inherent in ever larger and more sophisticated systems of nuclear weapons, but there was the correlative danger of a shipwrecked economy. Since the Soviet economy is less developed and weaker than that of the West, a greater proportion of its productive capacity must be devoted to arms in order to keep up with the West in the arms race.

Gorbachev has been forced to face the fact of his economy's vulnerability. And he has been forced to face the rising need to counter the apathy and revitalize the sagging spirits of the peoples of the Soviet

Union. He has also inherited the opportunities presented by the growing awareness of the threat to survival posed by the increasing numbers and sophistication of nuclear weapons and by the imminent proliferation of weapons systems to many other countries. He seems anxious to find answers.

Gone are expectations of communist revolutions everywhere. Gone are expectations of overtaking and surpassing the West economically. Gone as well is the guarded siege mentality that cynically strove for any and every advantage, even to the detriment of the USSR's real interests. Security in stark economic and military terms is now a major preoccupation. The Kremlin appears at last to perceive that security at a fundamental level demands a united world effort to control the Bomb.

Turmoil and instability in Eastern Europe, especially in Poland, is an inherent danger to that security. On the other hand, an attempt to lure Western Europe away from its close military and political ties to the United States is always attractive. Russia enjoys playing the big wheel in Europe and, given the present circumstances, would like to enlarge its role as much as possible. So the situation in Europe for the Soviet Union remains volatile—full of potential sudden dangers, as in Poland, and irresistible opportunities, as in West Germany. It is a situation full of possibilities for the unthinkable to happen. To reduce the volatility may well be to the USSR's growing actual and perceived interests, rendering its leaders amenable to a new geopolitical settlement.

The United States, for its part, will not extend its nuclear umbrella to the countries of Eastern Europe; nor will it commit its armed forces in their defense to protect them from Russian armies. This seems a virtual certainty, given the historical record of the past forty years. In 1956, one should recall, the Hungarians called on the West for assistance in vain. Quite early on in the rebellion the State Department sent messages of reassurance to the Kremlin through Marshal Tito denying any intention on the part of the United States to exploit the conflict against Soviet interests. Eisenhower made his position clear shortly thereafter. "We have never," he said, "urged or argued for any kind of armed revolt. . . . The U.S. does not now and never has advocated open rebellion by an undefended people."[38] American policy for Eastern Europe must proceed along political and not military lines.

But does the United States have a vital interest in Eastern Europe? On the surface, it would not seem to be so. But the United States does have a vital interest in Western Europe—for reasons of culture and civilization, for reasons of economic advantage, and for strategic, geopolitical reasons. But for these same reasons the United States has a deeper, almost hidden, concern for the countries of Eastern Europe. Not only are the latter the staging ground for the deployment of Soviet troops, but, equally important, they are also a breeding ground for turmoil and instability. The combination is filled with potential for frightening and lethal consequences for all of Europe, for America, and for the Soviet Union.

In addition, Western Europe is a continuing worry to the United States, partly because of Eastern Europe. Washington has found it necessary to refuse to renounce a first-strike nuclear response should Russian armies begin any movement into Western Europe. This is a heavy risk physically to the United States and may therefore not even be credible. The countries of Western Europe are not totally happy with this arrangement or with any arrangement for their defense that seems to embroil them automatically in a nuclear shooting match between the two superpowers. Many in Europe therefore would like to opt out, a psychological disposition that the Soviets might like to take advantage of.

It is doubtful that Washington could contemplate with equanimity a serious move by Western Europe to "go it alone" or denuclearize itself. Washington can rely on the apparently dominant social forces in Western Europe to prevent moves in this direction. Yet, increasingly, Western Europe periodically gets into an uproar over the issue. The dominant thinking still seems to be, however, that without the United States an independent Western Europe would be too vulnerable and weak in the face of the Big Bear. It could only with great difficulty withstand the constant threat, if not the actuality, of its embrace. And the threat is itself enough to disincline Western Europe from cutting its military ties with the United States. And on reflection it does not make sense to trade the present uncertainty for what might be an even greater uncertainty. The risks of war would not be lessened if Western Europe were to go it alone. Nor would the situation in Eastern Europe be helped one bit by the neutralization of Western Europe. Indeed it could only be worsened. Repression, for one thing, would only intensify.

So the world does seem to be locked into the unhappy standoff that is in place, and thus Poland, as one of the centerpieces in this international chess game, seems locked in as well.

But once again the analysis must be pushed beyond the usual interpretation of the facts to those same facts seen in their life-sized dimensions. Both the United States and the Soviet Union are exposed, each in its own way, to the volatility of Europe—both Eastern and Western Europe. It must become over time increasingly to their interest to find ways to reduce the volatility. But neither can accomplish this goal unilaterally. They will have to seek out ways, together, to temper an otherwise chronically and endemically explosive situation.

It is not just the threat of annihilation that hangs over their heads, though that should be enough to push them into a common strategic settlement. There is also the daily irritation of dealing with refractory states that become a drag on the policies of the superpowers elsewhere in the world. Latin America, Africa, North Africa and the Near East, South Asia, East Asia—these areas are claiming more and more of the attention of the superpowers. Given such factors as the growth of terrorism and the increasingly deadly threat of nuclear proliferation, there are forces loose in the world that will tax the energy, attention span, and resources of the leaders of both the United States and the USSR. Relatively, the "European fixation" of both will decline. At the same time, the willingness of Eastern and Western European countries to follow the initiatives of their respective patrons and protectors will also decline.

The central point is that Eastern and Western Europe must be thought of together, by both sides together, for solutions to be found. Leaders of both the right and the center in the United States have recently indicated a need to address anew the question of the strategic balance of political forces in Europe—to rethink the kind of Europe compatible with security and with the desire of the various nations to live free of domination by others. President Reagan asserted, on the occasion of the fortieth anniversary of the Warsaw uprising against the Nazis, that the United States "rejects any interpretation of the Yalta Agreement that suggests American consent for the division of Europe into spheres of influence."[39] Reagan, of course, was thinking of the Russian domination of Eastern Europe, but by raising the Yalta issue, he invited scrutiny of the relationship between Western Europe and the United States.

Zbigniew Brzezinski, former President Carter's foreign policy adviser, opened the can of worms wider in a provocative article in *Foreign Affairs* entitled "The Future of Yalta."[40] Although on one level the article is a tiresome reiteration of cold war anxieties and anger, on a deeper level it calls for a bold, new look at Europe as a whole. His recommendations for the future—though angled in a manner to suggest an ultimate absorption of Eastern Europe into Western Europe in the name of a new united Europe—do include the unification of Germany into a loose confederation. Whether his scheme is the "right" one or if some other might be better is less important than that the policy debaters and policy makers do more strategic thinking. The answers will then begin to suit the changing realities of European and world politics. Those changing realities suggest clearly a fundamental modification of the East-West conflict—a move away from a zero-sum mentality and toward strategic accommodation in Europe.

In May, 1987, Jaruzelski, in an address to representatives from the Communist parties of several European nations, put forward a plan for disengagement of both nuclear and conventional weapons in four Eastern European and five Western European countries. He called for the "gradual and mutually agreed withdrawal" of both nuclear and conventional weapons from Poland, Czechoslovakia, East Germany, and Hungary, within the Warsaw Pact, and from Western Germany, Belgium, the Netherlands, Luxembourg, and Denmark, within NATO.[41]

Jaruzelski's proposal, made at the dais by him alone, unaccompanied by any of his Warsaw Pact allies, seemed to signal for Poland a new independence within the Soviet-led alliance, presumably with the blessing of Soviet leader Gorbachev. The proposal reveals the evolutionary character of the political forces in East-West relations. Positions are not cast in stone. Consideration of strategic options does take place on both sides. Such thinking may lead to new policies and new patterns of political life for both sides.

LINKING IRONY AND ACTION

Solutions that give satisfaction, and steps toward them, will come more readily in proportion to the degree to which the sides in the historic East-West conflict perceive that Eastern Europeans, and Western Europeans, too, have their own agendas, whether the two sides like it or not. It is true that the sides can try to meet the problem of "control" with the usual instruments of realpolitik, aimed at each other and at their clients. But given the enormous fact of the Bomb and the correlative likelihood that the "force and fraud" components of realpolitik must end in the use of the Bomb or the gradual attrition of national treasuries or both, it becomes daily more questionable if threats of violence, threats of the withdrawal of the nuclear shield, and related tactics of deceit are still useful as mainsprings of state policy. In such a changing world, it seems that a growing emphasis must be put on finding, through political means and gradually over time, strategic settlements.

Writing in the New York *Times* in early 1987, Michael Mandelbaum and Strobe Talbot described superpower behavior vis-à-vis nuclear weapons as evincing a "peculiar exercise in sublimation." They wrote, "Instead of using these weapons to fight, the two countries have used them to maneuver for political advantage and, at the same time, to diminish the danger of catastrophic military conflict." They called this, with deliberate irony, "the turning of Clausewitz's famous maxim on its head, so that now politics becomes the conduct of war by other means."[42]

The likelihood is strong that this new irony in world affairs will continue. It offers a growing latitude for a political frame of mind, one clearly dominant over the military mind, and for policies that strike new balances.

That is one factor. A second is the growing presence in many European countries of pressures on the regimes in power for significant changes. Poland's Solidarity movement is the leading example, though not the only one. The forces poised in conflict throughout Europe are not that disproportionate in actual power, either externally (between nations) or internally (within nations). Given the stake nearly everyone has in keeping the lid on violence, this juxtaposition of forces can lead to situations of evolving political change—not stability, or war either, but change. And even more important, it can lead to the evolution toward new frameworks within which change can take place consistent with responsibility and participation.

This seems to be especially true of today's Poland. As the years pass since the days of Gdansk in 1980, the major forces within Poland are not too disproportionately matched. The conflict of these "nicely poised" forces has hitherto led to stalemate and to much suffering. But in the absence of recourse to violence, their nicely poised situation must evolve. And it *is* evolving.

The Communist regime in Warsaw (along with its mentor in Moscow) is scraping away some of its harder totalitarian features, even though it is clearly determined to hang on to Party supremacy. On the other hand, the political opposition under the leadership of the central core of Solidarity's councils has has matured under the impact of its experiences, which have included much suffering. It has cast aside extreme tendencies, or shown that it can master them, in order the more resolutely and effectively to persevere in the struggle for genuine forms of economic and political protection and participation for the ordinary person.

Evolution has occurred. A gap remains. But that gap exists within a context of real evolution. Thus action, continued action, is possible. No fate decrees a frozen future. The irony of the Bomb, the irony of forces nicely poised in conflict, the irony of small changes—such ironies ironically invite the liberation of the will. The gap can be closed. Ordinary people can win what Walesa calls a structural security within whose channels a renewed life can flow, a genuine life of the people. This is a worldwide challenge, a worldwide project. The challenge that Walesa poses, that Poland poses, is to win for ordinary people both economic rights and political rights, both social guarantees and civil liberties. Embedded in this challenge is an additional critical point—to seek these rights, and their effective integration, through a transformative, constitutionalizing, nonviolent process. The contexts are different in different parts of the world. In some contexts there are social and economic rights but no political and civil rights. In other contexts the reverse is true. And in still others there are no rights at all. But whatever the context, the challenge is the same. Poland challenges a divided world.

Appendix
The Gdansk Accord

Subsequent to consideration of the Twenty-one Demands put forward by the workforces striking on the Coast, the Government Commission and the Interfactory Strike Committee have reached the following decisions:

With regard to Point One: 'To accept free trade unions, independent of the Party and employers, in accordance with ILO Convention 87 concerning free unions, ratified by Poland', it was established:

1. Trade unions in the Polish People's Republic have not lived up to the hopes and expectations of employees. It is necessary to form new, self-governing trade unions, as authentic representatives of the working class. The right to remain in the present unions is not questioned and we envisage cooperation between unions.

2. The Interfactory Strike Committee declares that the new, independent, self-governing trade unions will accept the bases of the Polish Constitution. The new trade unions will defend the social and material interests of employees and do not intend to act as a political party. They accept the principle of the social ownership of the means of production on which the existing socialist system in Poland is based. While acknowledging the leading role of the Polish United Workers' Party in the state and not questioning the established system of international alliances, their purpose is to provide working people with appropriate means for exercising control, expressing their opinions and defending their own interests.

The Government Commission declares that the government will guarantee and ensure full respect for the independence and self-government of the new trade unions, both as to their organisational structure and to their functioning at all levels of their activity. The government will ensure the new trade unions have every opportunity to fulfil their basic function of defending employees' interests and meeting their material, social and cultural needs. It also guarantees that the new unions will not be subject to any discrimination.

3. The creation and operation of independent, self-governing trade unions accords with ILO Conventions 87 on Freedom of Association and Protection of the Right to Organise and 98 on the Right to Organise and to Collective Bargaining, both ratified by Poland. The increase in the number of trade unions and other bodies representing employees, will necessitate changes in legislation. In particular, the government undertakes to introduce appropriate amendments to the laws on trade unions and workers' self-management and to the Labour Code.

4. The existing strike committees are free to become bodies representing factory employees, such as: workers' or employees' committees, workers' councils or founding committees of the new, self-governing trade unions. The Interfactory Strike Committee, as the Founding Committee of these unions, has a free choice over which form of a single union or association on the Coast to adopt. The founding committees will continue to function until elections of new officials under their statutes. The government undertakes to provide conditions for registration of the new trade unions outside the Central Trade Union Council register.

5. The new trade unions should have a genuine opportunity to express their opinion in public on the major decisions which determine the living standards of working people: the division of the national product between consumption and accumulation; the allocation of the social fund amongst various sectors (health, education and culture); the basic principles for calculation and determination of wages, including that of automatic increases to compensate for inflation; long-term economic planning; the directions of investment and price changes. The government undertakes to provide conditions for fulfilment of these functions.

6. The Interfactory Committee is establishing a centre for social and professional studies. This will undertake objective research into the circumstances of employees, welfare conditions of working people and ways in which employees' interests can best be represented. It will conduct detailed research into wage and price indexing and propose means of compensation. The centre will publish the results of its investigations. The new unions will also have their own publications.

7. The government will ensure observance of the 1949 Law on trade unions, which states in Article One, Paragraph One, that workers and employees have the right of free association in trade unions. The newly-created trade unions will not join the association represented by the Central Trade Union Council. A new law will incorporate this principle. Participation by representatives of the Interfactory Strike Committee or founding committees of self-governing trade unions and other bodies representing employees in drawing up this new law is assured.

With regard to Point Two: 'To guarantee the right to strike and personal safety for strikers and their supporters', it was established:

The right to strike will be guaranteed by the law on trade unions now in preparation. It should lay down conditions for declaring and organising a strike, methods of resolving disputes and liability for breaches of the law. Articles 52, 64 and 65 of the Labour Code will not be used against strikers. Prior to adoption of the law the government guarantees the personal safety of strikers and their helpers, together with their present positions at work.

With regard to Point Three: 'To uphold freedom of expression and publication as guaranteed by the Constitution, not to suppress independent publishing, and to grant access to the mass media for representatives of all denominations', it was established:

1. The government will submit a draft law to the *Sejm* on the control of press and publications within three months. It will be based on the principles that censorship should protect: the state's interests, that is preservation of state and economic secrets which will be more closely defined by law; matters of state security and its major international interests; religious feelings and those of non-believers; and should prevent dissemination of morally damaging material. The draft law will also provide a right of appeal to the Supreme Administrative Court against decisions taken by bodies controlling the press and publications. The right of appeal will also be incorporated into the Code of Administrative Procedure.

2. Religious associations will be granted access to the mass media as part of their religious practice, once various essential and technical questions have been resolved between the organs of state and religious associa-

tions concerned. The government will allow the radio transmission of Sunday mass, in accordance with detailed arrangements to be made with the Episcopate.

3. Broadcasting, the press and publishing should express a diversity of ideas, opinions and evaluations. They should be subject to social control.

4. The press, like members of society and their organisations, should have access to public documents such as administrative acts and social, economic or similar plans issued by the government and its subordinate organs. Exceptions to the principle of openness in administrative activity will be defined by the law, in accordance with sub-point 1.

With regard to Point Four: '(a) To reinstate all those dismissed for participation in the strikes of 1970 and 1976 to their previous positions, and those students expelled from studies for their beliefs or opinions; (b) To release all political prisoners, including Edmund Zadrozynski, Jan Kozlowski and Marek Kozlowski; (c) To cease repression for beliefs or opinions', it was established:

(A) There will be an immediate review of the grounds for dismissals from work after the strikes of 1970 and 1976. In all cases where injustices are confirmed, there will be immediate reinstatement, if desired, recognising any qualifications gained in the meantime. This will also apply to the expelled students, where appropriate.

(B) The cases of persons mentioned in sub-point (b) will be referred to the Minister of Justice for review. He will take the necessary steps within a fortnight. Those persons named who are in prison, will be released pending completion of the judicial procedure.

(C) The bases for detention will be reviewed and persons named in the appendix will be released.

(D) There will be complete observance of freedom of expression and opinion in public and professional life.

With regard to Point Five: 'To put information in the mass media about the formation of the Interfactory Strike Committee and to publish its demands', it was established:

This proposal will be met by publishing the present protocol in the national mass media.

With regard to Point Six: 'To take definite steps to lead the country out of its present crisis by (a) giving the public full information about the social and economic situation and (b) enabling all social groups to participate in discussion of a reform programme', it was established:

We consider it vital to speed up work on economic reform. The authorities will define and publish the basic assumptions of this reform within the next few months. There should be wide public participation in discussing the reform. Trade unions should be involved in the preparation of laws on socialist economic organisations and workers' self-management. The reform of the economy should be based on a radical increase in the independence of enterprises and genuine participation by workers' self-governing institutions in management. There should be appropriate legislation to guarantee that trade unions are able to fulfil the functions defined in Point One of this Agreement.

Only an aware society, well-informed about reality, will be able to initiate and implement a programme for putting our economy in order. The government will radically increase the range of social and economic information made available to the public, to trade unions, and to economic and social organisations.

The Interfactory Strike Committee proposes further: creation of lasting prospects for the development of private peasant farming, the basis of Polish agriculture; equal treatment for the private, state and cooperative sectors of agriculture in access to all the means of production, including land; creation of conditions for the revival of rural self-government.

With regard to Point Seven: 'To pay all employees taking part in the strike wages equivalent to vacation pay for the duration of the strike, and out of Central Trade Union Council funds', it was established:

Members of the workforces on strike will receive 40 per cent of normal wages for the duration of the strike and, on return to work, additional amounts equivalent to 100 per cent of wages for vacation pay, calculated on the basis of an eight-hour day. The Interfactory Strike Committee appeals to the workforce to increase productivity, to economise on raw materials and energy and to improve labour discipline at all levels, in cooperation with the directors of enterprises, workplaces and institutions, once the strike has ended.

With regard to Point Eight: 'To raise the basic pay of every employee by 2000 zlotys a month, to compensate for current cost of living increases', it was established:

The wages of all groups of employees will gradually be raised, above all those of the lowest paid. It was agreed in principle that wages will be raised by individual factories and sectors. They will continue to be implemented as at present, according to specific jobs and trades, by increases of one point on the scale or its equivalent in other elements of wage calculation. For white-collar workers in industry, the increase will consist of one point on the scale. Increases still under discussion will be agreed according to sector and implemented by the end of September this year.

After analysing all sectors, the government, with the agreement of trade unions, will present a programme for increasing the wages of the lowest paid, with particular attention to large families. This will be put forward by 31 October 1980 and come into force on 1 January 1981.

With regard to Point Nine: 'To guarantee automatic wage increases that keep up with price rises and a fall in the value of money', it was established:

It was deemed necessary to halt price increases on basic goods through greater control over the socialised and private sectors and in particular by putting a stop to 'hidden' inflation. The government will do research into determinants of the cost of living. Similar studies will be conducted by trade unions and research institutes. The government will work out a method of compensation for cost of living increases by the end of 1980. After public discussion and acceptance, this will be implemented. The method chosen should take into account the *social minimum*.

With regard to the related points: Ten, 'To supply sufficient food for the domestic market, exporting only and exclusively the surpluses', Eleven, 'To abolish commercial prices and sales for hard currency in shops for *Internal-Export*'; and Thirteen, 'To introduce ration cards for meat and meat products—food coupons—until the market is stabilised', it was established:

Meat supplies will be improved by 31 December 1980 as the result of greater incentives for agricultural production, reduction of meat exports to a minimum, additional meat imports and other measures. A programme for improved meat distribution, including the possibility of introducing rationing, will be presented by the same date.

Foreign currency shops (PEWEX) will not stock Polish products in short supply. Information will be published about decisions and measures taken in regard to market supplies, by the end of the year.

The Interfactory Strike Committee proposes that commercial shops should be closed and the price of meat and meat products be regulated and standardised at an average level.

With regard to Point Twelve: 'To introduce the principle that people in leading positions are chosen on the basis of qualifications rather than Party membership. To abolish privileges of the militia, security service and Party apparatus by equalising family allowances and closing special shops, etc.', it was established:

It is accepted that people in leading positions will be selected on the bases of qualifications and ability, whether they are Party members, members of allied parties or unaffiliated. The government will present a programme for equalising the family allowances of all professional groups, by 31 December 1980. The Government Commission states that shops and cafeteria for their employees are identical to those at other workplaces and offices.

With regard to Point Fourteen: 'To lower the retirement age for women to fifty and for men to fifty-five. To allow retirement of those who have worked continuously in Poland for thirty years for women and thirty-five years for men, regardless of age', it was established:

The Government Commission considers that this proposal cannot be fulfilled in the present economic and demographic circumstances. It may become a subject for discussion in the future.

The Interfactory Strike Committee proposes this be investigated by 31 December 1980. The possibility of retirement five years early for those working in difficult or arduous conditions, after thirty years for women and thirty-five for men, should be considered. In the case of particularly arduous work, retirement should be advanced by at least fifteen years. Early retirement should take place only at the employee's request.

With regard to Point Fifteen: 'To increase pensions and annuities of the old portfolio to present levels', it was established:

The Government Commission declares that the lowest pensions and annuities will be raised annually, within the limits of what the economy can afford and taking account of the increase in lowest wages. A government programme to implement this will be presented by 31 December 1980. The government is working out a scheme by which the lowest pensions and annuities will be raised to the level of the *social minimum*, defined by appropriate research institutes, whose findings will be made public and subject to trade union control.

The Interfactory Strike Committee emphasises the extreme urgency of this matter, reiterates its proposal for the increase of pensions and annuities of the old portfolio to present levels and adds that increases in the cost of living should be taken into account.

With regard to Point Sixteen: 'To improve working conditions in the health service, so that full medical care can be provided for all employees', it was established:

It is recognised that an increase in the building capacity available for health service investment, improved supply of medicines through additional imports of raw materials, higher wages for health service employees (a change in the pay-scale for nurses) and implementation of governmental and regional programmes for the improvement of public health, are urgently needed. Other steps in this direction are appended:

1. Introducing a Charter of Rights for health service workers.

2. Providing an adequate supply of cotton protective clothing.

3. Reimbursing the cost of purchasing protective clothing, from the material cost fund.

4. Awarding special bonuses from the wage fund to all those who distinguish themselves at work.

5. Granting progressive wage supplements to those who have completed twenty-five and thirty years' service.

6. Making extra payment for work in difficult or unhealthy conditions and introducing a bonus for non-medical shift workers.

7. Restoring the supplement for work with patients suffering from contagious diseases, or with contagious biological material and increasing the rate of pay for nurses on night duty.

8. Classifying spinal ailments as an occupational disease of dentists.

9. Allocating high-quality fuel to hospitals and crèches.

10. Paying nurses who lack complete secondary education bonuses equal to those received by nurses with diplomas.

11. Introducing a seven-hour working day for all specialist employees.

12. Introducing free Saturdays which do not have to be made up later.

13. Paying double time for Sunday and holiday duties.

14. Supplying free medicines to health service employees.

15. Enabling part repayment of housing loans from the social fund.

16. Increasing the number of flats allocated to health service workers.

17. Allowing single nurses to be allocated flats.

18. Converting the bonus fund into a thirteenth monthly salary.

19. Granting six weeks' holiday for those with twenty years' service and granting them paid leave for health improvement, like teachers.

20. Allowing four weeks' paid leave for those doing doctorates and two weeks' for those training to become specialists.

21. Guaranteeing doctors the right to a day off after an all-night duty.

22. Five-hour shifts for employees in crèches (as in kindergartens) and free food.

23. Allocating cars to employees of the basic health service and paying a mileage allowance or lump sum for professional journeys.

24. Nurses with higher education are to be regarded and paid the same as other employees with higher education.

25. Forming special maintenance teams in Area Health Authorities to protect health service buildings from further deterioration.

26. Raising the spending-limits on pharmaceuticals from 1138 zlotys to 2700 zlotys per hospital patient since this is the real cost of treatment, and raising the food allowance.

27. Issuing food coupons for the chronically sick.

28. Doubling the supply of medical vehicles in order to meet already existing needs.

29. Ensuring clean air, soil and water, especially along the Coast.

30. Opening new housing estates with health centres, pharmacies and crèche facilities already provided.

With regard to Point Seventeen: 'To provide sufficient crèche and nursery places for children of working mothers', it was established:

The Commission fully supports this proposal. The regional authorities will present the necessary programme by 30 November 1980.

With regard to Point Eighteen: 'To grant paid maternity leave for three years while a mother brings up her child', it was established:
An analysis of whether the economy can afford this will be carried out by 31 December 1980, in cooperation with trade unions. The size and length of paid maternity leave for mothers whose leave is unpaid at present will be determined.
The Interfactory Strike Committee proposes the allowance be the equivalent of full pay for the first year and half pay for the second, but not less than 2000 zlotys a month. The proposal should be implemented in stages from the first half of 1981.

With regard to Point Nineteen: 'To reduce the waiting-time for flats', it was established.
The regional authorities will put forward a programme to improve the housing situation by shortening the waiting-time for flats, by 31 December 1980. The programme will be opened to general public discsussion in the region. There will be consultation with such bodies as the Polish Society of Town Planners, the Association of Polish Architects and the Chief Technical Organisation (NOT). The programme should involve both full utilisation of existing housing factories and a further increase in the building industry's capacity. The same steps will be taken in the rest of the country.

With regard to Point Twenty: 'To increase travelling allowances from 40 to 100 zlotys, plus compensation for separation from family', it was established:
Travelling allowances and compensation for separation from family will be increased from 1 January 1981. The government will present proposals for this by 31 October 1980.

With regard to Point Twenty-one: 'To make all Saturdays work-free. Employees on a three-shift and a four-brigade system will be compensated for the loss of free Saturdays by extension of annual leave or other paid days off, it was established:

Ways of introducing a programme for paid, work-free Saturdays, or some other method of regulation to shorten working hours, will be drawn up and presented by 31 December 1980. The number of paid, work-free Saturdays will start to increase in 1981. Other steps in this direction are included in an appendix.

After the above had been agreed, the government undertakes:

to guarantee the personal safety and present working conditions of participants in the present strike and their helpers;

that the ministries concerned will consider the specific problems of the branches put forward by the workforces on strike;

immediate publication of the full text of the present Agreement in the mass media (press, radio and television).

The Interfactory Strike Committee undertakes to end the strike on 31 August 1980 at 5 P.M.

Notes

CHAPTER 1

1. Both passages are quoted in the *Washington Spectator*, VIII (February 1, 1982), 2.
2. Interview with Jan Radomysky, cofounder of the Polish section of the British Broadcasting Corporation, October 16, 1986.
3. Interview with Jerzy Wiatr, then director of the Marxist-Leninist Institute of the Polish United Workers party, April, 1983.
4. Jeff Frieden, "Poland's Debt: Why the Big Banks Love Martial Law," *Nation*, January 23, 1982, pp. 13–14.
5. Czeslaw Milosz, *The Captive Mind* (New York, 1981), 104.
6. Leszek Szymanski, *Candle for Poland: 469 Days of Solidarity* (San Bernardino, Calif., 1982).
7. New York *Times*, October 26, 1984.
8. A. M. Rosenthal, "The Trees of Warsaw: A Return to Poland," *New York Times Magazine*, August 7, 1983, p. 26.
9. *Ibid.*, 31.

CHAPTER 2

1. Michael T. Kaufman, "For Poles, the Hand Is To Be Kissed," New York *Times*, June 23, 1984.
2. "The Pope in Poland," *Poland Watch*, No. 3 (1983), 1–10.
3. *Crisis and Conflicts: The Case of Poland, 1980–81*, Volume III, No. 2, of *Sisyphus Sociological Studies* (Warsaw, 1982), 174–226; *Poland Watch*, No. 3 (1983), 109–32.

CHAPTER 3

1. Friedrich Nietzsche, *The Use and Abuse of History*, trans. Adrian Collins (Indianapolis, 1977).
2. Hannah Arendt, *Eichmann in Jerusalem* (New York, 1977).
3. Its full name is *Sisyphus Sociological Studies*.
4. Quoted in Claus Offe, "The Greens of Germany," *New Political Science*, No. 11, (Spring, 1983), 14.

CHAPTER 4

1. "To see life steadily and see it whole" is from Thomas Carlyle. But I first encountered these words in lectures on English literature by Professor Henry Zylstra when I attended Calvin College. He quoted it often and inspired me to keep that goal always in mind.
2. Henry Norr, "Solidarity and Self-Management, May–July 1981," *Poland Watch*, No. 7 (1985), 97–122. I have also had the privilege of reading Mr. Norr's later work on the same subject, which he plans to publish in book form.
3. Andrzej Bryk and Kazimierz Dadek, "The Self-Governing Republic: A Critical

Review of the Major Reforms Proposed by Solidarity," *Review of Socialist Law*, No. 11 (1985), 309–31.

4. Jerzy Wiatr, "Polish Society," in *Poland: A Handbook* (Warsaw, 1977), 126–46.

5. "Interview with Jaroslaw Nanowski: Rural Solidarity," *Poland Watch*, No. 5 (1984), 33–42.

6. Anthony Kemp-Welch (ed.), *The Birth of Solidarity: The Gdansk Negotiations, 1980* (New York, 1983), 25.

7. For a sensitive explanation of KOR's ideas, one that sharply refutes Western stereotypical interpretations of intellectuals in popular social movements, see Jan Jozef Lipski, "The Ethos of KOR," *Poland Watch*, No. 3 (1983), 44–78. A work that provides a good background on the evolution of intellectuals in the opposition in Poland is Peter Raina, *Political Opposition in Poland, 1954–1977* (London, 1978).

8. George Sanford, *Polish Communism in Crisis* (New York, 1983), chs. 4–5, cites numerous instances of various technical, professional, and intellectual groups asserting their demands for autonomy after the Gdansk Accord.

9. New York *Times*, August 19, 1983.

10. A trenchant statement of Poland's geopolitical dilemma is offered by J. T., "Realpolitik—The Politics of Realities," in Abraham Brumberg (ed.), *Poland: Genesis of a Revolution* (New York, 1983), 263–71.

11. For this section, in addition to my interviews with government officials and economists in Poland, I rely on several scholarly and interpretative works, including Richard Portes, *The Polish Crisis: Western Economic Policy Options* (London, 1981); Jean Woodall, *The Socialist Corporation and Technocratic Power: The Polish United Workers Party, Industrial Organization, and Work Force Control, 1958–80* (Cambridge, Mass., 1982); Wlodzimierz Brus, *The Economics and Politics of Socialism* (London, 1973); Janusz G. Zielinski, *Economic Reforms in Polish Industry* (London, 1973); Maurice D. Simon and Roger E. Kanet (eds.), *Background to Crisis: Policy and Politics in Gierek's Poland* (Boulder, 1981).

12. George Schopflin, "Stability Through Weakness in Poland," *Conflict Studies*, No. 187 (June, 1986), 1–19.

13. James C. Davies, "Satisfaction and Revolution," in David H. Everson and Joann Poparad Paine, *An Introduction to Systematic Political Science* (Homewood, Ill., 1973), 158–90.

14. Oliver MacDonald, "The Polish Vortex: Solidarity and Socialism," in Tariq Ali (ed.), *The Stalinist Legacy: Its Impact on Twentieth-Century World Politics* (New York, 1984), 456–515; W. W. Adamski, "Structural and Generational Aspects of a Social Conflict," in *Crisis and Conflicts: The Case of Poland 1980–81*, Volume III of *Sisyphus Sociological Studies* (Warsaw, 1982), 49–57.

15. Christopher Cviic, "The Church," in Brumberg (ed.), *Poland: Genesis of a Revolution*, 68–91.

16. On this point of burying one's dead, I have read with profit Fred Jacobs' "Culture and the State: The Dilemmas of Polish Theater," a paper presented at the annual meeting of the American Political Science Association, Washington, D.C., August 30–September 2, 1984.

17. Lawrence Goodwyn, "Building a Democratic Movement: An Interpretation of KOR," paper presented at Harvard University's symposium entitled "KOR: Intellectuals in Democratic Movements—The Polish Experience," February 23, 1985.

CHAPTER 5

1. There is a large literature that questions these dichotomies. E. A. Burtt's *The Metaphysical Foundations of Modern Phycisal Science* (Rev. ed.; London, 1932), though not well known, is an excellent introduction. I especially recommend the following rich and varied works: Hegel's *Preface to the Phenomenology of Mind*, a good edition of which is

the translation by J. B. Baillie (New York, 1967); Georg Lukacs, *History and Class Consciousness*, tr. Rodney Livingstone (London, 1971), esp. the long essay "Reification and the Consciousness of the Proletariat," 83–222; Eric Voegelin, *The New Science of Politics* (Chicago, 1987); John Dewey and Thomas Bentley, *Knowing and the Known* (1949; rpr. Westport, Conn., 1976); Karl Marx, "The German Ideology," in Robert Tucker (ed.), *Marx-Engels Reader* (New York, 1972), 155–86; A. J. Polan, *Lenin and the End of Politics* (Berkeley, 1984); C. S. Lewis, *That Hideous Strength* (New York, 1968); Robert Pirsig, *Zen and the Art of Motorcycle Maintenance* (New York, 1974); Fritjof Capra, *The Tao of Physics* (New York, 1975); Gary Zukav, *The Dancing Wu Li Masters: An Overview of the New Physics* (New York, 1980); Gregory Bateson, *Steps to an Ecology of Mind* (Northvale, N.J., 1987); Joseph Wood Krutch, *The Modern Temper* (New York, 1956); R. G. Collingwood, *Autobiography* (Cambridge, England, 1939); Alfred North Whitehead, *The Function of Reason* (Boston, 1958); and Jurgens Habermas, *Knowledge and Human Interests*, tr. Jeremy J. Shapiro (Boston, 1971). For a work on Poland whose analysis is free of these dualisms and 'that locates the cultural in its material context, see Jeffrey C. Goldfarb, *On Cultural Freedom: An Exploration of Public Life in Poland and America* (Chicago, 1982).

2.   It is likely that Solidarity would respond positively to Gene Sharp, *The Politics of Non-Violent Action* (Boston, 1974), which presents realistic, matter-of-fact arguments for nonviolence.

3.   Vladimir Ilich Lenin, "What Is to Be Done? Burning Questions of Our Movement," in Robert Tucker (ed.), *The Lenin Anthology* (New York, 1975), 12–114.

4.   W. W. Adamski, "Structural and Generational Aspects of a Social Conflict," in *Crisis and Conflicts: The Case of Poland, 1980–81*, Volume III of *Sisyphus Sociological Studies* (Warsaw, 1982), 49–57.

5.   *Cf.* Lipski, "The Ethos of KOR," and Adam Michnik, "Letter from Mokotowski Jail," both in *Poland Watch*, No. 3 (1983), 44–78.

6.   Tadeusz Kawalik, "Experts and the Working Group," in Anthony Kemp-Welch (ed.), *The Birth of Solidarity: The Gdansk Negotiations, 1980* (New York, 1983), 145.

7.   Chapters 4 and 5 of Alaine Touraine *et al.*, *Solidarity: The Analysis of a Social Movement: Poland, 1980–1981*, tr. David Denby (Cambridge, England, 1983), discuss attempted conceptualizations of Solidarity's actions and intentions.

8.   Ewa Hauser, "Censorship and Law," *Poland Watch*, No. 5 (1984), 43–62; Kemp-Welch (ed.), *The Birth of Solidarity*, 1; Adam Michnik, "Statement of Elections and Trial," *Uncensored Poland News Bulletin*, No. 14 (July 19, 1984), 11–14.

9.   Kemp-Welch (ed.), *The Birth of Solidarity*, 48.

10.   Christopher Cviic, "The Church," in Abraham Brumberg (ed.), *Poland: Genesis of a Revolution* (New York, 1983), 92–108.

11.   "The Pope in Poland," *Poland Watch*, No. 3 (1983), 4–7. Italics added.

12.   Norman M. Naimark, *The History of the "Proletariat": The Emergence of Marxism in the Kingdom of Poland, 1870–1877* (New York, 1979), Chs. 4–7.

13.   Neal Ascherson, *The Polish August: The Self Limiting Revolution* (New York, 1982); Touraine *et. al.*, *Solidarity*; Jadwiga Staniszkis, *Poland's Self-Limiting Revolution*, ed. Jan T. Gross (Princeton, 1984).

14.   George Sanford, *Polish Communism in Crisis* (New York, 1983), 82.

15.   See Ayn Rand, *The Fountainhead* (Indianapolis, 1968) and *Atlas Shrugged* (New York, 1957).

16.   New York *Times*, July 18, 1984.

17.   Karl Marx, "Private Property and Communism," "The Meaning of Human Requirements," and "The German Ideology," all in Tucker (ed.), *Marx-Engels Reader*, 81–101, 155; Edmund Husserl, *Cartesian Meditations*, trans. Dorian Cairns (The Hague, 1960); Antonio Gramsci, *Selections from the Prison Notebooks*, trans. Lynne Lawner (New York, 1975).

18.   John Rensenbrink, "The Anti-Nuclear Phenomenon: A New Look at Fundamental Human Interests," *New Political Science*, No. 7 (Fall, 1981), 75–89.

CHAPTER 6

1. For this section I draw on my experience teaching courses on comparative Communist systems, in which a study of Party-state relations in the Soviet Union has been central. The following works are pertinent: John Armstrong, *Ideology, Politics and Government in the Soviet Union* (4th ed.; New York, 1978); Adam B. Ulam, *The Unfinished Revolution: Marxism and Communism in the Modern World* (Boulder, 1979); Jerry F. Hough and Merle Fainsod, *How the Soviet Union Is Governed* (Cambridge, Mass., 1979); Roy A. Medvedev, *On Socialist Democracy* (New York, 1975); David K. Shipler, *Russia: Broken Idols, Solemn Dreams* (New York, 1983); Chalmers Johnson (ed.), *Change in Communist Systems* (Stanford, 1970); H. Gordon Skilling and Franklin Griffiths (eds.), *Interest Groups in Soviet Politics* (Princeton, 1971); Skilling, "Interest Groups and Communist Politics Revisited," *World Politics*, XXXVI (October, 1983), 1–27; Stephen F. Cohen, *Rethinking the Soviet Experience* (New York, 1985); Aleksander Zinoviev, *The Reality of Communism*, tr. Charles Janson (London, 1985); Richard Pipes, *Survival Is Not Enough* (New York, 1985); Eugene Huskey, "Limits to Institutional Autonomy in the USSR: The Case of Audokatura," *Soviet Studies*, XXXIV (April, 1982), 200–27; Alexander Shtromos, "Dissent and Political Change in the Soviet Union," *Studies in Comparative Communism*, XII (Summer–Autumn, 1979), 212–43.

2. In my interviews in Poland I especially sought information about and interpretation of the significant events in the period of Solidarity's legal existence—from August, 1980, to Jaruzelski's military takeover in December, 1981. These interviews provoked in me a process of questioning that led to the understanding of Solidarity's political evolution presented in the rest of this chapter. Reading Volume III of the *Sisyphus Sociological Studies* in Poland was an important experience. Particularly important also were Solidarity's twenty-one demands (see Appendix) and the transcription of tape recordings of the negotiations leading to the Gdansk Accord in Anthony Kemp-Welch (ed.), *The Birth of Solidarity: The Gdansk Negotiations, 1980* (New York, 1983). Also significant was "the Program of the Independent Self-Governing Trade Union Solidarity Adopted by the First National Congress of Delegations, 1981" (pamphlet in author's possession), which emerged from Solidarity's congress in September–October, 1981. During my return visit to Poland in June, 1985, I picked up the threads of conversations with scholars, journalists, and activists whom I had interviewed before and also interviewed other persons. Especially helpful were conversations with Professors Jan Jerschina and Andrzej Bryk of the Jagiellonian University. In addition, the following works are insightful on the march of events from the August days to the December trauma sixteen months later: Kevin Ruane, *The Polish Challenge* (London, 1982); Lawrence Weschler, *The Passion of Poland: From Solidarity to the State of War* (New York, 1984); Alain Touraine *et al.*, *Solidarity: The Analysis of a Social Movement: Poland, 1980–1981*, tr. David Denby (Cambridge, England, 1983); George Sanford, *Polish Communism in Crisis* (New York, 1983); Abraham Brumberg (ed.), *Poland: Genesis of a Revolution* (New York, 1983); Jadwiga Staniszkis, *Poland's Self-Limiting Revolution*, ed. Jan T. Gross (Princeton, 1984); Jerry F. Hough, *The Polish Crisis: American Policy Options* (Washington, D.C., 1982); Neal Ascherson, *The Polish August: The Self-Limiting Revolution* (New York, 1982); Jean Yves Potel, *The Promise of Solidarity*, tr. Phil Markham (New York, 1982); Stanislaw Starksi, *Class Struggles in Classless Poland* (Boston, 1982); Timothy Garton Ash, *The Polish Revolution: Solidarity* (New York, 1984); Leszek Szymanski, *Candle for Poland: 469 Days of Solidarity* (San Bernardino, Calif., 1982); Bogdan Szajkowski, *Next to God . . . Poland: Politics and Religion in Contemporary Poland* (New York, 1983); Martin Myant, *Poland: A Crisis for Socialism* (London, 1982); Oliver MacDonald (ed.), *Polish August: Documents from the Beginnings of the Polish Workers' Rebellion* (Seattle, 1982); Jack Bielasiak and Maurice D. Simon (eds.), *Polish Politics: Edge of the Abyss* (New York, 1984); John Hennig *et al.*, *New Foundations: The Polish Strike Wave of 1980–81* (Kent, Ohio, 1981); Michael Checinski, *Poland: Communism, Nationalism, Anti-Semitism*, translated in part by Tadeusz Szafer (New York, 1982).

3. Ruane, *The Polish Challenge*, 71–75; Szajkowski, *Next to God . . . Poland*, 105–108.

4. Henry Norr, "Solidarity and Self-Management, May–July 1981," *Poland Watch*, No. 7 (1985), 97–122.

CHAPTER 7

1. "Program of the Independent Self-Governing Trade Union Solidarity Adopted by the First National Congress of Delegations, 1981" (pamphlet in author's possession). The quotations are from the first section, "Who Are We and What Are Our Aspirations?"

2. Underground publications by the Promienisci group, such as Marian Pilka's "Deformation of History in High School Textbooks," were included in an exhibit on Polish underground activity in the Widener Library at Harvard in December, 1985.

3. *Uncensored Poland News Bulletin*, No. 22 (November 14, 1985), 11–12.

4. New York *Times*, October 11, 1985.

5. The statements from *Tygodnik Mazowsze* were translated and published in *Uncensored Polish News Bulletin*, No. 18 (September 12, 1985), 16–22. The relevant issues of *Tygodnik Mazowsze* are No. 137 and No. 138, August 8 and 15, 1985.

6. *Tygodnik Mazowsze*, No. 136 (July 25, 1985). The interview was translated and published in *Uncensored Poland News Bulletin*, No. 19 (September 26, 1985), 13–15.

7. *Polska Mlodziez* (Polish Youth) (Warsaw, 1985), 94–95. The figures were reported in *Uncensored Poland News Bulletin*, No. 13 (July 1, 1986), 13–14.

8. Michael T. Kaufman, "Polish Echoes—and Ironies," *New York Times Magazine*, August 25, 1985, p. 28.

9. *Ibid.*, 38.

10. For an example of a conventional scholarly conception of revolution, consult Mark N. Hagopian, *The Phenomenon of Revolution* (New York, 1974), a leading text.

11. "Program of the Independent Self-Governing Trade Union Solidarity, 1981"; "Poland Five Years After August." The latter is available from the Coordinating Office Abroad of Solidarity, Brussels. Excerpts, including the foreword by Lech Walesa and the Summary of Conclusions, appeared in *Uncensored Poland News Bulletin*, No. 20 (October 9, 1985), 8–13, and No. 21 (October 24, 1985), 14–18.

12. Eric Voegelin, *The New Science of Politics* (Chicago, 1987).

13. Albert Camus has touched on the relation of violence and ideology in *The Rebel*, trans. Anthony Bower (Harmondsworth, England, 1962). An interesting recent work on this question is A. J. Polan, *Lenin and the End of Politics* (Berkeley, 1984).

14. Many authors either assume or overtly proclaim the end of ideology, especially in the United States. They refer to the substitution of materialist values for "idealistic" or "millenarian" constructions of future bliss. Leading figures are Daniel Bell and Seymour Martin Lipset.

15. Milan Kundera, *The Unbearable Lightness of Being*, trans. Michael Henry Heim (New York, 1984), 100.

CHAPTER 8

1. New York *Times*, October 29, 1984, December 17, 1984.

2. *Uncensored Poland News Bulletin*, No. 17 (August 29, 1985), 12–13.

3. Bogdan Szajkowski, *Next to God . . . Poland: Politics and Religion in Contemporary Poland* (New York, 1983), 218.

4. *Uncensored Poland News Bulletin*, No. 11 (May 22, 1985), 10.

5. *Ibid.*, No. 4 (February 20, 1986), 12–13.

6. *Ibid.*, No. 13 (July 1, 1986), 7, and No. 3 (February 3, 1987), 6.

7. *Ibid.*, No. 19 (September 29, 1987), 10.

8. *Ibid.*, No. 21 (October 30, 1987), 10–11.

9. *Ibid.*, No. 20 (October 9, 1985), 11.

10. *Ibid.*, No. 5 (March 5, 1984), 22.

11. These and the quotations by Hall that follow are from Adam Bromke, *Eastern Europe in the Aftermath of Solidarity* (New York, 1985), 195–98.

12. "An Interview with KOS, the Committee for Social Resistance," *Poland Watch*, No. 5 (n.d.), 131–41; "Message of KOS (Committee for Social Resistance) to END [European Nuclear Disarmament] Convention in Amsterdam, 29 June 1985," *Uncensored Poland News Bulletin*, No. 15 (July 25, 1985), 17; "Underground Society: Draft Manifesto of the Interim Coordinating Committee of the NSZZ Solidarnosc, July 28, 1982," *Communist Affairs: Documents and Analysis*, II (April, 1983), 250–51.

13. *Uncensored Poland News Bulletin*, No. 15 (August 2, 1984), 36.

14. *Ibid.*, 29–42.

15. It is sometimes bemusing to hear the often uncritical claims made for the West by otherwise intelligent Polish authors and activists. To assert, as does the Independence group in their declaration, that the West practices these principles is to invite the raised eyebrow. They might have said the West *strives* to practice such principles, but to assert that it actually practices them is naïve.

16. *Uncensored Poland News Bulletin*, No. 3 (January 31, 1985), 34.

17. *Ibid.*, No. 20 (October 9, 1985), 27.

18. *Newsweek*, September 2, 1985, p. 33.

19. *Uncensored Poland News Bulletin*, No. 22 (November 30, 1986), 30–31.

20. *Ibid.*, No. 17 (August 29, 1985), 12–13.

21. *Ibid.*

22. *Ibid.*, No. 22 (November 14, 1985), 22.

23. New York *Times*, August 31, 1985.

24. Boston *Globe*, April 4, 1985.

25. *Uncensored Poland News Bulletin*, No. 13 (July 1, 1986), 14–15.

26. For Szezepanski's statement and Szajkowski's response see Szajkowski, *Next to God . . . Poland*, 187. See also Dieter Bingen, "The Catholic Church as a Political Actor," in Jack Bielasiak and Maurice D. Simon (eds.), *Polish Politics: The Edge of the Abyss* (New York, 1984), 212–40.

27. "Cardinal Stefan Wyszynski to the Members of the Main Council of the Polish Episcopate, Warsaw, 22 May 1981," in Szajkowski, *Next to God . . . Poland*, Appendix II.

28. Professor Jerschina presented a lecture in Krakow on the cultural values of Polish youth to the Seminar on Contemporary Poland for visiting American professors in June, 1985, a seminar sponsored jointly by Jagiellonian University and the Institute for European Studies. From the lecture, from extended conversations with him later, and from his paper entitled "Catholicism and the Political Ethos of Poland," I gained a deeper sense of the impact of the Catholic church, not only in slowing the loss of faith and spiritual values that seems consequent on the industrialization of society, but in promoting a new and creative integration of "rationality" and "spirit," especially among the young people of Poland.

29. William Beecher, "Farm Aid Pitfalls in Poland," Boston *Globe*, July 22, 1983.

30. "Has Walesa Been Dumped?" *Newsweek*, July 11, 1983, p. 27.

31. "The Pope in Poland," *Poland Watch*, No. 3 (Spring–Summer, 1983), 1–10.

32. New York *Times*, July 1, July 29, September 5, November 19, December 5, December 20, 1983, January 7, 1984.

33. Boston *Globe*, January 20, 1984; New York *Times*, January 28, 1984. One may imagine the hard bargaining among the bishops and the resolute caution of Glemp at work in the sessions that produced this statement.

34. *Ibid.*, February 16, February 21, February 22, 1984.

35. *Ibid.*, March 9, March 10, March 14, March 15, March 17, March 31, April 4, April 7, 1984.

36.   *Ibid.*, March 13, August 16, August 27, August 6, August 9, October 1, August 30, 1984.

37.   Michael Kaufman, "Polish News: Provided (and Made) by Jerzy Urban," *New York Times*, March 23, 1985.

38.   Dawid Warszawski, "The Strategy of Provocation," *Uncensored Poland News Bulletin*, No. 2 (January 17, 1985), 20–22. The article originally appeared in the underground publication *KOS*, No. 63 (November 5, 1984). Glemp's words are taken from an interview that appeared in the Italian publication *Famiglia Cristiana*, No. 47 (1985), and was translated for publication in *Uncensored Poland News Bulletin*, No. 1 (January 2, 1986), 30–32. The part of the interview dealing with the primate's relations with Popieluszko was printed by the official weekly *Polityka*, No. 49 (December 7, 1985).

39.   *New York Times*, January 17, February 8, 1985.

40.   *Portland Press Herald*, April 25, 1985; *New York Times*, May 2, May 21, June 7, 1985.

41.   *New York Times*, September 16, 1985; *Uncensored Poland News Bulletin*, No. 17 (August 29, 1985), 9.

42.   *Uncensored Poland News Bulletin*, No. 18 (September 12, 1985), 7–8, and No. 21 (October 24, 1985), 29; *New York Times*, September 16, 1985.

43.   *Uncensored Poland News Bulletin*, No. 21 (October 24, 1985), 8.

44.   *New York Times*, November 5, 1984.

45.   "Program of the Independent Self-Governing Trade Union Solidarity adopted by the First National Congress of Delegations, 1981" (pamphlet in author's possession); "Poland Five Years After August," *Uncensored Poland News Bulletin*, No. 20 (October 9, 1985), 8–13.

46.   *Uncensored Poland News Bulletin*, No. 15 (July 25, 1985), 3.

47.   *Ibid.*, No. 18 (1985), 7–8, 33–35.

48.   *Ibid.*, No. 16 (August 8, 1985), 5. For an earlier and much-cited report on the environmental crisis, see Eugeniusz Pudlis, "Poland's Plight: Environment Damage from Air Pollution and Acid Rain," *Ambio*, XII (1983), 65–83.

49.   *Uncensored Poland News Bulletin*, No. 15 (July 25, 1985), 36–37.

50.   *New York Times*, May 20, 1986.

51.   *Ibid.*, September 24, 1985.

52.   This information is from my notes on lectures on Poland's agriculture by Polish scholars at the Seminar on Contemporary Poland held in Krakow in June, 1985.

53.   Szajkowski, *Next to God . . . Poland*, 216.

54.   In June, 1985, I conducted several interviews with scholars involved in this project.

55.   Walesa, in a dramatic and pointed way, in December, 1983, contributed his Nobel Peace Prize award (about $200,000) to the church-sponsored agricultural fund, to be held in escrow until the time it was established. Unfortunately, the protracted negotiations for the fund collapsed in September, 1986. A truncated version of such a fund, however, was established after negotiations between the government and the church in the fall of 1987.

CHAPTER 9

1.   *Uncensored Poland News Bulletin*, No. 18 (September 12, 1985), 16.

2.   *New York Times*, August 30, 1984.

3.   A high official in the prime minister's office gave the figure of 20 percent to those of us participating in the Seminar on Contemporary Poland held in Krakow in June, 1985.

4.   Seminar on Contemporary Poland, Krakow, June, 1985.

5.   *Uncensored Poland News Bulletin*, No. 22 (November 14, 1985), 11.

6.   *Tygodnik Mazowsze*, No. 146 (November 14, 1985), quoted in *Ibid.*, No. 24 (December 19, 1985), 17–18; "TKK's Plenipotentiary, Konrad Bielinski, on the Methodol-

ogy Employed by Solidarity," interview in *Tygodnik Mazowsze*, No. 142 (October 17, 1985), quoted in *Uncensored Poland News Bulletin*, No. 22 (November 14, 1985), 13–16.

7. *Uncensored Poland News Bulletin*, No. 24 (December 19, 1985), 18.

8. The TKK statement of October 22, 1985, was signed by Bogdan Borusewicz for the Gdansk region, Zbigniew Bujak for the Warsaw region, and Marek Muszynski for the Wroclaw region. Representatives of the Krakow and Upper Silesia regions also attended. *Ibid.*, No. 23 (November 29, 1985), 8. See also *Ibid.*, No. 22 (November 14, 1985), 16.

9. *Uncensored Poland News Bulletin*, No. 21 (October 30, 1987), 16.

10. New York *Times*, November 17, 1987.

11. *Uncensored Poland News Bulletin*, No. 21 (October, 30, 1987), 11.

12. New York *Times*, December 1, 1987.

13. *Ibid.*

14. A complete translation of the article appears in *Uncensored Poland News Bulletin*, No. 22 (November 13, 1987).

15. Bernard Crick, in his engaging book *In Defense of Politics* (New York, 1964), makes an important distinction between diplomatic language on one hand and full political speech between citizens in a republic on the other. The former occurs between those in mutually exclusive spheres, *e.g.* separate sovereign nations. The latter can occur only in a mutually inclusive sphere of action and decision, though it does not always do so. Diplomatic speech may foreshadow political discourse, but at best it is only anticipatory of such discourse. See especially chapter 1 of Crick's book.

16. New York *Times*, November 28, 1983.

17. Michael Kaufman, "Polish News: Provided (and Made) by Jerzy Urban," New York *Times*, March 23, 1985.

18. The New York *Times* gave front-page coverage to Walesa's Nobel lecture. New York *Times*, December 12, 1983. See also Portland *Press Herald*, December 6, 1983.

19. New York *Times*, December 8, December 9, 1983.

20. Boston *Globe*, January 20, 1984; New York *Times*, January 21, 1984.

21. Boston *Globe*, January 20, 1984; New York *Times*, January 20, 1984.

22. New York *Times* and Washington *Post* interviews with Jaruzelski, September 29, 1985.

23. *Ibid.* Two days after the election Urban said that as of election day there were 327 political prisoners.

24. *Uncensored Poland News Bulletin*, No. 20 (October 9, 1985), 5.

25. New York *Times*, November 11, 1985.

26. *Uncensored Poland News Bulletin*, No. 21 (November 16, 1986), 13.

27. *Ibid.*, No. 19 (October 14, 1986), 10.

28. Michael Kaufman, "Underground, an Illicit Polish Press Flourishes," Bath-Brunswick *Times-Record*, September 13, 1985.

29. See the analysis in Stephen F. Cohen, "The Friends and Foes of Change: Reformism and Conservatism in the Soviet Union," *Slavic Review*, XXXVIII (June, 1979), 187–203.

30. *Time*, September 9, 1985, p. 29.

31. New York *Times*, December 18, 1986, January 29, 1987, January 27, 1986.

32. In Hungary in 1956 the situation may have been turning in the direction of a greater role for industrial workers in the leadership of the opposition, but Russian tanks precluded any further such development. See Chris Harman, *Class Struggles in Eastern Europe, 1945–1983* (2nd ed.; London, 1983).

33. J. T., "Realpolitik—The Politics of Realities," in Abraham Brumberg (ed.), *Poland: Genesis of a Revolution* (New York, 1983), 264-71; Roger E. Kanet, "The Polish Crisis and Poland's 'Allies': The Soviet and East European Response to Events in Poland," in Jack Bielasiak and Maurice D. Simon (eds.), *Polish Politics: Edge of the Abyss* (New York, 1984), 319-20.

34. Jacek Jedruch, *Constitutions, Elections, and Legislatures of Poland, 1493–1977: A Guide to Their History* (Washington, D.C., 1982). Jedruch highlights the development of Poland's legislative institutions and provides a clear understanding of the significance of that long legislative tradition for contemporary Polish society. On this topic see also Norman Davies, *God's Playground: A History of Poland* (2 vols.; London, 1981); and Aleksander Gieysztor *et al.*, *History of Poland* (2nd ed.; Warsaw, 1979).

35. Sarah M. Terry, "Theories of Socialist Development in Soviet–East European Relations," in Terry (ed.), *Soviet Policy in Eastern Europe* (New Haven, 1984), 221–54.

36. Paul Marer, "The Political Economy of Soviet Relations with Eastern Europe," in Terry (ed.), *Soviet Policy in Eastern Europe*, 169. See also Alec Nove and H. H. Holiman, *The East European Economies in the 1970s* (London, 1982), 155–88.

37. New York *Times*, November 5, 1987.

38. Harman, *Class Struggles in Eastern Europe*, 161.

39. New York *Times*, August 18, 1984.

40. Zbigniew Brzezinski, "The Future of Yalta," *Foreign Affairs*, LXIII (Winter 1984–85), 279–302.

41. New York *Times*, May 9, 1987.

42. Michael Mandelbaum and Strobe Talbot, "What Arms Control Is All About," New York *Times*, January 30, 1987.

Selected Bibliography

BOOKS AND ARTICLES IN BOOKS

Althusser, Louis. "Marx's Immense Theoretical Revolution." In *The Structuralists from Marx to Levi-Strauss*, edited by Richard and Fernande De George. Garden City, N.Y., 1972.

Arendt, Hannah. *Eichmann in Jerusalem*. New York, 1977.

———. *The Human Condition*. Chicago, 1959.

Armstrong, John A. *Ideology, Politics and Government in the Soviet Union*. 4th ed. New York, 1978.

Ascherson, Neal. *The Polish August: The Self Limiting Revolution*. New York, 1982.

Ash, Timothy Garton. *The Polish Revolution: Solidarity*. New York, 1984.

Bateson, Gregory. *Steps to an Ecology of Mind*. Northvale, N.J., 1987.

Bialer, Seweryn. *Stalin's Successors: Leadership, Stability, and Change in the Soviet Union*. New York, 1980.

Bielasiak, Jack, and Maurice D. Simon, eds. *Polish Politics: Edge of the Abyss*. New York, 1984.

Blazyca, George. *Poland to the 1990's: Retreat or Reform?* Special Report No. 1061 by the *Economist* Intelligence Unit. London, 1986.

Bloch, Alfred, ed. *The Real Poland: An Anthology of National Self-Perception*. New York, 1982.

Brinton, Crane. *The Anatomy of Revolution*. New York, 1965.

Bromke, Adam. *Eastern Europe in the Aftermath of Solidarity*. New York, 1985.

Brumberg, Abraham, ed. *Poland: Genesis of a Revolution*. New York, 1983.

Brus, Wlodzimierz. *The Economics and Politics of Socialism*. London, 1973.

Brzezinski, Zbigniew. *The Soviet Bloc*. Cambridge, Mass., 1967.

Burtt, E. A. *The Metaphysical Foundations of Modern Physical Science*. Rev. ed. London, 1932.

Camus, Albert. *The Rebel*. Translated by Anthony Bower. Harmondsworth, England, 1962.

Capra, Fritjof. *The Tao of Physics*. New York, 1975.

Casals, Felipe Garcia. *The Syncretic Society*. Translated by Guy Daniels.
White Plains, N.Y., 1980.

Checinski, Michael. *Poland: Communism, Nationalism, Anti-Semitism*. Translated in part by Tadeusz Szafer. New York, 1982.

Cohen, Stephen F. *Rethinking the Soviet Experience*. New York, 1985.

Collingwood, R. G. *An Autobiography*. Cambridge, England, 1939.

Crick, Bernard. *In Defense of Politics*. New York, 1964.

Curry, Jane Leftwich, ed. and trans. *The Black Book of Polish Censorship*.
New York, 1984.

Czaplinski, Wladyslaw, ed. *The Polish Parliament at the Summit of Its
Development (16th–17th Centuries)*. Translated by Janina Dorosz.
Warsaw, 1985.

Davies, James C. "Satisfaction and Revolution." In *An Introduction to
Systematic Political Science*, edited by David H. Everson and Joann
Poparod Paine. Homewood, Ill., 1973.

Davies, Norman. *God's Playground: A History of Poland*. 2 vols. New
York, 1982.

Dewey, John, and Thomas Bentley. *Knowing and the Known*. 1949;
repr. Westport, Conn., 1976.

De Weydenthal, Jan, Bruce D. Porter, and Kevin Devlin. *The Polish
Drama, 1980–1982*. Lexington, Mass., 1983.

Experience and the Future Discussion Group. *Poland Today: The State
of the Republic*. Translated by Michael Vole *et al*. Armonk, N.Y.,
1981.

Friere, Paulo. *Pedagogy of the Oppressed*. Translated by Myra Bergman
Ramos. New York, 1970.

Gati, Charles. *The International Politics of Eastern Europe*. New York,
1976.

Gieysztor, Aleksander, *et al*. *History of Poland*. 2nd ed. Warsaw, 1979.

Goldfarb, Jeffrey C. *On Cultural Freedom: An Exploration of Public Life
in Poland and America*. Chicago, 1982.

Gomulka, Stanislaw. *Growth, Innovation, and Reform in Eastern Europe*. Madison, 1986.

Gramsci, Antonio. *Selections from the Prison Notebooks*. Translated by
Lynne Lawner. New York, 1975.

Habermas, Jurgen. *Knowledge and Human Interests*. Translated by Jeremy J. Sharpiro. Boston, 1971.

Hagopian, Mark N. *The Phenomenon of Revolution*. New York, 1974.

Hann, C. M. *A Village Without Solidarity: Polish Peasants in Years of Crisis*. New Haven, 1985.

Harman, Chris. *Class Struggles in Eastern Europe, 1945–1983*. 2nd ed. London, 1983.

Hegel, Georg Wilhelm Friedrich. *Philosophy of Right*. Translated by T. M. Knox. Oxford, 1949.

――――. *Preface to the Phenomenology of Mind*. Translated by J. B. Baillie. New York, 1967.

Hennig, John, *et al. New Foundations: The Polish Strike Wave of 1980–81*. Kent, Ohio, 1981.

Hough, Jerry F., and Merle Fainsod. *How the Soviet Union Is Governed*. Cambridge, Mass., 1979.

Husserl, Edmund. *Cartesian Meditations*. Translated by Dorion Cairns. The Hague, 1960.

Hutchings, Robert L. *Soviet-East European Relations, 1968–1980*. Madison, Wis., 1984.

Jedruch, Jacek. *Constitutions, Elections, and Legislatures of Poland, 1493–1977: A Guide to Their History*. Washington, D.C., 1982.

Johnson, Chalmers, ed. *Change in Communist Systems*. Stanford, 1970.

Jones, Christopher D. *Soviet Influence in Eastern Europe*. New York, 1981.

Kemp-Welch, Anthony, ed. *The Birth of Solidarity: The Gdansk Negotiations, 1980*. New York, 1983.

Koraszewski, Andrzej. *Najslabsze Ogniwo*. Stockholm, 1985.

Korbonski, Andrzej. *Politics of Socialist Agriculture in Poland, 1945–60*. New York, 1965.

Korbonski, Andrzej, and Roman Kolkowicz, eds. *Soldiers, Peasants, and Bureaucrats: Civil-Military Relations in Communist and Modernizing Societies*. London, 1982.

Krutch, Joseph Wood. *The Modern Temper*. New York, 1956.

Kundera, Milan. *The Unbearable Lightness of Being*. Translated by Michael Henry Heim. New York, 1984.

Lenin, Vladimir Ilich. "What Is to Be Done? Burning Questions of Our

Movement." In *The Lenin Anthology*, edited by Robert C. Tucker. New York, 1975.

Lewis, C. S. *That Hideous Strength*. New York, 1968.

Lukacs, Georg. "Reification and the Consciousness of the Proletariat." In Lukacs, *History and Class Consciousness*, translated by Rodney Livingstone. London, 1971.

MacDonald, Oliver. "The Polish Vortex: Solidarity and Socialism."In *The Stalinist Legacy: Its Impact on Twentieth-Century World Politics*, edited by Tariq Ali. New York, 1984.

———. ed. *Polish August: Documents from the Beginnings of the Polish Workers Rebellion*. Seattle, 1982.

Marer, Paul. "The Political Economy of Soviet Relations with Eastern Europe." In *Soviet Policy in Eastern Europe*, edited by Sarah M. Terry. New Haven, 1984.

Medvedev, Roy A. *On Socialist Democracy*. Translated and edited by Ellen de Kadt. New York, 1975.

———. *On Soviet Dissent*. Translated by William A. Packer and edited by George Saunders. New York, 1980.

Michnik, Adam. *Letters from Prison and Other Essays*. Translated by Maya Latynski. Berkeley, 1985.

Miliband, Ralph. *The State in Capitalist Society*. New York, 1969.

Milosz, Czeslaw. *The Captive Mind*. New York, 1981.

Montias, John M. *Central Planning in Poland*. New Haven, 1962.

Mur, Jan. *A Prisoner of Martial Law: Poland, 1981–1982*. Translated by Lillian Vallee. San Diego, 1984.

Myant, Martin. *Poland: A Crisis for Socialism*. London, 1982.

Myslek, W. *Kosciol, Katolicki w Polsce w Latach, 1918–39*. Warsaw, 1966.

Naimark, Norman M. *The History of the "Proletariat": The Emergence of Marxism in the Kingdom of Poland, 1870–1877*. New York, 1979.

Nietszche, Friedrich. *The Use and Abuse of History*. Translated by Adrian Collins. Indianapolis, 1977.

Nove, Alec, and H. H. Holiman, eds. *The East European Economies in the 1970's*. London, 1982.

Pateman, Carole. *Participation and Democratic Theory*. Cambridge, England, 1970.

Pipes, Richard. *Survival Is Not Enough*. New York, 1985.

Pirsig, Robert M. *Zen and the Art of Motorcycle Maintenance.* New York, 1974.

Polan, A. J. *Lenin and the End of Politics.* Berkeley, 1984.

Polonsky, Anthony. *Politics in Independent Poland, 1921–1939.* Oxford, 1972.

Portes, Richard. *The Polish Crisis: Western Economic Policy Options.* London, 1981.

Potel, Jean Yves. *The Promise of Solidarity.* Translated by Phil Markham. New York, 1982.

Raina, Peter. *Political Opposition in Poland, 1954–1977.* London, 1978.

Rand, Ayn. *Atlas Shrugged.* New York, 1957.

Rensenbrink, John. "How Change Does and Does Not Take Place: Innovation and Recurrence in Educational Reform Programs." In National Institute of Education—Educational Resources Information Center, *Resources in Education.* Arlington, Va., 1977.

Rothman, Stanley, and George W. Breslauer. *Soviet Politics and Society.* St. Paul, 1978.

Ruane, Kevin. *The Polish Challenge.* London, 1982.

Sanford, George. *Polish Communism in Crisis.* New York, 1983.

Sarason, Seymour B. *The Culture of the School and the Problem of Change.* Boston, 1971.

Schon, David. *Beyond the Stable State.* New York, 1973.

Seidler, Grzegorz L. *In Search of the Dominant Idea.* Lublin, 1984.

———. *Essays in Polish History.* Lublin, 1982.

Sharp, Gene. *The Politics of Non-Violent Action.* Boston, 1974.

Shipler, David K. *Russia: Broken Idols, Solemn Dreams.* New York, 1983.

Simon, Maurice D., and Franklin Griffiths, eds. *Interest Groups in Soviet Politics.* Princeton, N.J., 1971.

Simon, Maurice D., and Roger E. Kanet, eds. *Background to Crisis: Policy and Politics in Gierek's Poland.* Boulder, Colo., 1981.

Solidarity. *Poland in 1985.* Approved by Lech Walesa. Brussels, 1986.

———. *On Reforming the Polish Economy.* Approved by Lech Walesa. Brussels, 1987.

Staniszkis, Jadwiga. *Poland's Self-Limiting Revolution.* Edited by Jan T. Gross. Princeton, N.J., 1984.

Starksi, Stanislaw. *Class Struggles in Classless Poland.* Boston, 1982.

Stehle, Hans J. *Eastern Politics in the Vatican, 1917–1979.* Athens, Ohio, 1984.

Strong, John W., ed. *The Soviet Union Under Brezhnev and Kosygin.* New York, 1971.

Szajkowski, Bogdan. *Next to God . . . Poland: Politics and Religion in Contemporary Poland.* New York, 1983.

Sztompka, Piotr, ed. *Masters of Polish Sociology.* Warsaw, 1984.

Szymanski, Leszek. *Candle for Poland: 469 Days of Solidarity.* San Bernardino, 1982.

Taras, Ray. *Poland: Socialist State, Rebellious Nation.* Boulder, 1986.

Tazbir, Janus. *A State Without Stakes: Religious Toleration in Reformation Poland.* New York, 1986.

Terry, Sarah M. "Theories of Socialist Development in Soviet-East European Relations." In *Soviet Policy in Eastern Europe,* edited by Sarah M. Terry. New Haven, 1984.

Touraine, Alaine, *et al. Solidarity: The Analysis of a Social Movement: Poland, 1980–1981.* Translated by David Denby. Cambridge, England, 1983.

Tucker, Robert. *Marx-Engels Reader.* New York, 1972.

Ulam, Adam B. *Dangerous Relations: The Soviet Union in World Politics, 1970–1982.* New York, 1983.

Voegelin, Eric. *The New Science of Politics.* Chicago, 1987.

Walesa, Lech. *A Way of Hope: An Autobiography.* New York, 1987.

Wedel, Janine. *The Private Poland.* New York, 1986.

Weschler, Lawrence. *The Passion of Poland: From Solidarity to the State of War.* New York, 1984.

Whitehead, Alfred North. *The Function of Reason.* Boston, 1958.

Wiatr, Jerzy. "Polish Society." In *Poland: A Handbook.* Warsaw, 1977.

Woodall, Jean. *The Socialist Corporation and Technocratic Power: The Polish United Workers Party, Industrial Organization, and Work Force Control 1958–1980.* Cambridge, Mass., 1982.

Zielinski, Janusz G. *Economic Reforms in Polish Industry.* London, 1973.

Zinoviev, Aleksandr. *The Reality of Communism.* Translated by Charles Janson. London, 1985.

Zukav, Gary. *The Dancing Wu Li Masters: An Overview of the New Physics.* New York, 1980.

PERIODICALS

Across Frontiers, I–III (1984–1987).

Bryk, Andrzej, and Kazimierz Dadak. "The Self-Governing Republic: A Critical Review of the Major Reforms Proposed by Solidarity." *Review of Socialist Law,* No. 11 (1985), 309–31.

Brzezinski, Zbigniew. "The Future of Yalta." *Foreign Affairs,* LXIII (Winter, 1984–85), 279–302.

Cohen, Stephen F. "Friends and Foes of Change: Reformism and Conservatism in the Soviet Union." *Slavic Review,* XXXVIII (June, 1979), 187–203.

Crisis and Conflicts: The Case of Poland, 1980–81. Volume III of *Sisyphus Sociological Studies.* Warsaw, 1982.

Frieden, Jeff. "Poland's Debt: Why the Big Banks Love Martial Law." *Nation,* January 23, 1982, pp. 8–11.

Huskey, Eugene E., Jr. "Limits to Institutional Autonomy in the USSR: The Case of Audokatura." *Soviet Studies,* XXXIV (April, 1982), 200–227.

"Interview with Gorbachev." *Time,* September 9, 1985, pp. 22–29.

Kostecki, Marian J. "Revolt of the Incapacitated: Inter- and Intra-organizational Consequences of the Polish Summer 1980." *Journal of Peace Research,* XIX, No. 2 (1982), 143–60.

Kostecki, Marian J., and Krzysztof Mrela. "Workers and Intelligentsia in Poland: During the Hot Days and in Between." *Media, Culture, and Society,* No. 4 (1982), 225–41.

Offe, Claus. "The Greens in Germany." *New Political Science,* No. 11 (Spring, 1983), 45–46.

Poland Watch, No. 1–8 (1982–1986).

Rensenbrink, John. "The Anti-Nuclear Phenomenon: A New Look at Fundamental Human Interests." *New Political Science,* No. 7 (Fall, 1981), 75–89.

Rosenthal, A. M. "The Trees of Warsaw: A Return to Poland." *New York Times Magazine,* August 7, 1983, pp. 24–31.

Schell, Jonathan. "Reflections: Poland." *New Yorker*, February 3, 1986.
Schöpflin, George. "Stability Through Weakness in Poland." *Conflict Studies*, No. 187 (June, 1986), 1–19.
Shtromas, Alexander. "Dissent and Political Change in the Soviet Union." *Studies in Comparative Communism*, XII (Summer–Autumn, 1979), 212–43.
Skilling, H. Gordon. "Interest Groups and Communist Politics Revisited." *World Politics*, XXXVI (October, 1983), 1–27.
Survey: A Journal of East and West Studies, XVII–XXVIII (1971–1984).
Uncensored Poland News Bulletin. July, 1984, to December, 1987.
"Underground Society: Draft Manifesto of the Interim Coordinating Committee of the NSZZ Solidarnosc, July 28, 1982." *Communist Affairs: Documents and Analysis*, II (April, 1983), 250–51.
Wanless, P. T. "Economic Reform in Poland, 1973–79." *Soviet Studies*, XXXII (January, 1980), 28–57.
Washington Spectator, Vol. 8, No. 2, February 1, 1982.
Wiatr, Jerzy. "Sources of Crises." *Polish Perspectives*, XXV (Autumn, 1982).

NEWSPAPERS

Beecher, William. "Farm Aid Pitfalls in Poland." Boston *Globe*, July 22, 1983.
Interview with Wojciech Jaruzelski. Washington *Post*, September 9, 1985.
New York *Times*. 1982–1987.
Solidarnosc News (Brussels). 1982–1987.
Tygodnik Mazowsze. No. 137 (August 8, 1985), No. 138 (August 15, 1985), No. 142 (October 17, 1985).

Index